The Best American CRIME REPORTING
2008

The Best American CRIME REPORTING

Editors

2002: NICHOLAS PILEGGI

2003: JOHN BERENDT

2004: JOSEPH WAMBAUGH

2005: JAMES ELLROY

2006: MARK BOWDEN

2007: LINDA FAIRSTEIN

The Best American
CRIME REPORTING

2008

Guest Editor
JONATHAN KELLERMAN

Series Editors
OTTO PENZLER AND
THOMAS H. COOK

AN ecco BOOK

HARPER PERENNIAL

NEW YORK • LONDON • TORONTO • SYDNEY • NEW DELHI • AUCKLAND

HARPER PERENNIAL

Permissions appear on pages 327–329.

HarperCollins books may be purchased for educational, business, or sales promotional use. For information please write: Special Markets Department, HarperCollins Publishers, 10 East 53rd Street, New York, NY 10022.

FIRST EDITION

Library of Congress Cataloging-in-Publication Data is available upon request.

ISBN 978-0-06-149083-5

08 09 10 11 12 WBC/RRD 10 9 8 7 6 5 4 3 2 1

Contents

Preface

CRIME IS BY TURNS COMIC AND TRAGIC. This year's *Best American Crime Reporting* reflects these critical extremes, along with much that lies in between.

On the side of comedy there is "I'm with the Steelers," Justin Heckert's hilarious account of an improbable impostor. What man might imagine that he could convince a woman that he was a well-known and often-photographed player for the Pittsburgh Steelers, do this in, of all places, Pittsburgh—a football town if there ever was one—and pull it off not once but repeatedly?

But if evidence—even photographic evidence—is a weak weapon against wishful thinking, so too is critical thinking when confronted with the awesome power of reputation. Malcolm Gladwell's "Dangerous Minds" takes one of modern law enforcement's sacred cows, the criminal profile, and argues—with real rather than fanciful evidence—that it is little more than a sideshow hustle.

Calvin Trillin's "The House Across the Way" is the tale of an island upon which good fences would indeed make good neighbors . . . if they had any.

These stories, along with Tom Junod's "Mercenary," a tale of personal mythmaking that truly knew no bounds, and Mark Bowden's "The Ploy," in which flattery works better than waterboarding on a vain terrorist operative, form the comic boundary of this year's collection of the best of American crime reporting.

Unsurprisingly, personalities, both comic and tragic, sprout like hothouse plants in the worlds of both crime and punishment. In "Dean of Death Row," Tad Friend chronicles the life and work of one of America's premier death row administrators, while Charles Graeber's "The Tainted Kidney" records an evil man's effort to do at least one good deed. Or was it just an effort to seem good?

Crime, like politics, makes strange bedfellows, and even evil men have buddies, as James Renner makes clear in "The Serial Killer's Disciple," though in this case evil appears to get the friendship it deserves. The genuinely good deed of a witness determined to give testimony and the terrible penalty he paid is the subject of Jeremy Kahn's harrowing "The Story of a Snitch." The thugs who took his life are surely deserving of "The Caged Life," whose daily deprivations are revealed in Alan Prendergast's look inside one of America's foremost super-maximum prisons.

When crime darkens, it does so by degrees, of course, but it rarely seems more sinister than when it is carried out in accordance with state policy, as reported in Jonathan Green's "Murder at 19,000 Feet"; or by the due authorities of the state, as is argued by Pamela Colloff in "Badges of Dishonor"; or even by what amounts to irrational popular will, in this case, of rabidly anti-American sentiment, as chronicled in Dean LaTourrette's scary "A Season in Hell."

Two stories round out this year's *Best American Crime Reporting*. Nick Schou's "Just a Random Female" darkly demonstrates just how random a random murder can be, while D. T. Max's "Day of the Dead" suggests that even the most celebrated of human crimes can disappear into a fog of mood, insinuation, and coincidence, where the facts remain as unknowable as the human mind itself.

This is the seventh edition of *Best American Crime Reporting* (once titled *Best American Crime Writing* but retitled last year to avoid confusion with *Best American Mystery Stories*, as many readers thought both volumes contained fiction), and we are indebted to Jonathan Kellerman for agreeing to be the guest editor this year. Dr. Kellerman, the bestselling author of the Alex Delaware mystery series, has written one of the most interesting and provocative introductions that the series has enjoyed.

While on the subject of guest editors, it seems appropriate to express our profound gratitude to the previous authors who filled that role so admirably, helping to establish this series as the most prestigious of its kind: Nicholas Pileggi (2002), John Berendt (2003), Joseph Wambaugh (2004), James Ellroy (2005), Mark Bowden (2006), and Linda Fairstein (2007).

In terms of the nature and scope of this collection, we defined the subject matter as any factual story involving crime or the threat of a crime that was written by an American or Canadian and first published in the calendar year 2007. Although we examine an enormous number of publications, inevitably the preeminent ones attracted many of the best pieces. All national and large regional magazines were searched for appropriate material, as were nearly two hundred so-called little magazines, reviews, and journals.

We welcome submissions for *The Best American Crime Reporting 2009* by any writer, editor, publisher, agent, or other interested party. Please send the publication or a tear sheet with the name of the publication, the date on which it appeared, and contact information for the author or representative. If first publication was in electronic format, a hard copy must be submitted. All submissions must be received no later than December 31, 2008; anything received after that date will not be read. This is neither arrogant nor capricious. The timely nature of the book forces very tight deadlines that cannot be met if we receive material later than that date. The sooner we receive articles, the more favorable will be the light in which they are read.

Please send submissions to Otto Penzler, The Mysterious Bookshop, 58 Warren Street, New York, NY 10007. Inquiries may be sent to me at ottopenzler@mysteriousbookshop.com. Regretfully, materials cannot be returned. If you do not believe the U.S. Postal Service will actually deliver mail and prefer to have verification that it was received, please enclose a self-addressed stamped postcard.

Thank you,
Otto Penzler and
Thomas H. Cook
New York, March 2008

Introduction

A SMALL PROPORTION of human beings—perhaps 1 percent of any given population—is different from the rest of us in ways that wreak havoc on the rest of us.

The cardinal traits of this bunch include superficiality; impulsiveness; self-aggrandizement to the point of delusion; callousness; and, when it suits, outright cruelty. Truth and principle don't intrude upon the world of the disruptors. When they don't lapse into tell-tale glibness, the more socially adroit among them come across as charming, sometimes overwhelmingly charismatic.

They project a preternatural calm that isn't an act. Their resting pulse rate tends to be low, they don't sweat readily—literally and figuratively—nor do they react strongly to pain and fear.

Because of their eerily quiet nervous system, they don't learn readily from experience.

If anyone can fool the polygraph, they can.

Intellectually, they understand the necessity for rules and regulations, but only for others. *They* are exempt from all that nonsense because *they* are special.

The smarter ones among them eschew violence. Not because they abhor bloodletting, but because they realize violence is usually a counterproductive strategy. Some of the cleverest among them run successful Ponzi schemes or engage in hugely profitable insider securities trading. Others rise to the boards of corporations where they coordinate felonies of a subtler nature.

The most ambitious and, arguably, the most dangerous among them fix their eyes on the Oscar of amorality known as political power. Chameleons adroit at tailoring their behavior to the needs of others, they often win elections. Sometimes they simply take by force. In either event, when one of them runs a country, things really get ugly.

The stupid ones, on the other hand, opt for offenses that range from petty to horrific and rarely pan out. They're more likely to end up behind bars.

The disruptors don't comprise the majority of incarcerated criminals. That distinction belongs mostly to people who make poor choices due to bad habits.

When the nasty 1 percent do commit crimes, the offenses are frequently stunningly audacious, cold-blooded, vicious, and terrifying to the rest of us. Because their actions are beyond our ken, we are sometimes seduced into believing the circular logic of their defense attorneys:

Anyone who could chop up six women has to be insane.

Anyone who could poison her own children for insurance money must be crazy.

Wrong.

Insanity—a legal, not a medical concept—simply refers to the inability to understand the essential wrongness of one's acts. The disruptors understand damn well.

They just don't care.

People who get paid to produce jargon have termed the disruptors psychopaths, sociopaths, possessors of antisocial personalities.

For the most part, the labels are interchangeable and emanate from political points of view.

Psychopath implies an internal mental state. Jargonmeisters who favor an emphasis upon individual responsibility go for that one.

Those who prefer to blame an external force, typically that nebulous bogeyman known as "society," prefer sociopath.

Antisocial personality is a stab at sounding medically diagnostic without giving away one's bias.

"Bad Guy" would be just as good of a label.

Foolish bad guys commit the crimes that bore us.

High-level bad guys—who view crime as a job—begin their iniquitous careers with misdemeanors, but they learn quickly, zipping up the criminal ladder, because they're smart but lack an effective stop mechanism.

The most evil among us commit outrages that enthrall, capturing our attention precisely because the internal world that motivates them is so chillingly barren that they might as well have been reared on Pluto.

The most evil among us do the stuff covered by the media genre known as "true crime."

Back in the good old days, "true crime" meant delightfully lurid and judgmental pulp magazines, frequently marketed with covers depicting scantily-clad women in the grips of slavering brutes. Think *Thrilling Detective*. A secondary outlet was true-crime books, generally paperback originals, with authorial and editorial emphasis on the bloody and ghastly.

The occasional masterpiece of reporting that ventured beyond ghoulish explication of body fluids and viscera to skillfully explore the events, persona, and sometimes the sick-joke happenstance leading to "senseless" crime, did occasionally elbow its way above the slush pile. (Think the books of the late Jack Olsen.) But that was the exception; this was low-rent territory.

That hasn't changed, but the vehicle of delivery has. Nowadays, "true crime" most frequently refers to that ironically cruel

Grand Guignol mislabeled "reality TV." And since television is a cheap, quick high for those simply interested in a violence fix, it has achieved rapid dominance. (A fact that might also be explained by the prevalence of amoral, even psychopathic, individuals in what's known in my hometown, L.A., as "The Industry." What better way to capture psychopaths than to have their portraits painted by other psychopaths?)

The pulps and softcover originals may not have been refined, but they did possess a certain shameless charm. Sadly, they've been wounded grievously, perhaps incurably, by trash TV. But the occasional full-length true-crime print masterpiece continues to surface and thrive for the same reason that high quality crime novels seem impervious to the video onslaught and remain staples of any bestseller list: a great book is able to plumb the depths of human motivation in a way that TV and movies—essentially impressionistic vehicles—cannot.

For the most part, though, the best true-crime writing of today appears on the pages of magazines.

This book showcases the best of the best.

While the ultimate goal of crime-beat reportage—understanding what drives people toward evil—is eons away from being achieved and may in fact never be achieved, the stories in this book will satisfy you intellectually and emotionally because you will be moved to think, feel, puzzle, and sometimes to self-examine.

Every one of these gems is penned by an individual with a strong, distinctive voice, leading to a varied and fascinating lot, stylistically and contextually. And the topics are a deliciously eclectic mix. Sure, there are a few serial lust killer tales. How could there not be? But each has something especially provocative to say about that most terrible of patterns.

At times, the accounts in this book explore crime in the highest of places, reminding us that a geopolitical focus should not obscure the fact that evil deeds emanate from evil people. Particularly fascinating is an account of the strategic planning leading to the capture of Islamo-fascist kingpin Abu Musab al-Zarqawi—a tale that is unquestionably one of the finest police procedurals ever written.

The always provocative essayist Malcolm Gladwell has produced a compelling examination of a topic near and dear to my heart: exposure of the confidence game that is criminal profiling. But even if I didn't agree with him completely, I'd love the piece because it's witty, incisive, and beautifully written.

The eminent humorist Calvin Trillin abandons any pretense of levity in his fascinating look at the genesis of violence on an isolated Canadian island—one of those obscure locales, struggling for its very existence in the face of a rapidly changing world, that few of us are likely to visit. And even if we did ferry over, we couldn't capture the place, or the people, the way Trillin does.

Two of the stories deal with life in prison. One illuminates the perspective of a complex man who's spent a good part of his life on death row—as a custodian of the condemned. The other allows us a peek into the mind of one of the most dangerously violent offenders in the United States and offers a hint of what it might be like to occupy his private hell.

There's a great unsolved mystery—an eerily suggestive psychological autopsy exploring the death of an emotionally tortured, one-shot-wonder master novelist, that manages to leave the reader grandly satisfied. Two unforgettable portrayals of habitual liars, one of whom just might be telling the truth when the truth is most devastating, will leave you thinking about them long after you've read their final paragraphs.

The morally complex account of the painful intersection between public outrage and the attempt, by an undeniably evil man, to do something good leaves us with more questions than answers, but they are questions that need to be faced.

All in all, a page-turning look at the myriad faces of evil.

This is the new face of quality true crime.

Bad guys at their worst, writers at their best.

—Jonathan Kellerman

The Best American Crime Reporting

2008

Jeremy Kahn

THE STORY OF A
SNITCH

FROM *The Atlantic Monthly*

JOHN DOWERY JR. was happy to be working again. He had recently spent 11 months cooped up, a prisoner in his own home. In November 2003, two officers investigating the sound of gunfire in East Baltimore had arrested him after a car and foot chase. They said that Dowery, who had been riding in the back of a blue Mitsubishi, had jumped out of the car, placed a loaded .38-caliber handgun on the ground, and tried to flee. A 36-year-old heroin addict with a felony drug conviction, Dowery was facing federal prosecution and the prospect of up to eight years without parole. While he awaited trial, he had been "put on the box"—confined to his house, his whereabouts monitored by a transmitter locked around his ankle.

Staring down almost a decade behind bars can change a man, make him long for a second chance. And now it seemed Dowery had been given one. In October 2004, he had cut a deal, agreeing to become a witness in a murder trial. In exchange for his testimony, and as a result of good behavior, the feds had eased the terms of his pretrial detention. He had entered a drug-treatment program and landed a job working the graveyard shift at a condiment factory in the suburbs. For the first time in years, he was clean and sober, and life was looking up.

Each night, Dowery rode the commuter rail from the city to the plant; each morning, he rode it home again. He didn't mind the odd hours; having worked as a baker, he was accustomed to being nocturnal. Shortly after dawn on October 19, 2005, he got off the train as usual. It was a brisk morning, with clouds dappling the sky but no hint of rain. He decided to skip the bus and walk the mile to his house on Bartlett Avenue.

He ambled past the massive Board of Education building, with its columns, and headed down North Avenue to Greenmount Cemetery. There he turned left, passing the abandoned row houses where the "corner boys" were already opening for business, hoping to find a junkie in need of a morning fix. Farther on, past still-shuttered hair salons and check-cashing outfits, he turned down East 24th toward Bartlett. Just after seven o'clock, he reached his front porch and called out for his girlfriend, Yolanda, to let him in. Then he sensed something behind him.

He spun around to find two men dressed in black standing in his small front yard. One held a gun. As Dowery scrambled for his neighbor's porch, the man pulled the trigger. Dowery leaped from the porch and raced around the side of his house, the two men close behind him, the gunman firing the whole way. He managed to stagger through his back door before his legs gave out. The attackers, believing their work accomplished, took off. A neighbor would later tell police that she heard one of them say, "We busted his motherfucking ass."

Dowery had been shot in the back and in both arms and legs—six times in all. Only the skilled hands of the surgeons at Johns Hopkins spared his life. And yet, in the eyes of many people in the blocks around Bartlett, John Dowery had gotten what was coming to him.

IN MANY BALTIMORE NEIGHBORHOODS, talking to the law has become a mortal sin, a dishonorable act punishable by social banishment—or worse. Prosecutors in the city can rattle off a litany of brutal retaliations: houses firebombed, witnesses and their relatives shot, contract hits on 10-year-olds. Witness intimidation, they say, badly hampers their ability to fight crime, and it affects nearly every murder case they try.

Prosecutors in most major U.S. cities tell similar stories. Two years ago in Philadelphia, a drug kingpin was convicted of witness intimidation after he was taped threatening to kill those who testified against him. Five relatives of one witness in the case had already died, in a house fire that prosecutors believe was the drug lord's doing. Last year in San Francisco, two gang members beat a murder rap after the state's star witness turned up dead. Several years ago in Denver, a key homicide witness was sexually assaulted in what prosecutors believe was a "contract" attack designed to frighten him out of testifying.

Police and prosecutors have been contending with reluctant witnesses for decades. But according to law-enforcement experts, the problem is getting dramatically worse, and is reflected in falling arrest and conviction rates for violent crimes. In cities with populations between half a million (for example, Tucson) and a million (Detroit), the proportion of violent crimes cleared by an arrest dropped from about 45 percent in the late 1990s to less than 35 percent in 2005, according to the FBI. Conviction rates have similarly dropped. At the same time, crime has spiked. Murder rates have risen more or less steadily since 2000. Last December, the FBI voiced concern over a jump in violent crime, which in 2005 showed its biggest increase in more than a decade.

The reasons for witnesses' reluctance appear to be changing and becoming more complex, with the police confronting a new cultural phenomenon: the spread of the gangland code of silence, or *omerta*, from organized crime to the population at large. Those who cooperate with the police are labeled "snitches" or "rats"—terms once applied only to jailhouse informants or criminals who turned state's evidence, but now used for "civilian" witnesses as well. This is particularly true in the inner cities, where gangsta culture has been romanticized through rap music and other forms of entertainment, and where the motto "Stop snitching," expounded in hip-hop lyrics and emblazoned on caps and T-shirts, has become a creed.

The metastasis of this culture of silence in minority communities has been facilitated by a gradual breakdown of trust in the police and the government. The erosion began during the civil-rights era, when informants were a favorite law-enforcement tool against groups like the Black Panthers. But it accelerated because of the war on drugs. David Kennedy, the director of the Center for Crime Prevention and Control at the John Jay College of Criminal Justice, in New York, told me: "This is the reward we have reaped for 20 years of profligate drug enforcement in these communities." When half the young black men in a neighborhood are locked up, on bail, or on parole, the police become the enemy. Add to this the spread of racialized myths—that crack was created by the CIA to keep blacks in their place, for example—and you get a toxic mix. Kennedy thinks the silence of many witnesses doesn't come from fear, but from anger.

The growing culture of silence helps to legitimize witness intimidation. At the same time, criminals have become more adept at enforcing the code, using increasingly sophisticated methods to bribe, intimidate, and harm witnesses. Defendants and their surrogates have obtained witnesses' supposedly confidential grand-jury testimony and tacked it to their doors, along with threatening notes. They have adopted new technology like cell-phone cameras and text-messaging to spread the word about who is snitching; threats have even been text-messaged to the phones of sequestered witnesses. And every incident in which a witness is assaulted or murdered heightens the climate of fear and mistrust—the sense that the law either can't or won't protect ordinary people.

On October 13, 2004, a year before he was shot while returning home from work, John Dowery was still electronically shackled to his house. Sometime after 3 p.m. that day, he looked out his front window and saw his friend James Wise coming up the street. Dowery and Wise, whom everyone called Jay, shared a love of basketball—and of heroin. Today Jay was with a younger man Dowery didn't recognize. They stopped outside the chain-link fence around Dowery's front yard. Jay called to Dowery, then came up to the door. He seemed nervous. He wanted Dowery's advice.

Jay said the other man had a gun. They were planning to rob an old drug dealer named Reds, who operated from a vacant lot a few doors down. Dowery told him it was a bad idea. At 40, Jay was no innocent, but neither was he an experienced stickup artist. Even if the two men could pull off the robbery, stickup boys in East Baltimore don't usually live long: On the street, robbing a dealer is a capital offense. "I told him basically not to do it," Dowery would later say. "But he ain't listen."

Dowery looked on from his front door as the two men walked down the street and entered the "cut" where Reds worked. He watched a flock of dope fiends suddenly flee the alley, like ducks flushed from the reeds. Seconds later, Reds darted out too. Then Jay and his partner emerged and raced down the street.

The two had timed their escape poorly. Sauntering up the street just then was Tracy Love, an athletic 20-year-old with cornrows and a meticulously trimmed beard and mustache, whom everyone knew as "Boo-Boo." Prosecutors later alleged that Boo-Boo oversaw the Bartlett Avenue drug operation. Jay and his accomplice brushed right past him. As Dowery watched, Boo-Boo pivoted and began to follow them down the hill.

Fifteen minutes later, Dowery heard the wail of police sirens and the *thump-thump* of a helicopter overhead. Boo-Boo strode back up Bartlett with his younger half-brother, Tamall Parker, who went by "Moo-Moo." "I got that motherfucker, six times in the chest," Dowery later recalled Boo-Boo shouting—ostensibly to his crew down the street, but loudly enough that anyone out on the block could hear. "Next time, one of y'all gonna do it. I'm tired of doing this shit."

According to police and prosecutors, this is what happened after Jay and his partner, a man police would identify as Joseph Bassett, robbed Reds and left Bartlett Avenue: Boo-Boo went to find Moo-Moo. They got into a white Lexus with sparkling chrome hubcaps and began cruising the neighborhood, hunting for Jay and Bassett. Unaware they were being pursued, Jay and Bassett met up with a couple of prostitutes a few blocks away. Jay knew one of them, Doris Dickerson. He told her about the robbery and offered her drugs. She said she would catch up with him in a minute, and walked into an alley. Bassett also left for a few minutes. Just as Doris and Jay were about to meet back up, at the corner of Bonaparte and Robb, Boo-Boo and Moo-Moo spotted Jay. Boo-Boo let Moo-Moo out of the car, then drove around the corner and waited. Moo-Moo tugged the hood of his sweatshirt up around his face, approached Jay, and pulled out a 9-mm handgun. He opened up, firing at least 13 times. The bullets punched holes in Jay's chest and abdomen; at least one smashed into his skull.

James Sylvester Wise Jr. was dead—the 229th murder of the year in a city that would rack up 278 by the end of December. Although 10 people called 911 to report the shooting, many refused to give their names. Six told the emergency operators that they did not want to talk to the police when they arrived. One caller, John Craddock, said he had seen a man running down the street and jumping into a white Lexus. He could not see the man's face, but he thought he could make out part of the license plate—a blue-and-white temporary tag with the numbers *3, 4,* and *9*. Police dispatchers put out a description of the car, but to no avail. Officers canvassed the block but turned up no additional witnesses or information. None of the three who knew the most about the killing—Dowery, Bassett, or Dickerson—came forward.

A MAN GUNNED DOWN on a busy street. No identifying witnesses; no suspects. In this, James Wise's murder was typical. Colonel Frederick Bealefeld III, Baltimore's chief of detectives, says the police used to be able to rely on people's consciences and sense of civic duty to generate leads in murder investigations. But today, few witnesses are willing to offer information, even anonymously. "How hard is it for someone to get on the phone and say . . . 'The guy who shot up this block—it is wrong, here's who that person is'?" Bealefeld asks. "Yet we don't get a ton of those kinds of calls. And if we graphed it out, if we tracked it over the years, you would see a very clear decline."

A 26-year veteran of the force and the grandson of a cop, Bealefeld has seen these changes firsthand. His grandfather walked a beat on Greenmount Avenue, not far from Bartlett. In 30 years with the department, he fired his gun exactly once in the line of duty. "No way he could walk that beat and do that now," Bealefeld says. "He took it for granted that the community respected him. Today's police can't take that for granted." By the time Bealefeld joined the force, in 1980, things had become much more dangerous for both the police and the citizens of Baltimore. But during the '80s, working narcotics, he could still find confidential informants with relative ease. Over time, that too started to change.

Bealefeld says he does not want to underestimate the fear people feel on the streets, or their lack of trust in the law. But he thinks witness intimidation has also become a cover for indifference. "How do I separate your intransigence to take part in a civic responsibility, and a moral responsibility, from your alleged fear?" he asks, the anger rising in his voice. "'I am not doing it, because I am afraid'—that is easy to say. You may not be doing it because you are a jerk and don't care about anybody but yourself and have no love for your fellow man."

Bealefeld is right that disentangling fear from other factors is not easy. But when I spoke with people in the blocks near where James Wise was murdered, it was the fear that was most palpable. "Round here it's not a good idea to talk to the police," Jacob Smith, a thoughtful 13-year-old walking home from school in East Baltimore, told me. "People, they like, if they know you talk to the police, they don't be around you. And if people talk on them and they get locked up, their friends come up on you and hurt you or something." (The ostracism and retaliation he spoke of got wide airing as a plotline last season in HBO's *The Wire*, set in Baltimore and created by David Simon, a former crime reporter, and Ed Burns, a former police officer: A teenager thought by his peers to have snitched was beaten, and eventually his house was firebombed.)

All over Baltimore, whenever I asked people about cooperating with the law, I got the same response. "Why would you talk to the police? All you are doing is putting a label on yourself," said Barry Nelson, a 42-year-old part-time handyman who was waiting for a meal from a charity the day I met him. "They ain't going to be back to protect you after you done told on some cats." Randolph Jones, a retiree who was sweeping leaves from the sidewalk in front of his house in Northwest Baltimore, said he would call the police if something happened on *his* block. But the drug dealing and shootings on the next block over? He won't pick up the phone. Jones said the police try, but as soon as they arrest one corner boy, another moves in. "You got to live here, and the police can't do much," he said. "You don't want to end up like that family in East Baltimore, the Dawsons."

The Dawsons come up in almost every conversation about reluctant witnesses in Baltimore. Angela Dawson had tried to shoo drug dealers away from the sidewalk outside the East Baltimore row house where she lived with her husband, Carnell, and their five children. She had frequently called the police. The dealers decided to strike back. In October 2002, the Dawsons' house was firebombed. Angela Dawson and all her children were killed in the blaze; Carnell Dawson died in the hospital a week later. A drug dealer named Darrell Brooks was convicted of the crime and is serving life without parole. But the sentence has done little to reassure potential witnesses. More than four years later, the Dawsons still haunt the city.

JOHN DOWERY knew Boo-Boo and Moo-Moo had shot someone; he prayed that it wasn't Jay, that it was the other guy. But the next day's newspaper confirmed his fear about his friend. Jay's death shook Dowery. But it also made him more determined to get his life back on track. And in the tragedy of his friend's murder, Dowery sensed opportunity. If he told the police what he knew about the killing, perhaps he could get a lighter sentence on his gun charge. On the other hand, talking was dangerous: If Boo-Boo and Moo-Moo found out, they might come after him or his family. So Dowery struggled with the decision. A day went by, then a week. Then he picked up the phone and called his public defender.

On October 27, Dowery, along with his lawyer and the prosecutor handling his gun charge, met with Michael Baier, the Baltimore homicide detective assigned to Jay's murder. Dowery told Baier what he knew about the killing. He also said that Boo-Boo and Moo-Moo, who were still hanging around Bartlett, had ditched their distinctive white Lexus. His statement provided a crucial break in the case.

Another break came the following week, when Joseph Bassett, Jay's accomplice, was busted selling heroin to undercover cops. With his long rap sheet, Bassett knew he was in trouble. He tried offering up an illegal .32 he kept at home, in the hope that the officers would let him go in exchange for getting the gun off the street. When that failed, he said he might know something about a murder on Bonaparte. The officers brought Bassett downtown to homicide, where he told Baier about robbing Reds. He also said he had seen two men in a white Lexus circling the block, and that he saw the car stop and a man get out and shoot Jay. Baier showed him a photo lineup. Bassett identified Tracy Love as the driver of the car and Tamall Parker as the shooter.

Parker and Love were picked up two days later. Baier had several other pieces of evidence: The two suspects' mother had recently returned to the dealership a white Lexus with the temporary license tag 38491L. Video from a warehouse surveillance camera near the murder scene had captured what appeared to be a white Lexus circling the block in the minutes before Jay was killed. An analysis of Love's cell phone records determined that the phone had not left East Baltimore that day, a finding that directly contradicted Love and Parker's alibi: They said they had spent the day in their mother's hair salon, in West Baltimore.

Baier did not have a confession or a murder weapon, however. So at trial, a lot would depend on the testimony of Dowery and Bassett—convicted felons who had come forward at least in part because they were facing charges themselves. Eventually they would be joined by a third witness, also in trouble with the law: Doris Dickerson, picked up for prostitution, told police that she was heading toward Jay when she heard shots. She saw Jay fall to the ground and Moo-Moo run away. She too identified Parker as the killer from a photo lineup.

Witnesses of this sort would once have made a prosecutor

blanch. Now, they are usually all prosecutors have. One problem with such witnesses is that defense attorneys can use their records to attack their credibility. The fewer witnesses the state has and the more a defense attorney expects to be able to discredit them, the more likely she is to advise her client against a plea bargain. This means more cases go to trial, at significant expense to the state. And at trial, there is a decent chance—in Baltimore, about 50 percent in a nonfatal shooting, and 38 percent in a murder—that the defendant will walk.

Witnesses in the drug trade are also highly susceptible to being coerced into changing their stories or not showing up in court. If a witness goes missing, his prior statements generally aren't admissible. And a witness who "backs up"—legal slang for recanting—can create doubt, including reasonable doubt, in the minds of jurors.

Not surprisingly, defense attorneys have a different take. Elizabeth Julian, Baltimore's chief public defender, believes the problems of witness intimidation are overstated. She told me that the real issue is police tactics that encourage suspects to lie about their knowledge of other crimes, and she pointed out that it is perfectly legal for police to mislead potential witnesses into thinking they won't have to testify in court. "If you are being asked, and you are getting a 'Get Out of Jail Free' card tonight, people take it. That's human nature," she says. In her view, many witnesses who back up are telling the truth on the stand. It's their initial statements that were false—either outright fabrications or some mixture of fact and rumor. Julian jokes that the word on the street, rather than "Stop snitching," ought to be "Stop lying."

As it happened, Dowery decided to become a witness just as witness intimidation in the city was about to explode into a national story. The spark was an underground DVD titled *Stop Fucking Snitching* that began circulating in Baltimore in November 2004.

In it Rodney Thomas, a rapper known locally as Skinny Suge, talks about what he thinks should happen to informants: "To all you snitches and rats . . . I hope you catch AIDS in your mouth, and your lips the first thing to die, yo bitch." The DVD also includes numerous segments in which young men on the street rail against snitches.

In its subject matter, the DVD was more evolution than revolution. The slogan "Stop snitching" had been around since at least 1999, when it was popularized by the Boston rapper Tangg da Juice. The video would have remained a local curiosity except for one thing: It includes a cameo by Carmelo Anthony, a Baltimore native who became an NBA star with the Denver Nuggets. Anthony appears in only six of the film's 108 minutes, and spends most of that time poking fun at a former coach and a rival player. As he later told *The Baltimore Sun*, "I was back on my block, chillin'. I was going back to show love to everybody, thinking it was just going to be on the little local DVD, that it was just one of my homeboys recording." But his celebrity, combined with the DVD's charged subject matter, created a sensation.

For Baltimore's police, prosecutors, and judges, eager to raise awareness about witness intimidation, *Stop Fucking Snitching* was a gift. "Think how bold criminals must be to make a DVD," Baltimore Circuit Judge John M. Glynn told the local press. "It shows that threatening snitches has become mainstream." Patricia Jessamy, the state's attorney for Baltimore, had hundreds of copies made and distributed them to politicians and the national media. The publicity helped her win passage of a tougher witness-intimidation law, one the Maryland legislature had voted down the year before. The police department made a show of arresting the DVD's stars, including a man accused of carrying out contract killings, and created its own video, *Keep Talking*, to encourage future witnesses to come forward.

Stop Fucking Snitching was produced by Rodney Bethea, a 33-year-old barber and entrepreneur. I met him in his small West

Baltimore store, One Love Underground, which pulls double duty as a barbershop and a boutique from which he sells his own line of urban fashions. Bethea told me the authorities and media had misinterpreted the DVD. It was not intended to encourage violence against witnesses, he said; he had simply set out to make a freestyle documentary, and snitching happened to emerge as a major theme. He also said that the term *snitch* has a very specific meaning on the streets and in the video. "They are referring to people that are engaged in illegal activities, making a profit from it, and then when it comes time for the curtains to close—you do the crime, you do the time—now no one wants to go to jail," he told me, pulling on his goatee. "That is considered a snitch. The old lady that lives on the block that call the police because guys are selling drugs in front of her house, she's not a snitch, because she is what would be considered a civilian."

Bethea believes there is a double standard—and perhaps a tinge of racism—in law enforcement's criticism of the "Stop snitching" culture. "When you think about it, I mean, who likes a snitch?" he said. "The government don't like a snitch. Their word for it is *treason*. What is the penalty for treason?" He pointed out that the police have their own code of silence, and that officers who break it by reporting police misconduct are stigmatized in much the same way as those who break the code of silence on the street.

Bethea's argument has a certain elegance. But the distinction he draws between the drug dealer who flips and the civilian who is just trying to get dealers off her stoop has ceased to mean much. Just ask the Dawsons. Or Edna McAbier, a community activist who tried to clean up drugs in her North Baltimore neighborhood. The local chapter of the Bloods considered blowing her head off with a shotgun but settled for firebombing her house, in January 2005—not long after *Stop Fucking Snitching* made news. McAbier escaped with her life, and her house was not badly damaged; those responsible received long prison sentences. But though the gang members didn't succeed in killing her, they did silence her: She left Baltimore out of fear for her safety. And the city got the message: If you break the code, you are in danger—even if you are a "civilian."

BY THE TIME OF THE MCABIER FIREBOMBING, John Dowery was starting to reap the rewards of his decision to testify in the state's prosecution of Tracy Love and Tamall Parker. His own trial had been postponed indefinitely. He had been released from home confinement, his drug-treatment program was going well, and he had started working.

So far, Baier had kept Dowery's name out of the investigative records, referring to him simply as "a Federal Suspect" and "the Source" so the state would not have to disclose him as a witness until closer to the trial date. He had also deferred taking a taped statement from Dowery, out of concern for his safety. These were sound precautions: On several occasions, prosecutors have intercepted "kites"—letters from a defendant, smuggled out of jail—detailing the prosecution's witness list and instructing friends or relatives to "talk" to those on it. But Baier could not keep Dowery's name a secret forever. Sooner or later, the government would have to tell defense lawyers that he was going to testify. In the meantime, suspicions about Dowery had already begun to circulate in the neighborhood. "Somebody approached me saying, 'Yeah, you snitching on us,'" he told Baier.

The case against Love and Parker languished. A trial was set for early April 2005 and then postponed until May, and then postponed again, and then again—seven times in all. In Baltimore, as in most major U.S. cities, the large number of cases and the shortage of judges, courtrooms, and lawyers make such delays common. Some cases have been postponed more than 30 times and have dragged on for more than five years. And each postponement increases the risk that witnesses who were cooperative will cease to be so—that they will move and leave no forwarding address, change their stories, genuinely forget facts, or turn up dead. "The defense attorneys play this game," says Brian Matulonis, the lieutenant in charge of Baltimore's Homicide Operations Squad. "If the witness is not there, they are ready to go. If the witness is there, they ask for a postponement."

On May 20, 2005, Baier finally took a taped statement from Dowery. It was delivered to defense lawyers in June. Soon afterward, Dowery got a phone call from Love.

"That's fucked, man. Why you gonna do me like that?" the defendant seethed.

"I said I didn't know what he was talking about," Dowery would tell the jurors during the trial. "I was testifying the whole time. But I just act like I didn't know what he was talking about."

A few weeks later, Love called Dowery again. "He like, 'Man, the other guy, he say he ain't gonna testify. What about you?'"

Dowery again played dumb. "I say, 'Man, he lied. I don't know whatcha talking about. You cool." Love seemed satisfied. "It was, like, a friendlier conversation the second time," Dowery would testify.

Dowery was nervous about the calls and about becoming known in the neighborhood as a snitch. But he didn't believe he was in immediate danger. The trial kept getting pushed back. Summer gave way to fall. Then came the morning when two men met him at his front door with a gun.

ONE OF JESSAMY'S primary weapons against witness intimidation is her office's witness-assistance program. Unlike the federal witness-protection program—the one most people know about from the movies—Baltimore's program can't provide marshals to guard witnesses around the clock for years. It can't offer witnesses a new identity in some distant city. Instead, the Baltimore program— run by a staff of two, with an annual budget of $500,000—tries to get witnesses out of harm's way by putting them in low-budget hotels that serve as temporary safe houses. The average stay is 90 days. The program also helps witnesses relocate permanently, generally within Maryland, providing a security deposit or first month's rent, moving costs, and vouchers for food and transportation. If necessary, it helps with job placement and drug treatment.

In most cases, this is enough to keep witnesses safe. Few Baltimore drug gangs have much reach beyond a couple of blocks, let alone outside the city. Still, many witnesses refuse the help. Almost a third of the 255 witnesses whom prosecutors referred to the program last year did not even come to an initial meeting. Of the 176 who did, only 36 entered safe housing. "Many of these people have never left their neighborhood," says Heather Courtney, a witness-assistance coordinator. "A lot of people can't handle it. They just can't be out of that neighborhood. That is all they know."

Even after the shooting, Dowery did not want to leave East Baltimore. He had spent his whole life there. His entire family—aunts, uncles, cousins—lived nearby, most on or near Bartlett. This included many of his nine children. In a neighborhood of absentee fathers, Dowery doted on his kids. Two of them lived with him and Yolanda. And he tried to stay involved in the lives of the others.

Eventually the witness coordinators prevailed upon Yolanda, who in turn convinced Dowery that they should leave. After less than two weeks in a hotel, Dowery, Yolanda, and their five-year-old daughter moved to a house outside the city. Most of his relatives remained in the old neighborhood.

THE TRIAL OF Tracy Love and Tamall Parker for the murder of James Wise began on January 26, 2006, in the cramped courtroom of Baltimore Circuit Judge Sylvester Cox. During opening arguments, Christopher Nosher, the boyish assistant state's attorney prosecuting the case, appeared confident. Although Judge Cox had barred any reference to the shooting attack on Dowery, ruling that the defendants had not been definitively linked to the incident, Dowery would be allowed to testify about the phone calls from Love. For Nosher, this was a coup: Jurors can be instructed to interpret a threat against a witness as "consciousness of guilt." Evidence of intimidation can also help juries understand why witnesses may back up on the stand.

Nosher had another reason to be confident: He knew that all of his witnesses would show. John Craddock, the man who had caught three numbers of the Lexus's license plate, had never wavered during the long pretrial process. Bassett, Jay's accomplice, had been convicted of his drug charges and was serving a seven-year sentence, so he wasn't going anywhere. And both Dowery and Doris Dickerson had remained cooperative.

In this respect, the trial was unusual. Witnesses so commonly miss court dates in Baltimore, whether from fear or irresponsibility, that Jessamy's office has resorted to arresting them just to compel their appearance. Jessamy acknowledges that arresting witnesses is hardly ideal—it tends to make them hostile to the prosecution and more likely to back up, and it further sours police-community relations. "But if you've done everything you can to get them to come voluntarily, then you do what you have to do," she says.

That afternoon, Dowery took the stand. He had always been skinny, but in the witness box he looked gaunt. His long, loose-fitting black shirt covered a colostomy bag, a result of the October 2005 shooting. Dowery spoke in a deep, soft voice as Nosher walked him through the events he witnessed on the day James Wise was murdered.

As he began his testimony, a commotion electrified the hallway outside. Several friends of Boo-Boo and Moo-Moo tried to rush into the courtroom carrying cell phones, which they held near their thighs, fingers resting on the camera buttons. Detective Baier was also in the hall, awaiting his turn to testify. He spotted the cell phones and stepped in front of the men, barring their path to the door. "Whoa, you can't come in here," he told them. "It's a closed courtroom." This was not true, but it kept the men from entering. Then, for laughs, Baier took out his own cell phone and took pictures of them.

Incidents of intimidation at the courthouse are no longer aberrations. Gang members sometimes line the courthouse steps, forming a gantlet that witnesses and jurors must walk through. Family members of defendants have come to court wearing STOP SNITCHING T-shirts and hats. In a Pittsburgh case last year, a key (though hostile) prosecution witness came to court in STOP SNITCHING gear. He was ejected because his garb was considered intimidating to other witnesses, and without his testimony, the district attorney dropped the charges. At the close of a Baltimore trial two years ago, jurors were so frightened of the defendants and of gang members in the gallery that the forewoman refused to read the guilty verdict aloud; so did another juror asked to do so by the judge. The judge eventually read the verdict herself and, as a precaution, had sheriff's deputies accompany the jurors out of the building.

DOWERY ENDURED A WITHERING CROSS-EXAMINATION, but he escaped the stand largely undamaged. Nosher's two other eyewitnesses did not. Dickerson developed sudden memory loss, claiming not to recall key details of what she had seen. Then Love's lawyer got her to admit she was probably high on heroin when the shooting took place. As for Bassett, he backed up right away. "First, I would like to say I don't appreciate being here against my will," he said in a high, squeaky voice that seemed incongruous coming from a man of his bulk. He went on to say that he never saw Jay after the robbery, never saw anyone shoot Jay, never saw a white Lexus at the end of Bonaparte, and never told Baier that he had seen any of these things. When Nosher showed him the photo lineup he had signed, in which he had identified Parker as the shooter, Bassett said that Baier "basically picked the dude out for me." What about his taped statement? He had been forced to make it, he said. "I gave them the plot of the story; they put their own characters with it."

The jury heard from other prosecution witnesses: Craddock talked about seeing the Lexus and part of the license tag. Baier testified about the investigation, stating that he had not coerced Bassett or helped him pick photos from the lineup. A telecommunications expert testified about the location of Love's cell phone. Video from the warehouse surveillance camera was shown to the jury. The defense put on no witnesses of its own. But after two days of deliberation, the jury announced that it could not reach a unanimous verdict. Judge Cox was forced to declare a mistrial.

AT FIRST, the prosecutors planned to retry the case. But over the summer, the federal government decided to take over. (With Dowery's cooperation, it had already been working on a case against Love, Parker, and James Dinkins, a man police believe was involved in Dowery's shooting.) In late August, Parker, Love, and Dinkins were indicted on federal charges of conspiracy to distribute heroin. As of this writing, the trial is scheduled to begin in late March.

Federal prosecutions are one method cities are using to combat witness intimidation. A law passed by Congress last December explicitly makes witness intimidation in a state case grounds for federal prosecution. Rod Rosenstein, the U.S. attorney for Maryland, says the federal government has a big advantage over the states in breaking through the code of silence: leverage. Federal sentencing guidelines provide for long prison terms and, unlike the state system, do not allow for probation or parole. "We don't appeal to their sense of civility and morality," Rosenstein says. "We get a hammer over their heads. They realize that cooperating is the only way they can get out from under these hefty federal sentences."

Some states are looking to bring their laws into line with federal practices. The Maryland law Jessamy helped pass elevates witness intimidation from a misdemeanor to a felony punishable by a minimum of five years. It also allows prosecutors to introduce a witness's prior statements even if the witness isn't at the trial, if they can provide "clear and convincing evidence" that the defendant was responsible for the witness's absence. Still, Jessamy isn't satisfied. The new law excludes child-abuse and domestic-violence cases. And rarely can prosecutors obtain the kind of evidence of intimidation it requires. Even when they can, Jessamy says, trying to persuade judges to apply the law "is like pouring water on a stone."

Cities are also pushing to increase funding for witness assistance. The federal law passed in December allows the U.S. attorney general to dispense grants to states for witness protection. But Congress appropriated only $20 million annually for these grants through 2010. By contrast, a bill that Representative Elijah Cummings of Maryland introduced two years ago would have provided $90 million annually to support state witness-assistance programs; that bill died in committee. Since the start of the new congressional session, in January, several bills to strengthen the protection of witnesses in state cases have been introduced; as of this writing, they are all still in committee.

Federal prosecutions, new laws, more money—these are the blunt instruments of policy-makers. They might chip away at the edges of the problem. But to really reduce witnesses' reluctance to participate in the judicial process will require something beyond the abilities of cops and courts: a cultural transformation in America's inner cities. In Philadelphia, Boston, and Washington, D.C., authorities have tried to prohibit the sale of STOP SNITCHING clothing (they succeeded in Washington). But there is no indication that criminalizing a fashion and political statement will alter the underlying sentiment. Leonard Hamm, a long-serving Baltimore police officer who returned to head the city's department in 2004 after an eight-year absence, sees the problem this way: "I think that the community is going to have to get sick and tired of the shootings and the killings and the memorial services. And all we can do as police is be there when they say they are ready." But what if the community is never ready? Many inner-city neighborhoods have no community. The institutions that once held them together—the churches, the associations, the businesses—are shells of what they were, if they exist at all.

FOR DOWERY, the mistrial was unnerving. Yet in some ways it was better than a guilty verdict. He was still planning to testify for the federal government against Love, Parker, and Dinkins. This would further postpone his gun case. In addition, as a federal witness, he began receiving some token financial assistance from the FBI.

Dowery's family would visit him in the suburbs. Still, he missed them, and he missed his friends. So he occasionally sneaked back to the old neighborhood for a day or two, usually staying with his mother and trying to keep a low profile. In the spring, he proudly watched his two eldest sons graduate from high school. And he didn't want to skip Thanksgiving at his aunt's house, on Bartlett Avenue. "He was tired of hiding out," his aunt, Joyce Garner, told me.

On Thanksgiving night, more than 20 members of Dowery's family gathered for a feast. Dowery was in a good mood, reminiscing about old times. Garner remembers that he came to talk to her as she was cooking. She asked if he was worried about being back in the neighborhood. "He just talked about the Lord to us and gave us a big hug and said, 'God's got it,'" she recalled. Toward the end of dinner, Dowery excused himself. He wanted to run across the street to buy a pack of cigarettes and have a beer.

The sign over its beige stucco facade calls the Kozy Korner a "Cut-Rate & Lounge." Two doors separate the bar from the street. The first opens onto a grungy vestibule where a cashier sells beer and liquor from behind a bulletproof window. The second is locked; customers must be buzzed through. Once inside, they are greeted by a dark, narrow room. A Baltimore Ravens poster is affixed to one wall. A rendering of the Last Supper, with a black Jesus and black disciples, decorates the other. Three video gambling machines flash and hum.

When Dowery arrived, a dozen other patrons were packed into the space. He recognized one of them: a former girlfriend called Toot. They chatted inside the doorway while he smoked and sipped a beer. Just after 10 o'clock, the door opened, and two men entered. This time Dowery's sixth sense—the feeling that had told him to turn around on his porch that morning a year earlier—failed him. One of the men drew a gun, pointed it at Dowery's head, and fired. Then the other did the same. This time, the doctors couldn't save him.

And although the bar was crowded, no one has come forward to say they saw a thing. It's just another homicide in inner-city America, with no suspects, and no witnesses.

JEREMY KAHN *is an independent journalist whose work has appeared in* The Atlantic Monthly, Newsweek, *the* New York Times, *the* Boston Globe, The Guardian, Fortune, The New Republic, Smithsonian, Foreign Policy, *and* Slate. *Previously, he served as managing editor of* The New Republic *and was a staff writer at* Fortune. *He recently moved from Washington, D.C. to New Delhi, India.*

Coda

As a writer, you want all your stories to matter—you want them to be read, to have an impact. But in this case, that desire was particularly strong. I desperately wanted to wake people up, to make them think about the way in which witness intimidation reinforced the inequality of the American justice system—the way it put whole inner-city neighborhoods essentially beyond the reach of the law. I hoped that out of the tragedy of John Dowery's death, some good might come. But I have enough experience to know that merely exposing a wrong rarely rights it—that places like East Baltimore would not be the way they are if it were so easy to bring about change.

Since this story was first published in *The Atlantic Monthly*, the "stop snitching" ethos—some even call it a "movement"—has received increasing attention from the national media. African American columnists, commentators, and community activists have expressed outrage and dismay at the acceptance of this code of silence in America's inner cities, as well as anger at the hip-hop stars and professional athletes who condone and legitimize it. (Unfortunately, few white commentators or politicians have seemed as exercised.) But the marketing juggernaut that romanticizes "gangsta" culture shows no sign of changing course. So the rapper Cam'ron, without any hint of shame or guilt, freely admits to CNN's Anderson Cooper that talking to the police would "hurt my business." Never mind who else gets hurt—that's none of Cam'ron's business. Meanwhile, local police and prosecutors—whose business it is to see that justice is served—remain confounded by the epidemic of witness intimidation. In some cities, like Newark, prosecutors have stopped bringing cases in which there is just one witness because of the likelihood that intimidation will derail the prosecution. This policy keeps lone witnesses safe—sometimes—and it conserves the DA's precious budget, but it hardly makes neighborhoods safer or provides justice to victims' families.

When I wrote this story, I assumed John Dowery's murder would never be solved. Police and prosecutors were furious over his killing—determined to show that no one could execute a federal witness with impunity—but they had crashed into that familiar brick wall of silence. I wasn't optimistic they could break through. Still, Baltimore's entire law enforcement community—lead by the local FBI field office—was helping to work the case. And as U.S. Attorney Rod Rosenstein points out in this story, the feds can be pretty persuasive. Eventually, the wall cracked.

On November 20, 2007, almost a year to the day after Dowery was killed, federal prosecutors charged two men, Melvin Gilbert, age thirty-three, and Darron Goods, a twenty-one-year-old known on the street as "Moo-man," with his murder. Prosecutors allege that Gilbert ran an East Baltimore heroin, cocaine, and marijuana distribution ring that called itself "Special." Tracy Love, aka "Boo-Boo," and Tamall Parker, aka "Moo-Moo," were ranking members of Special, according to prosecutors, and Dowery was killed to prevent him from testifying against the gang. In addition to Dowery, prosecutors allege that members of Special killed at least four others, including at least one other witness. In January 2008, the U.S. Attorney's office announced that it would seek the death penalty against Gilbert. As of this writing, the case had yet to come to trial.

Dean LaTourrette

A Season in Hell

FROM *Men's Journal*

ERIC VOLZ WAS TRAPPED. a large crowd had gathered outside the small-town courthouse, screaming, *"Ojo por ojo!"*—an eye for an eye. Volz had just finished a preliminary hearing for the alleged rape and murder of his ex-girlfriend Doris Jimenez, and despite considerable evidence pointing to his innocence, the judge ruled to allow his case to go to trial. But the people in the town of Rivas, Nicaragua, wanted more than justice. They wanted revenge.

"We're not going to let you get away with it," they chanted in Spanish. "We're going to kill you." Looking out the window, Volz could see that the angry mob numbered well over 200, some of them waving sticks and machetes, their faces both enraged and excited at the prospect of violence against the gringo. His only protection was several local police officers, along with a U.S. embassy security officer named Mike Poehlitz. The plan was to escape via the back door, a scheme that evaporated moments later when a friend of Volz's called on his cell phone and said there was a man with a gun waiting outside.

The only option was to exit via the front, where a police pickup truck waited for them, right in the heart of the unruly crowd. As they hit the street and darted for the truck the driver sped away, and the horde closed in, throwing fists and stones. All but one of the cops also fled; the lone officer yanked at Volz's shirt and yelled, *"Corre!"* Run.

Though he was handcuffed and without shoelaces, Volz sprinted down the street with the officer and Poehlitz. Miraculously, they made it a block, then ducked into the doorway of a nearby gymnasium, where they barricaded the door and crept from room to room as protesters hunted for them outside. When an unmarked police truck finally arrived an hour later to escort them to the station, they dashed back outside. The crowd moved in, and people jumped on the car. The driver gunned it, hitting some protesters before speeding off toward the police station.

But Volz, a 28-year-old American who had come to Nicaragua with all of the best intentions, was far from free.

Four months later, in late March, Eric Volz sits inside a sweltering 6-by-10-foot cell at La Modelo prison, in Tipitapa, Nicaragua. He cannot feel the gentle breezes that groom and feather the incoming swells that first attracted him to Nicaraguan shores. If he serves his full 30-year sentence he'll catch his next wave when he's 57 years old.

The story of how Volz wound up here is every expatriate's worst nightmare. He was a well-known resident of the Pacific coast town of San Juan del Sur, a surfer's paradise that he'd helped promote. His ex-girlfriend Doris Jimenez, one of the prettiest girls in town, was found brutally strangled on the floor of her clothing boutique. Volz cooperated with the authorities, only to have them turn on him, he says, after he offended a local police officer. Despite numerous eyewitnesses who said that Volz was two hours away at the time of Jimenez's murder, and the fact that no physical evidence tied him to the scene, he was convicted and sentenced to 30 years in prison. The trial, many believe, was a travesty of justice that tests the bounds of the absurd.

"I'd say this was a case of guilty until proven innocent," says Ricardo Castillo, a well-known Nicaraguan journalist who was meeting with Volz at the time the murder allegedly took place.

"I was really angry that the judge would bend to public pressure so easily," Volz told *Men's Journal,* recalling the judicial farce that brought him here. "I did not kill Doris, absolutely not. And I had no connection to it."

Volz is handsome, with intense, dark brown eyes. He's six feet tall, and his muscular frame might make an assailant think twice, but he's already had to defend himself with his fists in prison. As an American convicted of raping and murdering a Nicaraguan woman, he got into scuffles with a former cellmate, and other inmates have menaced him daily.

"The threat is very real," he says. "It's very simple for Doris's family to pay $500 or $1,000 to send a message to one of these gangs to try and kill me."

Volz's imprisonment has sparked an unofficial diplomatic war. His parents and supporters have mounted a media campaign for his release that has resulted in segments on the *Today* show (among others), so far to no avail. Online, a handful of American and Nicaraguan blogs and websites offer their versions of the truth to the browsing masses. A seven-minute pro-Volz video on YouTube shows him being hustled off to the courthouse over a moody Radiohead soundtrack, while a competing version, by "Nicaraguan Films," also on YouTube, lingers on him blinking—guiltily, we're to assume—as the judge delivers her verdict. And *Men's Journal* has learned that Volz's family has hired private investigators to reexamine Jimenez's murder, which was poorly handled by police.

Volz's case is far more complex than that of an innocent abroad who got caught on the wrong side of a Third World justice system. At the time of his arrest he was anything but a carefree surf bum; he had fully embraced Nicaraguan culture, and his main pursuit wasn't leisure but publishing a bilingual magazine called *El Puente* (The Bridge), which sought to close the gap between Central and North American cultures. Instead, Volz has become a flashpoint for the tensions between Nicaragua's growing community of relatively wealthy Americans and locals who feel left on the sidelines of prosperity.

The trial left many questions unanswered—such as why anyone would want to harm Jimenez. How a man could be convicted of a murder that allegedly took place while he was on the phone and having lunch two hours away. Was Eric Volz singled out as part of an anti-American backlash—backed, perhaps, by the newly resurgent leftist Sandinista party? Or is the dream of surfing and living in paradise simply untenable? The only certainty is that no gringo in Nicaragua believed in that dream more than Eric Volz, and few have suffered a ruder awakening. "The more politically charged my case becomes, the more nervous I get," he says.

THE ROAD FROM MANAGUA to San Juan del Sur is like a metaphor for life in Nicaragua: lush and beautiful, but uneven and full of surprises. There are sections of fresh pavement where cars can zoom along, but for the most part it's a slow, potholed slalom course requiring serious navigation skills.

Once you reach the end of the road, San Juan del Sur sucks you in. Nestled by a horseshoe-shape bay, with fishing boats on the beach, the friendly and relaxed town of 18,000 is not far from some of the best surfing beaches in southern Nicaragua. There's a magical quality about the place that you just can't put your finger on, something that inspires first-time visitors to start dreaming about dropping out of the rat race.

"I've never once felt unwelcome by the locals; in fact, just the opposite," says Bryan McMandon, who quit his San Francisco job and moved here in 2004 after visiting on a surfing trip. "Everyone has bent over backwards to help me, especially when I first got here and didn't know a lick of Spanish."

Real estate offices line San Juan del Sur's main drag, and you can still find a beachfront lot for $75,000—a bargain compared to Costa Rica, just 20 miles to the south. "The first time we came here we asked Eric about buying property," says Volz's stepfather Dane Anthony.

A little more than 20 years ago, though, San Juan del Sur was a Cold War battlefield. In 1984 U.S. forces planted mines along the coast as part of the Reagan administration's effort to oust Sandinista leader Daniel Ortega—who was recently reelected president.

"It's real touchy, real delicate here," says Jane Mirandette, who founded and runs a local library program. "There are people who don't speak to their neighbor because of what happened in 1980. We have Contras, we have Sandinistas, we have everything in this town. Emotions run really deep, and people's fears run deep too."

Eric Volz first rolled into town on a backpacking trip in 1998. Like most young *norteamericanos*, he'd come for the surfing, but that wasn't the only reason. Despite the tabloid headlines calling him "the gringo murderer," Volz is only half gringo; his mother is Mexican. He spent a semester studying Spanish in Guadalajara and majored in Latin American cultural studies at the University of California-San Diego. "I think Eric always wanted to get in touch with that part of his heritage," says his mother. "And like everything else he does, he poured himself into it."

He moved to San Juan del Sur in early 2005 and took a job in the small but bustling local Century 21 office, earning as much as $100,000 a year selling beachfront lots and townhouse condos in developments that were beginning to dot the pristine coast. He began taking photos for *El Puente*, then a local newsletter, started by an expat named Jon Thompson.

It wasn't long before he met Doris Jimenez, a slender 25-year-old beauty who worked at the Roca Mar restaurant, where Volz usually ate lunch. Her parents had split up when she was young; her mother moved to Managua, and Jimenez was raised in San Juan del Sur by her grandmother and aunt. She was beautiful, with milky brown skin and a dazzling smile. "Everyone really liked her," says Gabriela Sobalvarro, Jimenez's best friend, who calls her a *coqueta*, Spanish for flirt. She was smart, too: According to one friend she was studying business administration at a university campus in Rivas, about 30 minutes away.

There's no such thing as casual dating in Nicaragua, at least for the locals. Couples are either *juntos* (together) or they're not, without much of anything in between. According to Sobalvarro, Volz and Jimenez hit it off, and after a few weeks of being friends the relationship turned romantic. They became *juntos*. "They got along really well," says Thompson, who, with his wife, shared a house with Volz and Jimenez in the latter half of 2005. "Doris was really chill, almost docile."

Once, when Volz went away for a few days, Jimenez decorated the house with balloons and streamers and baked a cake to welcome him back. "The guy was only gone a week," says McMandon, who lived with the couple in 2006.

Volz's mother first met Jimenez on a visit in November 2005. "She was gorgeous, and very sweet," she says. At the time, Volz was helping Jimenez open up a clothing store, called Sol Fashion, in San Juan del Sur, and his mother helped Jimenez design and decorate the space. "There was something about Doris where you almost wanted to take care of her," she says.

Jimenez's friends wondered if Volz returned her affections. "I didn't like him much," claims Sobalvarro. "He was always busy with his work and never had time for Doris. I also think he felt that he was superior to her."

Volz wasn't the type to go out drinking every night with the boys. He had greater ambitions; he was spending more and more time on *El Puente*, which he and Thompson now co-owned. Thompson wanted to keep *El Puente* local and grassroots, while Volz saw it growing into a glossy travel magazine covering sustainable tourism and development in Central America. In early 2006, he wrested control from Thompson in a messy split. "I would call Eric controlling, not just with Doris but in general," says Thompson. "He was very self-assured, very confident. I'd call him arrogant, but he probably thought he had reason to be."

In July 2006 the new (and so far only) issue of *El Puente* magazine was published. That same month Volz moved to Managua, and he and Jimenez broke up. They were separated for about a month, according to friends, but then he began to visit and they would be seen hanging out together. But Volz's main focus was in Managua, where he had an increasingly complex business. On Tuesday afternoon, November 21, 2006, Volz was working in *El Puente*'s Managua office with more than a half dozen others when he says he got the call from Jon Thompson's wife. Doris Jimenez had been murdered.

THE FIRST PERSON to discover the crime was Jimenez's cousin Oscar Blandón, who told the court he went to Sol Fashion around two in the afternoon and found her body in the back room. She had been gagged and strangled, her wrists and ankles tied. Blandón ran to get Gabriela Sobalvarro, who worked down the street. "When I entered the store, it was a mess," she says. "Doris was wrapped up in sheets like a mummy."

Sobalvarro called Volz. "He told me not to let anyone go into the crime scene, including the police, until he got there," she says. It was too late. A crowd had gathered, and at least 20 people traipsed in and out of the store, touching the body and possibly even moving it, before the police arrived about 20 minutes later and finally roped off the scene.

Although Jimenez was found fully clothed, the police removed her jeans and her shirt and took pictures of her. Marks on her body led them to conclude that she'd been raped, vaginally and anally, an explosive claim that soon found its way into print but was never substantiated. Jimenez wasn't known as a drinker, but she had a blood alcohol level of 0.30 percent—three times the DUI limit in most U.S. states. The coroner estimated the time of death between 11 AM and 1:45 PM, right during lunchtime, while people were eating at sidewalk restaurants.

"We didn't see or hear a thing," says Bob Merrill, whose pizza shop is directly across the street. "It just doesn't make any sense to me."

Meanwhile, Volz rented a car in Managua and set out for San Juan del Sur, stopping in Rivas to pick up Jimenez's father Ivan. When they arrived at the scene at around 6 PM there was still a crowd in front of the store, but police had the entrance blocked off. A take-charge sort of person, Volz demanded to be let in. The police refused; when Volz kept asking questions, he says, they turned hostile.

"I know the rules," says Volz. "You're not supposed to get involved here, you're not supposed to get hands-on with a police investigation. But Doris's family wasn't doing anything, the police weren't giving them any answers."

From this point on his actions would be carefully scrutinized. Spying Sobalvarro, he gave her a brief hug. "He was very cold, very unemotional," she says. "He didn't even cry. He asked me if I had eaten, if I was hungry. I thought that was strange."

The next day, Volz says he was in Rivas when a friend called, saying he'd received a threatening text message: "Your girlfriend, is next." Alarmed, Volz, his friend, and the girlfriend went into the police station to report it and spoke to a commissioner of investigations named Emilio Reyes. The meeting quickly turned sour. "You drink a lot, don't you Eric?" Reyes asked, according to Volz. "Do you get violent when you drink? How many times have you hit Doris? Are you a jealous guy? Are you jealous enough to kill someone if they cheated on you?"

Reyes also wondered aloud, "Why don't Americans take showers very often?"

That set Volz off. "I know my rights, and I stood up for them," he says. "I was like, 'I don't like the way you're talking to me. If you're going to accuse me of something, if you're implying something, do it directly. I'll get an attorney if I need to.'" He left in a huff, refusing to sign a statement Reyes had given him.

At Jimenez's funeral on Thursday, Volz helped carry the casket and cried at the grave site. Afterward the police asked him to come back to the station to resume his conversation with Reyes. Volz realized he was in trouble when the police put him in their pickup truck and paraded him slowly through the center of San Juan del Sur, as his friends and acquaintances gaped.

"It was a strategy to immediately build support [against me] and have people start spreading rumors," Volz says now. The police brought him to the Rivas station and charged him with murder. "I was totally shocked," says Volz. "I was not expecting that at all."

The police also charged three other men, including a wealthy student named Armando Llanes, whose father owns a nearby hotel, and who Doris had dated after she and Volz broke up. They also picked up two local hangabouts, Nelson Lopez Dangla, a known drug user, and Martin Chamorro, who had a long-standing crush on Jimenez and who had chided her publicly for dating Americans. Chamorro had scratches on his face, while Lopez had marks all over his body, including his penis. According to the police, the four had allegedly raped and killed her together, led by Volz. In a statement to police, Chamorro alleged that Volz and Llanes had paid him $5,000 to help them do the deed.

It wasn't long before all of the attention settled on Volz, especially, he says, after a local police official told Jimenez's mother that Volz had confessed to the crime (which he hadn't). A few days later the Sandinista paper *El Nuevo Diario* published a front-page story accusing Volz of leading a brutal gang-rape and murder of "this 'sirenita' of San Juan del Sur." The newspaper's version was accepted as gospel.

Jimenez's mother Mercedes Alvarado, 45, appeared often on TV, appearing to sob exaggeratedly—despite the fact that she and Jimenez had been estranged and rarely talked. A volunteer Sandinista organizer, she lives in a small house on a dirt street with a huge picture of President Ortega on the wall. She had met Volz only a few times, but that didn't stop her from relaying lurid tales of his disrespectful treatment of her daughter, from midnight booty calls to supposed beatings. (Jimenez in fact spent most nights at Volz's place when they were together, and roommates say they got along well.) Alvarado organized the truckloads of protesters who were brought in for Volz's preliminary hearing.

"This is my town, and these are my people," she says. "It was a show of solidarity and support from the people. We knew if the judge found him innocent, he would go free."

He ended up in El Chipote, the Sandinistas' notorious underground torture prison in Managua. Clad only in boxers and a tank top, Volz was thrown into a tiny, windowless concrete cell, which he shared with two scorpions and a tarantula. The lights stayed on 24 hours a day, and the dripping moisture bred mosquitoes that feasted on his exposed flesh.

Volz believes Emilio Reyes, commissioner of investigation for the Rivas police—the same man he thinks ordered his arrest and leaked his "confession"—may have sent him there.

MORE AKIN TO A FOURTH-GRADE classroom than a house of law, the Rivas courtroom seats about 25 people, on metal chairs, and testifying witnesses are within arm's length from both the judge and the court reporter. A large, colorful poster tacked on the courtroom door depicts a hand offering money to a faceless judge, with a stop sign in between. According to the U.S. State Department, judicial corruption is rampant in Nicaragua.

On February 14, the first day of his trial, Volz entered the courtroom wearing a brown long-sleeved parka zipped up to his chin that concealed a bulletproof vest. After the mayhem following the preliminary hearing, Volz and the police weren't taking any chances. The police took the further precaution of blocking off the streets around the courthouse.

There was no jury, only the judge, a woman from Rivas named Ivette Toruño Blanco. And the four initial suspects had been whittled down to two: Volz and Chamorro. On the day of the preliminary hearing in December, Llanes had shown up with his father and a lawyer and a paper showing he had been registering for classes on the day of the crime. After a closed-door meeting with the prosecutor he was let go. Charges against Lopez Dangla had also been dropped, and in an unlikely twist, he was now going to testify against Volz.

It appeared at first that Volz might have a fighting chance. The medical examiner and the police testified that there was no physical evidence linking Volz to the killing. None of the 100-plus hair samples matched his. There was no semen found in Jimenez's body, but because she had been embalmed, a full examination was not performed. And the only blood found at the crime scene besides Jimenez's was type O. Volz is type A. Also, Volz had signed credit card receipts for the rental car; the contract was printed at 3:11 PM. The only physical evidence the prosecution presented regarding Volz was photos of scratches on his back. (He claims they were from carrying Jimenez's casket.)

Soon it was clear that this was not going to be an orderly, *Law & Order*-style trial, but more of a theatrical performance. After she finished answering questions, Sobalvarro announced dramatically that Jimenez had confided that Volz had threatened to kill her if she went with another man. Jimenez's mother echoed that statement, adding that Volz's family had offered her $1 million to drop the charges against Volz, a claim Volz's family adamantly denies. At one point during the trial gunshots were fired outside—apparently by police trying to control the crowds—and while the judge retreated to chambers, Alvarado launched an impromptu news conference.

Things became even more bizarre when Lopez Dangla took the stand. According to defense attorney Fabbrith Gomez, he was "visibly incoherent" and "agitated" during his testimony, continually pleading his innocence to the judge even though he was not on trial. Lopez Dangla said he had seen Volz coming out of the victim's store at 1 PM, and that Volz had paid him about $3 to dispose of two black bags he was carrying. He did not mention Llanes. "I may be lazy and a drug user," he said, "but I'm not a liar." (Contacted by *Men's Journal*, Lopez Dangla said he stands by his testimony.)

Volz sat patiently through the testimony, consciously controlling his body language. By U.S. standards he had an airtight defense. Records from cell phone towers showed that he was in Managua at the time of the murder, as did testimony from several witnesses, including Ricardo Castillo, who said he had lunch with Volz that day. Several others had also seen him, but the judge disqualified them because they worked for him.

On Friday, February 16, the third day of the trial, Judge Toruño Blanco reached her decision. In open court she either discounted or dismissed most of the defense's evidence. She discredited the alibi witnesses, claiming they all had business relationships with the defendant, including the journalist Castillo. She dismissed the phone records saying there was no proof that Volz had actually made the calls. (The defense did not call witnesses who could confirm having spoken to Volz on his cell phone.)

She instead chose to accept Lopez Dangla's testimony, despite the fact that he was incoherent on the stand and had everything to gain by testifying against Volz. The scratches on Volz's shoulder constituted further proof that he had committed the crime, she said; no mention was made of Lopez Dangla's numerous scratches. "Nelson Dangla and [another witness] have all the credibility necessary," she asserted. She found Volz and Chamorro both guilty.

Volz stood blinking in disbelief. "Once I heard the initial part of the verdict, I stopped paying attention," says Volz. "I immediately started preparing for what was next. It was back to survival mode, focusing all my energy on staying alive."

Following his conviction Volz was sent to the El Modelo maximum-security facility. After fighting with his first roommate, he was paired with a 35-year-old man convicted of attempting to murder his wife. "He keeps the place clean, he respects personal space, he doesn't use drugs, and he's not gay," says Volz. "It's a good situation."

His parents have hired someone to bring him fresh vegetables and water to supplement the single plate of rice and beans he's allotted each day. Once a week he gets two hours in the yard; he spends the whole time running. He does yoga stretches in the morning and uses meditation and visualization to try to keep himself centered. "I don't really have time to spend with the other prisoners," he says. "Prison is a time to self-explore and really try to make sense of it all."

Volz isn't the only one trying to make sense of things. His mother and stepfather Dane Anthony have launched a media campaign on his behalf, beginning with a website, friendsofericvolz .com, that's regularly updated with news about his case, and lists of things that visitors can pray for if they choose.

The U.S. embassy is tight-lipped, but the embassy monitors his treatment in prison, and legal observers attended his trial. Volz's lawyers have appealed the conviction, in the hope that—barring further lynch-mob shenanigans—cooler heads will prevail. (Chamorro has also appealed.) "I don't think [the conviction] was politically motivated," says Castillo. "This type of thing happens to a lot of Nicaraguans, and it's really a problem. It needs to change."

Then again, cooler heads might not prevail. The media campaign has stirred up a backlash in San Juan del Sur; one American journalist had his tires slashed, and a photographer was threatened—by an expat. Local opinion seems to have solidified against Volz. A recent headline in *El Nuevo Diario* condemned "Pure Lies From the Volz Family." "I'd say about 85 percent of the Nicaraguans here think Eric Volz is guilty," says one San Juan del Sur native. "Maybe more."

To their minds, everything adds up. Volz and Jimenez had split, she was seeing someone else, and he was jealous. He also was said to show no emotion at the murder scene, which struck people as suspicious. He asked too many questions, acted too bossy, and dared to tangle with the cops, which any Nicaraguan knows is tempting fate. Something was up. And, finally, the judge found him guilty. "Justice was served," says Jimenez's mother.

In the short run some Nicaraguans might see the case as a victory against the rich Americans who are buying up the country, one quarter-acre beachfront lot at a time. "The locals are starting to realize how much money the gringos are making in Nicaragua," says one expat. "I don't think they really knew before. Maybe there is some animosity when a gringo buys land for $20K from a local and turns around and sells it for $50K to another gringo. The local made $20K for land they've owned their whole life and the gringo made $30K in five minutes. This has happened plenty, and I'm sure the locals have felt ripped off as a result."

"I think locals are starting to realize that they're getting left behind," Volz agrees. "There's been more crimes and other things that seem related to the social inequity. I think there's an underlying tone to the whole real estate boom, and me being a member of that community working for Century 21. They just chose to see this so-called privileged, moneyed real estate guy."

Volz is annoyed that fellow expats are keeping quiet about his case; he thinks they're afraid to spoil their budding boomtown, which local real estate websites liken to Cancun in the '60s. There are miles of unspoiled coastline waiting to be snapped up. One day there will be highways and condos, and the pristine kilometer-long beach that's listed for $2 million will seem like an incredible bargain. Or so they hope.

DEAN LATOURRETTE *is a freelance writer living, working, and surfing in San Francisco. He has written for* Men's Journal, San Francisco *magazine,* Sunset, *and* The Surfer's Journal, *among others. He is coauthor of* Time Off! The Upside to Downtime *and* Time Off! The Leisure Guide to San Francisco, *and considers himself a leisure connoisseur.*

Coda

Unlike most real-life crime stories, "A Season in Hell" actually has a happy ending. On December 21, 2007, after spending a harrowing year in a Nicaraguan prison for the reputed rape and murder of his ex-girlfriend, Eric Volz was released—his case having been overturned by a Nicaraguan appeals court. Thirteen months after Volz's nightmare first began, he enjoyed Christmas dinner in the United States with his family.

Volz phoned me out of the blue, about a month after his release. He would not divulge his location—he was still in hiding, fearing repercussions due to his release (a substantial portion of the Nicaraguan people still believe he's guilty). It was only the second time I had ever spoken to him, the first being within the walls of La Modelo maximum-security prison in Tipitapa, Nicaragua, in

March 2007. It was hard to believe the voice I heard on the other end of the phone belonged to the same individual I had interviewed in prison, when hope for a just outcome in his case was running thin. If speaking to him was surreal for me, I could only imagine how the implausible events of the prior year must have felt to him.

The absurdity surrounding the Volz case is difficult to describe. When I first learned about the story, I was convinced that there had to be more to the investigation than was first reported—that Volz somehow *was* guilty—and I set off for Nicaragua determined to dig up a smoking gun. That all changed, however, on my first day there, sitting in the courthouse, poring through the case files. What I found was shocking, as much for its incompetence as for its injustice. By U.S. legal standards, it was a slam dunk: The case should have been thrown out before it ever went to trial (in actuality it *was* originally thrown out, by a judge who was later "dismissed" from the case). But this wasn't the U.S. legal system; it was a relatively callow and unsophisticated Nicaraguan system finding its way. And this wasn't just any crime: it was the supposed rape and murder of a beautiful, innocent Nicaraguan woman, presumably by a rich and successful "gringo." In many ways it served as a metaphor for U.S.–Latin American relations over the past two hundred years, and Nicaraguans were not about to take things lying down. Did anti-American sentiment play a significant role in the trial? Absolutely. But so too did primitive police work, botched legal processes, and small-town justice.

In the end, despite the stirred up anti-Americanism and strained U.S.-Nicaragua relations; despite a bungled investigation, irresponsible media reporting, and a trial gone awry, some very brave Nicaraguans ultimately risked their reputations, their careers, perhaps even their lives—to step up and fight for justice.

And that's something Nicaragua should be proud of.

Justin Heckert

I'M WITH THE STEELERS

FROM *ESPN: The Magazine*

SHE COULD TELL. But she couldn't bring herself to believe it, even though the pictures she examined led to very simple observations: that the man in the photo had a head that wasn't as square, for instance, and a nose that was longer and not bowed slightly to the right. And that his neck was stout but his jaw too strong. And she noticed that the face wasn't framed by an almost horizontal hairline, like the one on the man she knew, the hair thinning and brown instead of a black flattop, thick and gelled back. This is what she thought, at first, that something was off, until he explained that pictures lie. Until he said the photographs of Steelers tight end Jerame Tuman that she found online were taken several years ago, when he arrived at training camp as a rookie with the features of a young man. Weathering those seasons had changed him, he said, and he was insulted, even a bit embarrassed, that she doubted him.

Kristin* didn't have much to go on but the pictures. The Jerame

---

* *The victims' names have been changed to protect their identities.*

Tuman she knew had a rounded stomach that fell below his waist, and arms and legs that weren't trim. But he was tall, so she slowly convinced herself that if he said he was an NFL tight end, then this is what an NFL tight end must look like. He had shown her a cell phone full of numbers, after all—Jerome Bettis, Hines Ward, Ike Taylor—and bragged about "his boys."

In the beginning, Kristin actually got a thrill from hanging out with him in the leather passenger seat of his white Denali, looking out the tinted windows as he navigated the nighttime traffic on the south side of the city, feeling the rap thrum from his extravagant speakers as he bounced in the driver's seat while speeding through red lights, saying, "Nobody in Pittsburgh is gonna arrest me, I'm a Steeler"—because, well, she was with a Steeler. And when he began to phone her twice a day to wish her good morning or to talk about the upcoming divorce from his wife, Molly, or the custody battle over his son, or to recount the sad story about his mother and his sickly uncle who raised him, she believed. And when he explained that he was changing his cell number every couple of weeks because he was "tired of dating this other girl on the side who only likes me for what I am, not who I am," she believed then, too. Because she thought he was confiding in her, because he was one of her best friends, and because he was sweet. He once called a 7-year-old family friend to wish him a happy birthday; "How's my little buddy doing?" he asked. He couldn't wait to show her his Super Bowl ring, and promised her season tickets, neither of which he followed through on. And she trusted him because while he was at times vapid, he wasn't above revealing weakness. He once rang her at 4 a.m. to say, "I'm not married anymore. I'm 30. What am I doing with myself?"

Kristin was a good and interested friend; she often bought him lunch and made him dinner, though he always canceled and gave her excuses about being held up by appointments. She overlooked it when he invited her and her girlfriends out on the town, saying he and Hines would take care of the bill, but never showed. She gave him keys to her apartment, though he didn't let her see his. When he told her he didn't have time to go to the mall to buy a new pair of shoes, she went for him and picked out a pair with a metallic silver swoosh on the side. And when he told her he lost his wallet, she lent him money. In fact, when he needed help paying rent for his "place on the waterfront," she obliged, believing him when he said his bank accounts had been frozen in the divorce. When he needed quick cash to go on a trip with some teammates, she asked no questions. And when he told her he wanted rims for his SUV but couldn't use his credit card because he was about to start paying alimony, she covered him then, too. Over four months in 2006, she loaned him $3,200. And with each loan, he told her not to ask if he was good for the money, reminding her that he could get anyone else to help him if he wanted.

It is because of her generosity that Kristin has been blamed for being gullible, stupid, an outright imbecile even, in a very public way, in a town where you're not part of the conversation if you don't love the Steelers. And though it is easy to stare at the same photos and wonder what she was thinking, it's also impossible to blame her—he was that good. It wasn't until after he had, in Kristin's words, "fallen off the face of the earth" for a month and a half that she got pissed and sent a Hallmark card to the Steelers' training facility, addressed to Tuman, asking for her money back as soon as possible; she'd given him her savings and was living paycheck to paycheck. Then, one day last August, Kristin, a tall, pretty woman with long, blond hair who majored in communications and anthropology at the University of Pittsburgh, was riding the bus home from work when she got a call from Steelers security director Jack Kearney. "I hate to break it to you," Kearney told her flatly. "But you've never met Jerame Tuman in your life."

Consider her surprise. Or humiliation. Consider her anger, if nothing else. If you don't live in Pittsburgh, the city at the confluence of steel-black rivers, a town that embodies its football team, you might empathize with Kristin. If you don't live where flags fly black and gold and the awnings of half the buildings bear the same industrial colors, where gift shops are stocked with candy and soda and Steelers commemorative hats, banners, shirts, baby clothes and not much else, you can probably understand, even as you find it hard to fathom. But if you're from Pittsburgh, there's a good chance you're aware that Kristin was one of three women over two years who were fooled by a man named Brian Jackson, a 32-year-old former car salesman who moonlighted as Steelers tight end Jerame Tuman, third-string quarterback Brian St. Pierre, and most curiously, Ben Roethlisberger. And you might deride Kristin, and have a good laugh over a cold Iron City at her expense. Even if you didn't know what Tuman looked like, you'd at least have been able to see that Jackson looked nothing like a football player. Pretty much, you'd have been smarter than she was.

"The Steelers are next to God here, so I don't see how someone impersonating one of them got away with it," says Anne Madarasz, director of the Western Pennsylvania Sports Museum.

"Oh god, the women were that gullible?" says a woman browsing Steelers towels at Mike Feinberg Co. store, "The Official Home of Steeler Nation."

"Everyone thinks it's funny," says Mike Katic, a bartender at the Buckhead Saloon at Station Square. "I guess as long as the guy had the build of a football player . . ."

It wasn't so funny for Tara,★ a 24-year-old part-time model who thought she'd met Ben Roethlisberger at a local pizza shop. Two years ago, a big guy wearing a backward Steelers hat and khaki shorts had strolled up to the table where she and a friend were sitting and announced confidently that he thought she "was hot," before explaining how famous he was and which famous friends he wanted her to meet. Tara and her friend ogled him over their slices, considering whether he was big or athletic enough to be a quarterback.

Though she didn't know it that day in July 2005, the guy she was staring at was really a middle-class man born and raised in Pittsburgh; a man who, Allegheny County courthouse records reveal, has a litany of traffic incidents, including one involving vehicular homicide, and who now has a July court date to face felony charges of identity theft and theft by deception for impersonating Tuman, and for stealing money from Kristin in the process.

Two days after Tara met him, she spent a few very awkward, if memorable, hours on a date with "Big Ben"; hours she'd like to undo. Their activities included traveling to the Steelers' training facility, where the security guard who never stops anyone waved at the faux quarterback, letting him through to attend to "some business" while Tara sat in the car; signing a Steelers jersey for Tara's giddy neighbor and posing for a photo; telling her about his dog, Zeus, over a dinner *she ended up paying for* because he left his wallet somewhere; and an uncomfortable encounter in which he tried to touch her hand and lean in for a kiss, which freaked her out, because she wasn't attracted to him anyway.

Whispering recently from her bedroom because she's afraid her fiancé might hear, Tara says Jackson talked so much about himself as Roethlisberger that she barely got a word in. "He said he just got back from Miami, talked about his cars, about other players," she says. "He should be in prison, or in a mental hospital. I was leery, but hell, I didn't know. I didn't think he was telling the truth, but my friend thought I should give him a chance."

The day after the date, Tara's neighbor showed her a newspaper photo of Roethlisberger, and she quickly alerted the police and told Jackson never to call her again. But he persisted, demanding she return his calls and insisting on more dates. He had his friends call her, pretending to be Roethlisberger's friend or sister, to say Tara was breaking his heart. He sent her a signed football, which she has since "destroyed." Soon the story was out and she was the laughingstock of talk radio. "It was one of the worst parts of my life, and it wasn't even a full day," she says. "Being portrayed as an idiot, it was awful." Her neighbor asked the team for a replacement Roethlisberger jersey. He never got it.

"When I heard about it, I laughed," says the real Big Ben. "It was kind of flattering. Then again, feelings were hurt and that isn't funny. But I hear all the time that 'someone at a bar is trying to be you.' It's because all people talk about in Pittsburgh is the Steelers. Me, I don't really care. But it made Jerame uneasy. He's happily married with a family."

IT IS FAIR to say Brian Jackson thrived on the attention; that his escapades were born not only of malicious conjuring, but of his fantasy. He *was* Jerame Tuman when he wore his black-and-gold hat askew, sometimes pulled down to mask his eyes, and he *was* Ben Roethlisberger in his T-shirts and thick-legged sweats, and the official pair of football gloves he wore, sometimes while he drove, as though he'd just come from a long and successful practice. It is not supposition to say he felt comfortable when he dressed and acted the way he did, because his clothes and actions weren't part of a costume. His dreams had become his waking life. He *was* part of the team. It's what made him so convincing. He believed it was all real.

"He put almost incomprehensible thought into what he was doing," says prosecuting attorney Debra Barnisin-Lange. "He had an answer for any question that may have come up from the women. This type of scam is very embarrassing for the victims; several other women he did this to haven't come forward. It's the way all cons run. He said he was a Steeler, but in another instance someone might say, 'I won the lottery,' but they don't have a bank account to cash their check. Once you're in for a penny, you're in for a pound."

According to courthouse officials, he knew more than enough

about the Steelers to work a room with tales of the team. Those familiar with the case say he had an encyclopedic, nearly obsessive knowledge of the men he said he was: he knew where they were born, where they went to school, what they drove, the names of parents and wives and children and pets. And he could recall a player's TV highlights as if living inside the moments of another man's life. He regarded a woman he was trying to impress the same way an athlete might regard a trophy. According to the women, he was funny, at times charming and caring. He trolled the strip downtown near the practice facility on weekends in his Denali or black Impala or blue Mustang, and ate lunch at Nakama, the sushi place frequented by Steelers during the season.

Jackson put himself amid the passing drunks in Steelers jerseys and among the women who packed the sidewalks by Primanti Bros. and Cottage Jewelry and Sunny's Fashions, with the clothing racks out front and the black-and-gold Pittsburgh City Paper boxes at their waists. There were always more than enough fans around eager to celebrate in his presence. In the murk of a rowdy night, his sort-of-familiar face and confident stories—*Yeah, I'm waiting for Hines, he should be here any minute*—were truth enough.

"This city lives, eats, breathes Steelers," says detective Frances LaQuatra, a season ticket-holder. "They are always the news. The radio people get sick of talking about them all day, 12 months of the year. Working this case, I realized that when people hear something about the Steelers, they think, Why would someone lie about them?"

He was Brian St. Pierre. And he wooed Annie★ with stories about teammates and autographed footballs for kids in her neighborhood. When he suggested she look for him on the sideline, during a game, on TV, she took him up on the offer. But when the camera showed the real St. Pierre, their relationship took a sudden turn. After the game, she called him out as a liar and he called her "crazy" and, according to court documents, said she'd "be sorry" if she pressed charges. He even impersonated Roethlisberger in a phone call not long after, in which he vouched for himself as St. Pierre. Then he followed her home in different cars and materialized wherever she went, which, frankly, scared her to death. That was at the end of 2004, and she still won't speak of him. "She's moved on. I don't want her to relive it," says Annie's boyfriend. "She doesn't want to either."

Jackson didn't harass Kristin the way he did Annie or bother her the way he did Tara. No, one day he just went away. He stopped calling Kristin to say good morning or to ask for advice. He stopped picking her up at work so she could buy him fish sandwiches. When he changed cell phones, his old number was the last trace of a man who never existed.

She saved that number, and now it reminds her of that night in March 2006 when she was partying like everyone else on the south side and, after a few cocktails, had picked up her girlfriend's cell. She was interested and curious and—football fan's curse—attracted even though she'd never seen him. Like it would be with a lot of people, she says, her desire to talk to him took control. She wanted to find out what he might say, because, "Who doesn't want to talk to a Steeler?" She left him a message that went something like, "So, what's up? My girl tells me you're a Steeler, so . . ."

But Kristin isn't stupid. Maybe just a little naïve.

Is IT HIM? Well, yes, of course it's him, in a baggy gray hoodie and jeans that fall off his behind. He's been watching out the window of his redbrick house, the one with the unattached trailer in the front yard. He grudgingly opens the glass screen of his front door to greet the unwelcome company, and nearly slips when he steps on the porch.

He doesn't look so threatening as he clings awkwardly to the door frame. He looks like he hasn't slept, though, just as he looked when he turned himself in to Detective LaQuatra last year after Kristin came forward and his gig was up. He groveled to LaQuatra that day: "I can't help myself, I really can't." And he doesn't sound so cocksure now, as he didn't when he called Kristin right before she pressed charges, to offer this rambling admission: "I just idolize these guys and what they do, and the attention they get from women, and I just want that for myself, and I don't think I can do it on my own and I just want to be them."

On this February morning, Brian Jackson just looks angry or nervous or both, like a man about to face felony charges who doesn't want to be bothered. As the sun hits his face, he stares off to the side, eyes bloodshot-red like kindling.

Are you Brian Jackson?

"No. I'm his brother," he says.

Well, is your brother home, then?

"No."

Do you think he'd want to talk about. . .

"No, he wouldn't."

He's tall, all right, his head is square, his body sturdy. His voice is as heavy as lead, and standing in front of him, it is not only conceivable he could pass for a Steeler, but understandable, especially in a town that sanctifies the men who wear that uniform but are often unrecognizable without it.

This morning, the Denali with tinted windows is docked in the drive, without the rims. Taking a step back, Jackson shuts the screen door. He's not wearing his Steelers hat. But he does have on a nice pair of sneakers, with a metallic swoosh on the side.

JUSTIN HECKERT *is a native of Cape Girardeau, Missouri, and now lives in Atlanta. He is a contributing writer for* ESPN: The Magazine.

After graduating from the University of Missouri School of Journalism, he was a staff writer at Atlanta magazine for two years, where his narrative work was awarded the City and Regional Magazine Association's gold medal for Writer of the Year in 2005 and its silver medal in 2006. He has also written for Esquire, the Oxford American, the Los Angeles Times, the Washington Post, Vox magazine, the Columbia Missourian, and the Southeast Missourian.

Coda

He swindled other women, too. No one knows how many, but the number is probably a lot more than three. Though Kristin, Tara, and Annie all came forward and shared their stories about Brian Jackson with the Pittsburgh police, officials at the Allegheny County Courthouse postulated there were maybe a dozen more women who had been afraid to speak out, even when encouraged to. Not because they were afraid of his physically imposing presence, or his anger, or the thought of vengeance—but because they were much more scared of what something like this, in a relatively small city that thrives off its football team no matter the season, would do to their reputations. The Steelers wouldn't touch this story. Their PR people, the security director, the players, their agents—nearly all of my calls and requests went unanswered, no matter my vigilance. It was a coup to even get Ben Roethlisberger on the phone, finally, two days before the story was put to press. (When he did talk, he was lighthearted and seemed unbothered when reflecting about all of this trouble.) I walked around Pittsburgh, and drove across its bridges, and passed the empty stadiums, heading into the hills in the ice and cold to ask people if they knew about this. Nearly everyone remembered something about him, or had heard about him, or the women, or had some vague recollection of the guy who had pretended to be a Steeler. No one remembered his name. It was an important topic on local radio stations, but for the most part the hosts just mocked the women, ran bits about how stupid they were, and the sentiment from more than a few Steelers fans was that they deserved what they got, because they were "gold-digging" anyway. Kristin even sent me a recording of one station that (though they didn't have her name) was merciless in its excoriation of her. The women who did agree to speak with me—none of them had spoken on the record before, and getting to them involved a great deal of groundwork—provided invaluable insight into Jackson, and though none of them had ever spoken to each other, they all had pretty much the same things to say, despite the different experiences they had hanging out with him. While I doubt these women are perfect angels, I also know they're not the money-grubbing, gold-digging harlots the local radio made them out to be. I literally staked out Jackson's house to try and speak with him. His lawyers asked him, but he didn't want to talk. Every day in the morning I'd drive to Brentwood and sit for a few minutes by his driveway; I'd come back at lunch; then at night; and then I'd go again, to ask his neighbors if he still lived there and what times he might be home. I was always looking for the white Denali. It was only the last morning I was in town that I saw it there, finally. (Though he didn't speak to me when I approached his door, he had his lawyers call me just as the story was going to bed and we were able to print part of his confession in the magazine.) In August of last year, Jackson was sentenced to ninety days in prison and five years probation after pleading guilty to impersonating Tuman and taking $3,200 from Kristin. He gave back all the money he owed her, writing a $1,950 check and paying the rest in cash. He seemed very sorry for what he had done, as though it really had ruined his life. I have wondered if he'll do it again, though; if we'll be seeing another blurb in the paper, or on one of the news websites, like the one that originally sparked an interest in me to embark on this story. I've wondered if that old feeling, whatever's inside him, will rear itself, and if he'll put the gloves or jersey on and take the Denali out of the driveway and head back to the strip on the South Side of the city one night, and what might happen if he does. I asked Kristin what she thought about that. "I don't know. I think it's over," she said. "I've moved beyond it. Although, training camp has started here. You never really know."

Calvin Trillin

THE HOUSE ACROSS THE WAY

FROM *The New Yorker*

THE RESIDENTS OF CEDAR STREET, a thinly settled road on
the island of Grand Manan, would not have considered Ronnie
Ross an ideal neighbor even if they hadn't believed that he was
running a crack house. Ross was a slim, sporadically belligerent
man in his early forties who had grown up in Nova Scotia and
had worked from time to time on Grand Manan lobster boats. He
was a devotee of loud music and powerful speakers—both sometimes left on, the neighbors had come to believe, even if nobody
happened to be home. He often seemed high on something. Carter
Foster, a burly young fisherman who lived across the road with
his girlfriend, Sara Wormell, has recalled that one of the first conversations he had with Ross—about two years ago, a few months
after Ross moved into 61 Cedar—began with Ross stating that he
could see people up in the trees behind his house. Erin Gaskill,
who lived with her two small children in the house next to
Ross's, once saw Ross take a two-by-four and smash all the windows of a car parked in his driveway—a car that apparently belonged to his girlfriend. The people who congregated at Ross's

were a rowdy lot. The neighborhood children were so reluctant to walk past the house that the school-bus stop was moved so they wouldn't have to. Laura Buckley, the proprietor of the Inn at Whale Cove Cottages, who is known on the island for tart speech, recently summed up Ronnie Ross this way: "He had asshole issues that were much larger than just being a drug dealer."

The calm assumption that some people are just drug dealers is a phenomenon of recent decades on Grand Manan, which lies off the southeast coast of New Brunswick, in the Bay of Fundy. There are older people who remember the days when someone who wanted nothing more than a bottle of beer was faced with a trip to the mainland on the ferry, which runs to Blacks Harbour, New Brunswick, twenty miles away. Grand Manan always had more than its share of churches that take a stern view of drinking and carrying on. Whenever the question of opening a liquor store on Grand Manan was being debated in the provincial capital, an islander in his sixties said recently, so many stalwart Christians were so eager to testify in the negative that casual travellers to the mainland couldn't find space on the ferry. On the other hand, he added, there have always been a lot of people who believe that "the good Lord can't see you once you get past Blacks Harbour."

Although the needs of whale watchers and birders and people with vacation cottages provide some employment in the summer, most people on Grand Manan make their living from the sea, in jobs whose rigors and dangers predispose them to a robust celebration of, say, the arrival of Saturday night. From November through June, Grand Mananers haul lobster traps out of the frigid waters of the Bay of Fundy. Starting in the spring, some of them, including Carter Foster, tend weirs—towering herring traps that look like Richard Serra sculptures made of telephone poles and netting. Some drag for scallops or sea urchins. Some work as divers, maintaining the nets used in salmon farms or weirs. Some "wrinkle"—gather periwinkles from the rocks at low tide—or collect and dry dulse, a seaweed that is edible, or at least considered so in the Canadian Maritimes.

Grand Manan experienced a boom in the nineties, but in recent years there have been some economic reversals. The aquaculture industry, which had disease problems, has greatly shrunk. Two years ago, a large sardine factory closed down. A federal program to buy fishing licenses and turn them over to Indian tribes eventually drove the cost of a boat and a lobster license so high that young islanders found it difficult to enter the field as proprietors. Still, someone just out of high school can make a considerable amount of money in the fisheries if he's willing to work hard. There is not much to spend it on. Grand Manan is seventeen miles long. Since virtually nobody lives on what residents call the back of the island—the imposing cliffs whose shade helps produce high-quality dulse—just about all the houses and businesses are close to the one main road, officially New Brunswick Route 776, which runs from North Head through Grand Harbour to Seal Cove. Given the wait for the ferry and the drive on the mainland to St. John, New Brunswick's largest city, it's a three-hour trip to the bright lights. Activities for young people who aren't interested in church functions have always been in short supply on Grand Manan and so have drug-prevention programs. In the view of the Regional Crown Prosecutor, James McAvity, who is based in St. John, Grand Manan has almost laboratory conditions for a serious drug problem.

In the late sixties, a liquor store finally came to the island, and it wasn't long before liquor was supplanted by marijuana and hashish, as it was in small communities all over the Maritimes. Grand Mananers who came of age in that period are likely to be undisturbed by the sight of a fisherman lighting up a joint. That tolerance wavers around cocaine and tends not to extend to crack. People said they'd heard that Ronnie Ross was not simply selling crack but selling it to schoolchildren, and they wondered why he was never arrested. Law enforcement on Grand Manan is in the hands of a four-officer detachment of the Royal Canadian

Mounted Police. The Mountie who concentrated on drug enforcement had spent hours watching Ross's place from Carter
Foster's or Erin Gaskill's. A search warrant to go through Ross's
premises was executed, but the evidence required for a charge
wasn't found. One community activist thought of organizing a
sort of mothers' vigil in front of 61 Cedar to monitor the comings
and goings, until she heard that Ross kept some particularly nasty
dogs. Someone posted a sign, quickly torn down, warning people
who turned off Route 776 onto Cedar Street that they were about
to drive down a block that held a crack house. As time went on,
Ross seemed to grow more brazen. "People on the wrong side of
the law usually keep a low profile," a councillor in the Grand
Manan village government said recently, in discussing Ronnie
Ross. "He made himself out to be this big-time gangster."

The big-time-gangster image was fed by having plenty of visitors from the mainland. Grand Mananers are not as wary of people from away as they might have been in the days when just
about everyone on the island seemed to belong to one of the
families that had been there for generations. In recent years, there
has been turnover in the population. Some young people, like a
lot of other young people from Atlantic Canada, have moved to
British Columbia, which has an appealing climate, or to Alberta,
which has an appealing wages. (Carter Foster and Sara Wormell,
who are in their twenties, had been thinking about a move to
British Columbia themselves.) Some Newfoundlanders who came
to work in the sardine factory or the salmon farms have remained.
But the mainland still represents dangers that don't exist on an
island of twenty-five hundred people. Stolen goods, which would
be recognized in a community as small as Grand Manan, can easily
be fenced on the mainland, for instance, and last summer more
people reported missing property—especially power tools. It was
rumored that the stolen goods were being taken by Ronnie Ross's
crowd, or being accepted by Ross as payment for drugs. One of
Ross's regular visitors, Terry Irvine, a young man from St. John,

drove a G.M.C. Jimmy, and some people on Grand Manan began to see the Jimmy as a way of carrying stolen goods off the island and bringing drugs on. The stealing seems to have caused at least as much anger on Grand Manan as any drug dealing. "That's where it changed, I guess," Carter Foster later told the R.C.M.P. "When stuff started getting stolen." On the first weekend of July last year—the long Canada Day weekend, which is roughly equivalent to the Fourth of July—Irvine's G.M.C. Jimmy, parked in Ronnie Ross's driveway, was destroyed by fire.

ROSS ACCUSED CARTER FOSTER, AMONG OTHERS, OF HAVING burned Irvine's S.U.V. Foster pointed out that he hadn't even been on the island at the time of the fire. That assertion had no effect on Ross, who told Foster and Sarah Wormell that they had better sleep with their eyes open, because "a flaming ball of fire is going to come through your window." That evening, Ross piled some wooden palettes in his front yard, right next to the street, put a couple of propane tanks on top of the pile, started a fire, and, according to Foster, said that he was going to blow up the entire neighborhood. The R.C.M.P. constables who put the fire out were told by Ross that people at a community meeting had decided to burn his house down. During the next few weeks, various accusations were exchanged, including a claim by Ross that, even before the car fire, someone had thrown a propane tank through his living-room window. R.C.M.P. Constable Gerald Bigger had what sounds like a rather typical confrontation, in which Ross went from obscene gestures and obscene language to picking up a large rock and saying, according to the constable's report:

"I ought to drive this through you." I pulled my side arm from my holster, placed it by my side and told him if he raised the rock in my direction he'd be shot. Ronald threw the rock down. He continued to yell, call names and swear. Then, as quick as it started it was over. Ronald

jumped across the ditch, said he didn't like to be called a loser or laughed at. I told him that I didn't like to be called names. He said he only called me the names because he thought that I didn't like him. Ronald also accused me of conspiring with the community to burn him out. I told him that I wasn't part of any conspiracy and that I wasn't aware of any community meeting to burn him out. Before leaving, Ronald shook my hand and invited [me] to drop by his place anytime for a drink.

A lot of rumors went around the island, many of them about who might arrive from the mainland and what they intended to do to avenge the burning of Irvine's S.U.V. On Grand Manan, some rumor enhancement is taken for granted. It has always been said that if hailstones the size of mothballs start to fall in North Head they're the size of icebergs by the time the story reaches Seal Cove. Some of the rumors, though, were disturbingly specific. Larry Marshall, a wrinkler and dulse-gatherer, heard that Ross was importing people from the mainland to burn eight or ten houses, with Carter Foster's house at the top of the hit list. Marshall's brother, Harold, whom he customarily describes as "a bag of trouble with a capital 'T,'" hung around with Ross. The two of them, Larry Marshall told Foster, were "planning to have people come from away with dynamite and machine guns." A volunteer fireman later told the R.C.M.P., "I heard . . . that Ronnie Ross had some of his friends come down, supposedly from the Hell's Angels." It was said that on July 21st, a Friday, ten thugs were going to be arriving from St. John in an S.U.V., presumably the vehicle that would take them around to the houses on their hit list. The estimate quickly grew to twenty.

Not long after midnight on that Friday night, Constable Bigger stopped by Carter Foster's house. By that time, there were thirty or forty men in Foster's yard. A number of them were, in Foster's words, people "who'd had something stolen and knew where it went." Some were people who had come from a baseball game and were still in their uniforms. Some were older men who were saying that Carter Foster and his neighbors oughtn't to put up with Ronnie Ross. Constable Bigger informed Foster that the rumor about twenty hoodlums arriving from the mainland wasn't true. Irvine's new vehicle, a white G.M.C. Yukon, had been stopped by the R.C.M.P. when it left the ferry and had turned out to contain only three men and no weapons. Foster told Bigger that he had, in fact, spotted the three men at Ross's. According to the constable's report, Foster said that if the crowd at 61 Cedar started something, he and his friends were going to finish it. Sara Wormell, a polite young woman who likes to take photographs and keep journals, had put her dog and some family papers and favorite photographs in her car. "I thought for sure our house was going to be burnt down," she later said.

The talk on both sides of houses being burned down would have come as no surprise to one summer resident—Marc Shell, the Irving Babbitt Professor of Comparative Literature at Harvard, who recently completed research for a book called "Grand Manan; or, a Short History of North America." Shell concluded that on Grand Manan, which has always been lightly policed by officers sent from the mainland, "unpopular groups are often driven off island by fire" and "sometimes the only form of law enforcement is illegal police-enforced banishment." As far back as 1839, for instance, the Episcopal church was destroyed by fire, and any question about whether the blaze had been started by what a church statement called "a sacrilegious incendiary" was settled by a note at the scene containing, according to the same statement, "language which betokens premeditated malevolence and hostility against the Bishop of the Diocese, against the Rector of this Parish in particular, and four other persons of this County." All of the men brought to trial for the arson were acquitted.

"THE IDEA WAS to put the fear of God in 'em, get 'em on the boat, and get 'em the hell off the island," a lifelong Grand Mananer said recently. "But it got out of hand." On Friday the twenty-first,

Erin Gaskill was told that she might want to have her children sleep over at their grandmother's that evening. According to later court testimony, there had been hints, or perhaps more than hints, from the R.C.M.P. that calls involving Ronnie Ross would not draw a swift response. For a while, the people in Foster's yard seemed less like a group of aroused citizens than like a bunch of men attending a barbecue. Accounts of what happened when the trouble started are imprecise. It was dark. People on both sides of Cedar Street had been drinking. It's clear that the sides were not evenly matched—there were fewer than a dozen people at Ross's—and were not cleanly divided between outsiders and islanders. Some of the people at Ross's house were from Grand Manan and a few of the people on Carter Foster's side of the street may at times have tempered their outrage at drug dealers with a few purchases of their own. It's clear that at one point some of the men on Foster's side were carrying bats, and at least one of Ross's crew had a knife taped to a pole. Shortly after midnight, Carter Foster and several companions moved into Cedar Street to confront the men who had come out of Ross's house. "You're going to fucking get off the island!" Foster shouted at Ross. He and Ross began to fight. Foster, who was winning, had Ross in a choke hold when the shooting started.

The shots seemed to be coming from Ross's house. Foster let go of Ross, went back to his own house, and got his rifle—a high-powered sniper model that he is licensed to use on seals that get into the herring weirs. He climbed onto the roof and started shooting at the white Yukon parked in Ross's driveway. He fired at least once at Ross's porch light. "People in my group were saying, 'Shoot the shooter,'" Foster later told the R.C.M.P. "I can't do that. I couldn't even put a person in my sights. . . . So I proceeded to shoot the vehicle to disable it for our own protection, so they wouldn't take off and get out of there. And, at the same time this was all going off, some people on our side had rocket flares, pistol flares, different things like that." The exchange of gunfire went on for five or ten minutes. Remarkably, no one was hit by a bullet, although Ross was struck in the leg by a flare. By the time the three available R.C.M.P. officers arrived, the shooting had stopped and no one was in the street. Later, though, fights broke out that the Mounties seemed powerless to stop. Both Ross and Irvine were beaten up. At some point, a couple of young men from Foster's side of the street circled around behind Ross's house, poured out some fuel, and tossed in a match. Flames shot out the back wall, and the people inside the house rushed out the front door.

When the Grand Manan volunteer fire company arrived, the firefighters figured that they might have to reserve one of their hoses to protect themselves, since they could hear shouts of "Let it burn!" and "Off the island!" Rocks were falling near the fire-fighting equipment. Eventually, the firefighters were satisfied that the blaze was out and they returned to the fire hall. Ross and some of his friends were escorted away by the R.C.M.P., leaving the house empty. Then, at four-thirty or five in the morning, there were explosions inside the house and it burst into flames. When the firefighters arrived this time, they encountered a pickup truck parked across Cedar Street to bar their entry. After that had been cleared away, the fire trucks were blocked by half a dozen people, including Sara Wormell, linking hands across the road. Sooner or later, the firemen were allowed through, but it was too late. Ronnie Ross's house was beyond saving.

CANADA WAS STARTLED. There were headlines across the country about the normally serene fishing community of Grand Manan—in the normally law-abiding country of Canada—having resorted to vigilantism. Crown Prosecutor McAvity moved swiftly to bring charges against those who had broken the law, partly to demonstrate that the authorities were not going to tolerate what he called mob rule. The R.C.M.P. was not able to find out who had set the fire that actually destroyed Ronnie Ross's house, and Crown prosecutors eventually decided not to charge the people who had blocked the fire trucks or egged on the crowd. But five young men who worked in the fisheries were taken to jail on the mainland—arrested for offenses that could potentially lead to terms in the penitentiary. Two of the defendants were charged with having set the earlier fire, and three, including Carter Foster, were charged with participating in the shooting. (Ronnie Ross was charged with the same firearms violation and with having issued the fireball threat to Carter Foster and Sara Wormell.) A week or so after the incident, the R.C.M.P., apparently acting on tips that another person suspected of dealing drugs might be burned out, sent seventy officers to Grand Manan—a show of force that mainly just irritated the islanders. The mayor of Grand Manan, Dennis Greene, asked for an investigation of the R.C.M.P., which he claimed had spent a hundred thousand dollars on an after-the-fact invasion after years of saying that it didn't have a few thousand dollars in the budget to put a drug-sniffing dog on the ferry.

Overwhelmingly, islanders rejected the notion that the five incarcerated men were criminals. A sign went up at the ferry terminal in Grand Manan saying "Free Our Heroes." All around the island, red ribbons were displayed to show solidarity with the defendants, who came to be known on Grand Manan as The Boys. A public meeting called by the R.C.M.P. to hear residents' concerns turned into a dressing down of the police for lax drug enforcement and a pep rally for The Boys. When David Lutz, a New Brunswick criminal lawyer, went to the island to meet with some people about representing The Boys, he was asked what sort of retainer he'd need. He said twenty thousand dollars. The next evening, as he sat in his car waiting to get on the seven-o'clock ferry back to Blacks Harbour, a man he'd never met before handed him an envelope with cash and checks totalling just about twenty thousand dollars. The fund-raising efforts eventually included bake sales and the sale of T-shirts. The father of one defendant said later, "How many criminals are there that the community pays their legal bills?"

In November, when the trial of The Boys got under way on the mainland, a county weekly, the *Saint Croix Courier,* asked its readers about their sympathies, and eighty-two per cent of the respondents said that they backed the defendants. "These five men did what Mr. McAvity just said that they did," David Lutz said in his opening statement, after the Crown prosecutor had outlined what the jury would hear. "The issue is why they did what they did that night." Lutz's strategy was based on necessity: all five of the defendants under videotaped R.C.M.P. questioning, had admitted their roles in the gunfire or the arson. As the defense presented it, "They acted out of fear for their lives and the lives of others." Lutz portrayed the gathering at Carter Foster's house as a sort of "mobile neighborhood watch" that went "horribly wrong" when shots began coming from Ross's house.

If the crowd had gathered for the "peaceful intervention" that Lutz described, the Crown prosecutors replied, how come there were rifles at the ready? And what, they asked, does setting fire to someone's house have to do with self-defense? Although "the Crown is not here to support Mr. Ross's life style," Crown Prosecutor Randy DiPaolo said, the defendants "do not get an exemption from the criminal-justice system because they're fishermen or because they work hard."

Ronnie Ross's record, introduced into evidence, reflected that before he moved to Grand Manan he was convicted of crimes like extortion and assault. He had never been convicted of selling drugs, though, and there was only sketchy testimony about drug dealing at 61 Cedar Street—most of it concerning Terry Irvine. Ross admitted using crack, but, like Irvine, he denied being a dealer. When Lutz asked him why he bought so much baking soda, an ingredient of crack ("You're not a baker, are you? You don't make cookies and muffins"), Ross said that he used it to deodorize his refrigerator. The one person Ross identified as having been at 61 Cedar Street while crack was being smoked was one of the men on trial for trying to burn the place down because it was a crack house. Ross, who had testified that he'd lived on Grand Manan for ten years, said that the assumption that he was a crack dealer was caused by prejudice against outsiders: "Islanders stick together. If one person doesn't like you, no one likes you. They gossip and stories get twisted around." As for any plans to travel around in the Yukon burning down houses on a hit list, Ross's friends testified that they had gathered at his house that night for their usual Friday-night pastime of getting drunk or getting high. Terry Irvine, who, according to some witnesses, may have fired the first shot, testified that he'd been too drunk to remember much of anything about the evening.

The jury found those who admitted to shooting guns that night not guilty—in his charge, the judge had said "the law doesn't require somebody to run to the woods if they are being attacked"—but it found the two arson defendants guilty. Foster was also found guilty of the minor charge of unsafe storage of weapons, and another defendant was found guilty of firing a flare gun. The verdicts were not popular. There were tears in the courtroom, and the mood on the ferry going back to the island was sombre. The reaction softened a bit when, without objection from the Crown prosecutor, the judge handed down lenient sentences; the most severe, for the arsonists, included a form of house arrest. Editorialists tended to detect a sensible Canadian compromise between the requirements of lawfulness and mercy. "The island people were well satisfied that they didn't go to jail," one resident said recently. "If those boys had gone to jail for a year, I'd be scared to say what might have happened."

A COUNTRY SONG about The Boys has been posted on the Internet: "They were known as The Boys. And they were fishermen. Cared about their families. They cared about their friends. Looked out for the neighbors. Out on Grand Manan. They were known as The Boys. And they were fishermen." Some Grand Mananers, including some of those who were willing to contribute to the defense fund, feel a bit uneasy about The Boys' being portrayed as the equivalent of the peaceful farmers in a Western who finally rise up against the gunslingers hired by the wicked cattle baron. "They weren't exactly the churchgoing crowd," one islander said recently. There are, of course, some people on Grand Manan who have never felt even enough solidarity with The Boys to accept the term. ("They're not boys. They're grown men.") Some volunteer firemen, for instance, were shocked at the scene on Cedar Street that night; they are understandably accustomed to a different reception when they show up, at some risk and for no pay, to save a neighbor's house. "You can't carry out vigilante justice," one of them said not long ago. "If the drug dealers had had more people, Foster's home would have been burnt out." Such opinions, though, tend to be expressed privately.

By now, most of the red ribbons, many of them bleached pink by the harsh Maritime winter, have been taken down. Among the last to go were three or four bright-red towels that until recently were still draped around trees in the front yard of Carter Foster and Sara Wormell. They have decided to stay in Grand Manan for the time being, although they'd like to figure out a way to spend some of the winter months in British Columbia. By this time of year, tall stakes driven into the ocean floor have been connected with netting, a process sometimes called "suiting your weirs," and people like Foster are getting up at a quarter to five every morning hoping to find the nets full of herring. The shed in back of their house has been repainted, but Foster can put his fingers in two bullet holes. At times, he has said that he wished he hadn't been present on the night of the fights and the gunfire and the house-burning. He calls the twenty days he spent in jail awaiting bail the worst twenty days of his life. ("To me, that would have been a good enough sentence if I had done something really horrific.") He has said that he's haunted by the thought that he could have been killed or that he could have killed somebody else. On the other hand, he thinks that some good has come of the altercation with Ronnie Ross. "They're talking about a center for the young people, and a paintball field," Foster said recently. "There's going to be some recreation for the young kids. The only recreation I had growing up was to go get drunk."

Many islanders would agree with Carter Foster that Grand Manan is better off than it was before he and Ronnie Ross met in the middle of Cedar Street—or will be if the grants that the village has applied for come through. That opinion is often followed by "Of course, I don't condone violence," but it also might be followed by the observation that a smarter way to get rid of someone like Ronnie Ross would be to wait until he was out of the house some dark night, drop in a Molotov cocktail, and "run off into the woods like a rabbit." Although there are still drug dealers on the island, none of them are outsiders who make themselves out to be big-time gangsters. There seems to be more focus on doing something about the drug problem. Now that Terry Irvine is no longer making regular visits in one S.U.V. or another, islanders are more relaxed about leaving tools unguarded—even though no evidence was ever presented that Irvine and Ross were behind the thefts. In fact, Irvine is in jail. This spring, in St. John, he pleaded guilty to stealing several thousand dollars' worth of goods from three Atlantic Superstores, in full view of surveillance cameras—committing what his own lawyer summed up as "a rather stupid offense."

And Ronald Ross is no longer a menacing presence on Grand Manan. His house is gone. Where it stood, there is simply an empty lot with some charred rubble. People see the end of his Grand Manan sojourn in varying ways. The Crown prosecutors believe, of course, that a mob put itself in the place of legally constituted authorities, while most residents of Grand Manan prefer to believe that islanders, regrettably, had to do what the R.C.M.P. seemed unwilling or unable to do. If it is true that the R.C.M.P. offered to turn a blind eye or even encouraged the violence, the legally constituted authorities could be said to have used the islanders as an unregulated auxiliary to get rid of Ronnie Ross. One resident of Cedar Street told the R.C.M.P. that, despite all the talk of drug problems, the eruption of violence was essentially part of a "personal war" between Ross and his neighbors—another way of saying that what really got Ronnie Ross put off Grand Manan was what Laura Buckley called his "asshole issues."

At Ross's trial in April, he was found guilty of the "ball of fire" threat but not guilty on the gun charge. (The judge, who heard the case without a jury, said that in his opinion the islanders at Foster's assembled not for a peaceful intervention but in the hope that something would start so that they could finish it.) Ross, who had been confined to his father's house in Nova Scotia since the previous summer, was sentenced to time served. After the sentencing, he told reporters that he might go back to Grand Manan once he is no longer prohibited from returning by the terms of his probation. A lot of people took that as just more Ronnie Ross bravura—when Mayor Greene was asked about it recently, he laughed—but Laura Buckley says that some people who know Ross believe that "he will actually have the brass balls to return." Being an outsider and presumably not a student of history, after all, he may not realize that, in Marc Shell's formulation, he has been banished.

CALVIN TRILLIN *has been a staff writer for* The New Yorker *since 1963. For fifteen years, he did a* New Yorker *series called "U.S. Journal"— a three thousand word article from somewhere in the United States every three weeks. He is the author of twenty-five books, including* Killings *and* American Stories.

Coda

In the summer, I live on the South Shore of Nova Scotia, so I heard reports on CBC radio about the incident on Grand Manan Island, just across the Bay of Fundy, in July 2006. The South Shore has some cultural similarities with Grand Manan. People in the village I live in have traditionally made their living from the sea—mainly lobstering in recent years, as the supply of ground fish became depleted. Law enforcement is provided by the Royal Canadian Mounted Police, headquartered in the nearest town large enough to have a drugstore and a supermarket—although in thirty-five summers the only Mountie I can recall seeing in our village was the one in ceremonial dress who was always present for the blessing of the fleet that used to be held on the government wharf every August. In other words, the presence of a menacing neighbor would present the same sort of problem for our village as it did for the residents of Grand Manan.

One difference, though, is that the South Shore is not an island. I've always been intrigued by islands—particularly islands that are relatively remote from mainland population centers. I've also been attracted to situations that are, for want of a better word, murky—situations in which the rights and wrongs are not obvious. So a murky situation on an island, involving people much like my summertime neighbors, was irresistible.

Alan Prendergast

THE CAGED LIFE

FROM *Westword*

WHEN THE GOON SQUAD showed up at his place at five in the morning, Tommy Silverstein knew something was up. He wasn't accustomed to greeting guests at such an ungodly hour—much less a team of corrections officers, helmeted and suited up for action.

In fact, Silverstein wasn't used to company at any hour. His home was a remote cell, known as the Silverstein Suite, in the special housing unit of the federal penitentiary at Leavenworth, Kansas. He'd been cut off from other inmates and all but a few emissaries from the outside world for more than two decades.

He stayed in the Silverstein Suite 23 hours a day. His interactions with staff typically amounted to some tight-lipped turnkey delivering his food through a slot in the cell door. The only change of scenery came when an electronic door slid open, allowing him an hour's solitary exercise in an adjoining recreation cage. Visitors were rarely permitted, and entire years had gone by during which he never left the cell.

But this day was different. Silverstein could think of only a couple of reasons why so many well-padded, well-equipped officers would be at his door, ordering him to strip for a search. Cell shakedown? Time for a game of hockey, with Tommy as the puck? No, that was a captain leading the squad. Something big.

A transfer.

So it came to pass that on July 12, 2005, U.S. Bureau of Prisons inmate #14634-116 left his cage in Kansas for one in Colorado. Security for the move was tighter than Borat's Speedo—about what you'd expect for a former Aryan Brotherhood leader convicted of killing four men behind prison walls. (One conviction was later overturned; Silverstein disputes the second slaying but admits the other two.) The object of all this fuss didn't mind the goon squad. He was enjoying the view—and hoping that the move signaled the end to his eight-thousand-plus days of solitary confinement. Maybe, just maybe, his decades of uneventful good behavior had paid off.

"They said for me to keep my nose clean, and maybe one day it'd happen," he recalled recently. "So I foolishly thought this was it. If you saw me in that van, you'd think I was Disneyland-bound, smiling all the way."

But the smile vanished after Silverstein reached his destination: the U.S. Penitentiary Administrative Maximum, better known as ADX. Located two miles outside of the high-desert town of Florence, ADX is the most secure prison in the country, a hunkered-down maze of locks, alarms and electronic surveillance, designed to house gang leaders, terrorists, drug lords and other high-risk prisoners in profound isolation. Its current guest list is a who's who of enemies of the state, including Unabomber Ted Kaczynski, shoe bomber Richard Reid, plane bomber Dandenis Muñoz Mosquera, abortion clinic bomber Eric Rudolph and double-agent Robert Hanssen.

When it opened in 1994, ADX was hailed as the solution to security flaws at even the highest levels of the federal prison system. Much of the justification for building the place stemmed from official outrage at the brutal murders of two guards in the control unit of the federal pen in Marion, Illinois, during a single 24-hour period in 1983. The first of those killings was committed by Thomas Silverstein, who was already facing multiple life sentences for previous bloodshed at Marion. The slaying of corrections officer Merle Clutts placed Silverstein under a "no human contact" order that's prevailed ever since, and it gave the Bureau of Prisons the perfect rationale for building its high-tech supermax. Although he never bunked there until 2005, you could call ADX the House that Tommy Built.

What greeted Silverstein two years ago was nothing like Disneyland. His hosts hustled him down long, sterile corridors with gleaming black-and-white checkerboard floors that reminded him of *A Clockwork Orange* or some other cinematic acid trip. One set of doors, then another and another, until he finally arrived at the ass-end of Z Unit, on a special range with only four cells, each double-doored. His new home was less than half the size of the Silverstein Suite and consisted of a steel slab with a thin mattress, a steel stool and desk, a steel sink-and-toilet combination, a steel shower and a small black-and-white TV.

Stripped of most of his small store of personal belongings, Silverstein had little to do besides take stock of his eighty-square-foot digs. The Silverstein Suite was a penthouse at the Plaza compared to this place. There were steel rings on the sides of the bed platform, ready for "four-pointing" difficult inmates. A camera mounted on the ceiling to record his every move. If he stood on the stool and peered out the heavily meshed window, he could get a glimpse of a concrete recreation cage and something like sky. So this was his reward for all those years of following the rules—24-hour surveillance in his own desolate corner of the Alcatraz of the Rockies. He was no longer simply in the belly of the beast. He was, he would later write, "stuck in its bowels, with no end/exit in sight."

The double doors muffled sound from outside. But over time,

Silverstein realized that there was one other prisoner on the range. He shouted greetings. The man shouted back. He asked the man how long he'd been in the unit. Four years, the man said.

Silverstein told the man his name. His neighbor introduced himself: Yousef. Ramzi Yousef. Convicted of the 1993 World Trade Center bombing, the one that killed six people and injured a thousand. Nephew of Khalid Sheikh Mohammed, the al-Qaeda leader who recently confessed to planning that failed effort to bring down the towers as well as the 9/11 attacks.

His keepers had put Silverstein in the beast's bowels, all right— right next to the one man in the entire federal system more loathed than he was. Still, it was somebody to talk to. Shouting to Yousef was the first conversation with another inmate that Silverstein had managed in almost twenty years.

But talking wasn't allowed. Within days, a new barrier was erected in the corridor outside his cell, preventing any further communication between the two residents of the range. Inmate #14634-116's transfer to ADX was now complete.

Entombed, Terrible Tommy was alone again. Naturally.

In the late 1980s, Pete Earley, a former *Washington Post* reporter, persuaded Bureau of Prisons officials to grant him an unprecedented degree of access to inmates and staff at the Leavenworth penitentiary. Earley was allowed to walk the yard without an escort, to interview inmates without official monitoring, to talk candidly with veteran corrections officers about the dangers and frustrations of their work.

The resulting book, *The Hot House: Life Inside Leavenworth Prison*, is one of the most vivid works of prison reportage ever published. Among several unsettling portraits of career criminals and their keepers, the most memorable character is probably one Thomas Silverstein, who was then being housed, a la Hannibal Lecter, in a zoo-like cage in Leavenworth's basement, where the fluorescent lights stayed on around the clock to make it easier to watch him. Wild-haired and bearded—the BOP would not allow him a razor or a comb—Silverstein spent hours talking into Earley's tape recorder, describing his violent past and the petty torments he claimed the guards were putting him through in an effort to drive him insane.

Earley's book made Leavenworth's dungeon monster seem not only rational but quite possibly human. Granting a journalist un-fettered access to him was a public relations blunder the BOP has been unwilling to repeat. Silverstein hasn't been allowed to have a face-to-face interview with a reporter for the past fifteen years. When *Westword* recently asked to visit him, ADX warden Ron Wiley promptly denied the request, citing "continued security concerns." But then, Wiley and his predecessors haven't let any journalist inside ADX to interview any inmate since 2001 be-cause of "continued security concerns."

Although he readily agreed to an interview with *Westword*, Silverstein isn't a huge fan of the press, either. He remains friendly with Earley, but he's learned to be wary of hit-and-run tabloid writers following in his wake, eager to write about "the most dangerous prisoner in America." Most of what the outside world knows about him, if it pays any attention at all, is the fragmentary image presented in *The Hot House*; he's a captive of his own leg-end, like some prehistoric insect trapped in amber. His letters seethe with contempt for lazy "plagiarists" who have simply ap-propriated snatches of Earley's account as well as for those who've produced long magazine pieces or cheeseball cable programs about the Aryan Brotherhood that largely rely on the lurid tales of gov-ernment snitches.

"For some odd reason the media pees when Master snaps his fingers," he wrote recently. "I wouldn't call 'em 'mainstream' any more cuz there isn't anything mainstream about 'em. They're just lackeys for the powers that be."

Silverstein's response to the "injurious lies" spread about him

has been to launch his own information campaign at www
.tommysilverstein.com. That's right—America's most solitary
prisoner, a man who's been inside since before the personal computer was invented and has never been allowed near one, has his
own website, maintained by outside supporters who forward messages to him and post his responses.

"He's got a pretty impressive network," says Terry Rearick, a
California private investigator who has communicated with Silverstein by letter and phone over several years. After the two lost
touch for a time, Rearick got a call from a woman in England on
Silverstein's behalf.

The same woman posts regularly on the website, where Silverstein himself duels at length with his detractors. (A similarly
heated debate has ignited over the wording of Silverstein's entry
on Wikipedia; his defenders and his critics alternately revise the
account to suit their competing versions of his crimes.) Some
visitors to his site dismiss him as a textbook psychopath. But Silverstein contends that if people understood the grim context in
which the killings at Marion took place, the snitch games and
psychological warfare and organized violence of prison life, they
wouldn't be so quick to demonize him.

It's a strangely disconnected argument—a garbled dialogue
between cultures on different planets. Most of the visitors to his
website know little about Silverstein's world, just as he knows
little about theirs. He's been in prison for the past 32 years, and
much of what he's learned about life on the street since he was put
in solitary in 1983 has come from reading or watching television.
No American prisoner, not even Robert Stroud, the Birdman of
Alcatraz, has ever been condemned to such a walled-off existence
for such a long period of time. Many of Stroud's years of solitary
confinement were spent in relative ease at Leavenworth; he had
not only frequent visitors, but also a full-time secretary. Even his
seventeen-year stretch in Alcatraz allowed for much more daily
communication with others than Silverstein has had.

"I'm amazed that he's not stark, raving mad," says Paul Wright, the editor of *Prison Legal News*, who's corresponded with Silverstein for years and published some of his writing. "He's been in total isolation for almost 25 years. The only people I can think of that have been held in anything remotely like this in modern times are some of the North Korean spies held in South Korea."

Yet the no-contact conditions imposed on Silverstein are becoming less unique by the day. There are now 31 supermax prisons in the country, with more under construction, including Colorado's own 948-bed sequel to the current state supermax, known as Colorado State Penitentiary II. They are costly on several levels—the operational expense per cell can be double that of a less-secure prison, and the rate of mental illness in solitary confinement far exceeds that of the general prison population—but lockdown prisons are all the rage with a vengeful public. Increasingly, they are being used not for short-term punishment (disciplinary segregation) but for long-term confinement of hard-to-manage inmates (administrative segregation), whose privileges keep shrinking. Colorado, for example, no longer allows journalists to interview its supermax inmates except by mail.

"The phenomenon is disturbingly common," says David Fathi, a staff attorney for the ACLU's National Prison Project. "If it's disciplinary confinement, it's finite—when you're done, you're done. But with administrative segregation, there's a real lack of transparency about what a prisoner can do to earn his way out."

In the federal system, the past decade has seen the rise of "special administrative measures," or SAMs, which are imposed on terrorists or other inmates whose communications with the outside world "could result in death or serious bodily injury to persons." There are now at least two dozen SAMs cases in federal prisons, including Yousef and Zacarias Moussaoui, whose access to mail, phone calls, media interviews or other visits are extremely limited or banned outright. At present the restrictions must be approved by the U.S. Attorney General, but the Bush administration is considering changes that would allow wardens at ADX or other high-security prisons to designate inmates as terror threats and thus ban them from all media contact—even if they haven't been convicted on terrorism charges yet, Fathi notes.

Silverstein isn't a SAMs case. He still has his website and his mail (although he claims it's frequently withheld or "messed with" in other ways). But he may be the prototype of what the government has in mind for other infamous prisoners—to bury them in strata of supermax security to the point of oblivion.

Responding in letters to questions about the psychological impact of his isolation, Silverstein struggles to find the right words. "Trying to explain it is like trying to explain what an endless toothache feels like," he writes. "I wish I could paint what it's like."

In an article a few years ago, he called solitary confinement "a slow constant peeling of the skin, stripping of the flesh, the nerve-wracking sound of water dripping from a leaky faucet in the still of the night while you're trying to sleep. Drip, drip, drip, the minutes, hours, days, weeks, months, years, constantly drip away with no end or relief in sight."

IN A DARWINIAN WORLD, predators have to adapt or die, just like their prey. Tommy Silverstein arrived in the federal prison system at a critical phase of its evolution, when the number of inmate assaults on other inmates and staff was rising sharply and officials were looking at the idea of control units as a way to neutralize the growing threat posed by prison gangs. Silverstein quickly became a symbol of the problem—and the inadequacy of the proposed solution. It's not a stretch to say that the Marion control unit helped to make him what he became, just as the mayhem that erupted there helped to reshape the American prison system.

Before he reached the nether regions of the BOP, Silverstein's criminal career had been thoroughly unremarkable. Born in 1952 in California, he'd grown up in a middle-class neighborhood in Long Beach, but he was bullied by other kids who thought he was Jewish. (According to *The Hot House,* Silverstein's biological father was a man named Thomas Conway, whom his mother divorced when Tommy was four years old; she later married a man named Silverstein.) As a teenager, he ripped off houses for money to buy drugs; his sister, Sydney McMurray, says he was battling a heroin addiction and problems with his volatile, controlling mother.

"We were taught never to throw the first punch, but never to walk away from a fight," McMurray recalls. "My brother started getting into trouble because he was running away from a violent environment at home. Then he got into drugs, and he became a brother I never knew."

Silverstein graduated from burglary to armed robbery. He was soon arrested for a series of hold-ups—pulled with Conway and another relative—that yielded less than $1,400. He was sentenced to a federal prison for fifteen years. He was 23 years old, and his life on the streets was already over.

At Leavenworth, Silverstein became closely associated with Aryan Brotherhood members who allegedly controlled the heroin trade inside the prison—close enough that when convict Danny Atwell was found stabbed to death, supposedly because he'd refused to be a mule for the heroin business, Silverstein and two other AB members were charged with the murder. In 1980, he was convicted at trial on the basis of shifting testimony from other inmates and sentenced to life in prison. A federal appeals court later ruled that much of the testimony should never have been allowed and threw out the conviction. But by that time, Silverstein was in the Marion penitentiary and facing more murder charges.

Marion opened in 1963, the same year that Alcatraz closed. It was intended to be not just a replacement for the Rock but an improvement, with a more open design and modern rehabilitation programs. Yet by the late 1970s, it had the most restrictive segregation unit in the BOP; not coincidentally, it was also the most violent prison in America, a dumping ground for gang leaders and crazies. Between 1979 and 1983, the prison logged 81 inmate assaults on other inmates and 44 on staff; 13 prisoners were killed. BOP reports issued in 1979 and 1981 proposed turning the entire facility into a "closed-unit operation."

Confined to a one-man cell in the control unit 23 hours a day, Silverstein says he spent much of his time learning how to draw and paint. "I could hardly read, write or draw when I first fell," he explains. "But most of us lifers are down for so long and have so much time to kill that we actually fool around and discover our niche in life, often in ways we never even dreamt possible on the streets. We not only find our niche, we excel."

Prison officials worried that Silverstein was finding his niche in other areas, too. Long-simmering disputes between white and black gangs had a way of coming to a boil in the control unit. In 1981, D.C. Blacks member Robert Chappelle was found dead in his cell. He'd apparently been sleeping with his head close to the bars and had been strangled with a wire slipped around his neck, plied by someone exercising on the tier. Silverstein and another convicted killer, Clayton Fountain, received life sentences for the crime; inmates who testified for the prosecution claimed the two had boasted of it.

Silverstein has always denied killing Chappelle. (Another inmate later claimed to have done the deed, but investigators found his confession at odds with the facts.) Yet even if he hadn't been convicted in court, the suspicion that he was responsible was sufficient to trigger more violence. Shortly after the slaying, the BOP saw fit to transfer one of Chappelle's closest friends, D.C. Blacks leader Raymond "Cadillac" Smith, to the Marion control unit from another prison. Within days, Smith had tried to stab

Silverstein and shoot him with a zip gun. Silverstein and Fountain responded by cutting their way out of an exercise cage with a piece of hacksaw blade and paying a visit to Smith while he was in the shower. Smith was stabbed 67 times, in what Silverstein still describes as an act of convict self-defense.

"Everyone knew what was going on and no one did anything to keep us apart," he told Earley. "The guards wanted one of us to kill the other."

At the time, there was no federal death penalty for inmate homicides—and not much the system could do to Silverstein, who was already serving multiple life sentences in the worst unit of the worst prison the BOP had to offer. But some staffers, concerned about Silverstein's outsized rep among white inmates, apparently did their best to keep him in check. In the months that followed Cadillac's death, Silverstein began to regard Officer Merle Clutts, a bullheaded regular of the control unit, as his chief tormentor.

Silverstein has given different explanations about what Clutts did to deserve such attention. Clutts trashed his cell during shakedowns and withheld mail; he smudged his artwork and taunted him; he even tried to set him up for attack by other inmates, Silverstein has suggested. Silverstein claims he told Earley "the whole story," but only pieces made it into *The Hot House*. Earley won't comment, saying he no longer discusses Silverstein with other reporters because of past misunderstandings.

The BOP has denied that Clutts harassed Silverstein. Whatever the source of the feud might have been, there's no question that Silverstein became fixated on Clutts. One study by Harvard psychiatrist Stuart Grassian suggests that prisoners in control units sometimes experience "the emergence of primitive, aggressive fantasies of revenge, torture, and mutilation" of the guards who watch over them.

Silverstein thought about Clutts, and he thought about the difficulties involved in getting to his enemy when he was allowed out of his cell only one hour a day, shackled, escorted by three guards.

Locked down for life, he had a mountain of time to consider the problem.

ONE DAY IN SOLITARY is pretty much like another. Prisoners have different strategies for filling up their days, but there are always more days to come.

In his cell at Florence, 54-year-old Tom Silverstein usually rises before dawn, catches up on letters and reads, waiting for the grand event that is the delivery of his breakfast. He goes to rec for an hour, comes back to the grand event that is lunch, showers and cleans his cell. Time for some channel-flipping on the small black-and-white TV, in search of something fresh amid the religious chatter and educational programs he's watched over and over. More reading, some yoga. Then dinner, more TV—he's a sucker for *Survivor, Big Brother* and other "reality-type shows"—and so to bed.

When he was in the Silverstein Suite at Leavenworth, Silverstein had access to paintbrushes, pens and other art supplies. At ADX, he's only permitted pastels, colored pencils and "cheap-ass paper," he reports; consequently, he hasn't drawn a lick since he's been there. He says that every few weeks, he's moved from the cell with the heavily meshed window to one with no window at all, then back again a few weeks later. There are rare, glorious interruptions in the routine—a visit with sister Sydney last May, an occasional lawyer checking in. Visitors sit in a booth outside the cell and talk to him on a phone; he sits shackled on the other side of a glass partition and talks back. But these dazzling bursts of conversation quickly fade into a muddle. Did the last lawyers come before or after his sister? Silverstein isn't sure.

"It's all a blur, a dream state of mind," he writes. "Like my memories. When I venture back to my yesterdays, it's hard to distinguish fact from fiction."

Yet there is one memory, one day that stands out from all the rest—the day that started it all. Twenty-four years later, Silverstein is still in the position of analyzing, defending and regretting the act that has defined his fate. But nothing can explain away the act itself, a murder that was meticulously planned and ruthlessly executed.

Marion wasn't designed to be a supermax. Control unit prisoners had to be shackled and escorted to the shower every day, and the guards permitted them to have brief conversations with other inmates in cells along the way. On October 22, 1983, Silverstein was on his way back from his shower when another inmate in a rec cage called over one of his three escorts—Merle Clutts. Now flanked by only two guards, Silverstein paused at the cell of one of his buddies, Randy Gometz, and struck up a conversation.

Before the guards knew what was happening, Gometz had reached through the bars, uncuffed Silverstein with a hidden key—and supplied him with a shank. Silverstein broke away from the guards and headed toward Clutts, now isolated at the far end of the tier. "This is between me and Clutts!" he shouted.

He stabbed the officer forty times before the dying Clutts could make it off the tier. Hours later, Silverstein's friend Clayton Fountain pulled the same handcuff trick and attacked three more guards in the control unit, fatally wounding Robert L. Hoffman Sr.

Two federal officers slaughtered in one day, on what was supposed to be the most secure unit in the entire BOP, sent the system into shock. The bureau's response was to forge ahead with the long-considered plan to turn all of Marion into a control unit while whisking Silverstein and Fountain into even more restricted quarters. (Fountain died in 2004 at the age of 48.)

For years prison activists attempted to challenge the Marion lockdown in court, charging that the prison staff set about beating other prisoners and subjecting them to "forced rectal searches" as payback for the deaths of Clutts and Hoffman. In 1988, a federal judge ruled that the inmate accounts of staff brutality were simply not credible.

By that point, Silverstein and the bureau were already on the road that would lead to ADX—a place where communication among inmates, and physical contact between inmates and staff, could be strictly controlled and all but eliminated.

If the guard killings in Marion happened at any federal prison today, the perpetrators would almost certainly face the death penalty. Silverstein has suggested more than once that death would have been a more merciful option in his case.

"Even though we may not execute people by the masses, as they do in other countries, our government leaders bury people alive for life in cement tombs," he writes. "It's actually more human to execute someone than it is to torture them, year, after year, after year."

SILVERSTEIN'S LAST TASTE of some kind of freedom came in the fall of 1987. Rioting Cuban prisoners broke into his special cell in the Atlanta federal penitentiary and set him loose. For one surreal week, he was able to roam the yard while the riot leaders dickered with federal negotiators over the release of more than a hundred prison staffers who'd been taken hostage.

Then the Cubans jumped him, shackled him and turned him over to the feds. Surrendering Silverstein had been high on the BOP's list of demands for resolving the situation, right up there with releasing all hostages unharmed.

Contrary to the bureau's expectations, Silverstein didn't butcher any guards during his precious days of liberty. He didn't harm anyone. He suggests the episode shows that he's not the killing machine the BOP says he is, and that he could exist in a less restrictive prison without resorting to violence.

The bureau isn't convinced. He killed Clutts.

Terrible Tommy says he's changed. He claims to have gone 21 years without a disciplinary writeup. Other long-term solitaries go berserk, smearing their cells with feces and "gassing" their captors with shit-piss cocktails. Not him.

"The BOP shrinks chalk it up as me being so isolated I haven't anyone to fight with," he writes, "but they're totally oblivious to all the petty BS that I could go off on if I chose to. I can toss a turd and cup of piss with the best of 'em if I desired. What are they going to do, lock me up?

"But I just have more self-control now, after 25 years of yoga, meditation, studying Buddhism and taking some anger-management courses. All that goes unacknowledged."

McMurray says her brother has learned a great deal about patience and suffering over the years. "He's more like the brother I knew on the outside years ago," she says. "I have spoken with the guards who deal with him every day, and they don't have a bad thing to say about him. It's the ones in administration who are trying to make it as difficult as they can for him.

"But my brother has a spirit that is unbreakable. In Leavenworth, at least he could draw. It's been more of a challenge for him in this situation, but he hasn't let it break his spirit."

The bureau doesn't care about his spiritual progress. He killed Clutts.

Silverstein has told reporters that he wants to apologize to the families of the men he killed, "even though it was in self-defense." He has recanted some oft-quoted lines from his interviews with Earley about "smiling at the thought of killing Clutts" and feeling the hatred grow every time he was denied a phone call or a visit. He says he regrets the grief he's caused and no longer seethes with hatred.

The bureau is unmoved by his repentance. He killed Clutts.

Silverstein has been cut off from the operations of the Aryan Brotherhood for decades. His story is still told among the faithful, in an effort to keep his memory alive among the younger members, but he disputes that the group is a white supremacist organization. His own paintings include an ethnically diverse array of portraits. "I think it's worth noting that Tommy is no longer a racist, if he ever was," says *Prison Legal News* editor Wright.

The bureau could give fuck-all. He killed Clutts.

Twice a year, prison officials hold a brief hearing to review Silverstein's placement in administrative segregation. For many years, the hearings were held in the corridor outside the Silverstein Suite in Leavenworth. Silverstein stopped attending because the result was always the same: no change. At ADX, he's taken to filing grievances, claiming that the move has left him more isolated, with fewer privileges than ever before.

"I am being punished for good conduct under ploy of security reasons," he wrote last year in a formal appeal of his situation. "The goal of these units is clearly to disable prisoners through spiritual, psychological and/or physical breakdown."

In his response, Warden Wiley pointed out that Silverstein is provided with food and medical care, "daily contact with staff members" and access to television, radio and reading materials.

"It's ridiculous to call a nameless guard that shoves a food tray through the hole in the door . . . a source of meaningful 'human contact,'" Silverstein fired back. "I request placement in general population."

He took his appeal to the regional office, then to headquarters, where it was swiftly denied. "You are serving three consecutive life terms plus 45 years for bank robbery and murder, including the murder of Bureau of Prisons staff," an administrator noted. "You are a member of a disruptive group and an escape risk. Your heinous criminal and institutional behavior warrant a highly individualized and restrictive environment."

Wiley declines to comment on Silverstein's treatment at his prison. Last spring, a group from Human Rights Watch was allowed to tour certain areas of ADX. The group wasn't let in Z-Unit, where Silverstein lives, or anywhere near A-Unit—the "hole," where most disciplinary cases are housed. But they saw enough to realize that the staffers who bring meals "do not converse regularly, if at all, with the inmates." Despite claims that clinical psychologists checked on prisoners every other week, "several inmates said they had not spoken to a psychologist in many months," and such conversations tended to be brief.

The group also reported that many ADX prisoners are trapped in a catch-22 predicament—they've been sent there directly after sentencing but have never been provided any opportunity to "progress" to a less restrictive setting because of the nature of their crime. Every placement review finds that the "reason for placement at ADX has not been sufficiently mitigated."

"No matter how well they behave in prison, they cannot undo the past crimes that landed them in prison, generally, and then ADX, specifically," Human Rights Watch director Jamie Fellner wrote to BOP director Harley Lapin.

Some crimes, it seems, are beyond redemption.

Silverstein got a copy of the do-gooders' report and immediately fired off a letter to the group, suggesting that they come see him in Z-Unit if they want the real story about the government's "failed and draconian penal system."

No one from the group has come to see him yet. Silverstein waits for them in his box within a box. He knows that the bureau just wants to bury him and that he turned the key himself. But he also knows he didn't build that box all on his own.

His earliest possible date of release is eighty-eight years away. He has nothing but time.

ALAN PRENDERGAST *is a staff writer at* Westword *and author of* The Poison Tree: A True Story of Family Violence and Revenge. *He teaches journalism at Colorado College and has written about crime and punishment for* Rolling Stone, Outside, Los Angeles Times Magazine, *and other publications.*

Coda

I have written several stories about operations at ADX since the prison opened in 1994, but access has become a sore point since the September 11 attacks. The warden's refusal to permit a face-to-face interview with Tommy Silverstein prompted me to ask now many journalists had been allowed to visit prisoners there since 2001. No one at ADX would tell me, but after several months a Freedom of Information Act request provided the answer: zero. Shortly after I reported that every inmate press interview request had been denied for almost six years, prison officials organized a "media tour"—but steered the visitors clear of Silverstein and Z Unit.

In November 2007, student lawyers at the University of Denver's Sturm College of Law filed a lawsuit in federal court on Silverstein's behalf, claiming that his twenty-four years of solitary confinement amounts to cruel and unusual punishment. Silverstein and his supporters continue to protest his situation on his website, but his "no contact" status remains unchanged. In fact, he's never had a chance to read "The Caged Life." Warden Wiley denied him access to a copy of the article, claiming that its dissemination would compromise security because it mentions other inmates and contains information about escort procedures. I still receive letters from Silverstein, but it's hard to imagine a day when we might actually meet.

Pamela Colloff

BADGES OF DISHONOR

FROM *Texas Monthly*

BEFORE THE CASE OF Border Patrol agents Ignacio "Nacho" Ramos and Jose Alonso Compean became a cause célèbre—that is, before there were calls for congressional hearings, high-level resignations at the Department of Justice, and presidential pardons—*most* didn't make the newspaper at all. The facts of the story might never have come to light if not for a phone call between two middle-aged women who had grown up together in a village in Mexico. In late February 2005, Macaria Aldrete-Davila called her old friend Gregoria Toquinto from her home in Chihuahua and said that her son had crossed into the United States illegally near the West Texas town of Fabens. Border Patrol agents had pursued him, and he had fled on foot. An agent had shot him in the backside as he ran from them, toward the Rio Grande. Her son had managed to limp back to Mexico, but he still had a bullet lodged in his groin and was in need of medical attention. Gregoria, who was living in El Paso, listened to her friend's story. Then she called her son-in-law, who happened to be a Border Patrol agent.

So began a Department of Homeland Security internal investigation that uncovered what appeared to be a straightforward case of two federal agents shooting at a man as he ran away and then concealing their actions. Investigators found that Osvaldo Aldrete-Davila had put his hands in the air and tried to surrender, but Compean—instead of apprehending him—had swung at him with the butt of his shotgun. Aldrete-Davila had bolted, and as he ran, Compean and Ramos had fired at him fifteen times, with Compean stopping to reload his Beretta as he tried to hit his mark. Neither agent announced the shooting over the radio or informed his supervisor of what had happened; the official report about the pursuit made no mention of their firing their weapons. And rather than secure the area so that evidence could be preserved, Compean had retrieved most of his spent shell casings and tossed them into a ditch. Only when questioned by investigators a month later did he offer the explanation that he and Ramos had acted in self-defense; Aldrete-Davila had been "pointing something shiny" that "looked like a gun." A federal jury, which heard both agents' testimony, rejected their version of events and convicted them on five out of six criminal charges, including assault, obstruction of justice, and civil rights violations.

That might have been the last word on the case, except that when talk radio shows, CNN's *Lou Dobbs Tonight,* and conservative blogs picked up the story, they glossed over nearly all of the most damning facts presented at trial. Set against the backdrop of the national debate over immigration, a new narrative emerged, one in which Ramos and Compean were recast as "American heroes," unjustly persecuted by a government that cared more about amnesty for illegal immigrants than about border security. The story line advanced by pundits and bloggers focused on Aldrete-Davila's own illegal activity, since he had been ferrying a large load of marijuana when he had crossed paths with Ramos and Compean. (The agents had not known this when they fired their weapons; the marijuana was discovered only after the shooting, in a van Aldrete-Davila had abandoned when he fled.) The jury had taken this into consideration and had still chosen to hand down guilty verdicts. But the stark contrast between Aldrete-Davila's fate and that of Ramos and Compean inspired outrage. Two Border Patrol agents were being sent to prison, while a dope smuggler—who had been granted immunity by federal prosecutors in exchange for his testimony—walked free.

This seemingly perverse logic provoked a backlash from conservatives who had grown frustrated with the Bush administration's handling of border issues, prompting Ann Coulter to pen an acid assessment of the case titled "No Drug Smuggler Left Behind!" U.S. attorney Johnny Sutton, a Bush appointee, was excoriated for prosecuting the agents—and even branded "Johnny Satan" by Houston talk radio show host Edd Hendee—while bloggers hailed Ramos and Compean as "political prisoners" in a modern-day Dreyfus affair. Lou Dobbs opined about the case on more than one hundred broadcasts, calling it an "outrageous miscarriage of justice" and "an appeasement of the Mexican government." Anti-illegal immigration activists like the Minuteman Civil Defense Corps staged rallies and raised money for the agents' defense funds, and more than 370,000 Americans signed an online petition demanding presidential pardons. Republican congressmen known for their law-and-order credentials argued on the House floor that the agents were guilty of nothing more than "procedural violations" for failing to report the shooting, and U.S. representative Ted Poe, of Humble, commended them for their actions. "We ought to give both of these Border Patrol agents medals and send them out there to bag another one," he said.

Entangled in the heated politics of illegal immigration, the facts of what had actually happened down by the river were cast aside, and the victim's identity as a drug smuggler overshadowed the misconduct of the officers who had shot at him. Of the nearly 14,000 federal agents who patrol U.S. borders, it was Ramos and Compean who were held up as heroes. In an interview this summer, and in handwritten letters from prison that followed, Ramos was thoughtful and articulate about his time with the Border Patrol, longing for the days when he kept watch over the Rio Grande instead of a seven-by-thirteen-foot cell. Yet he was unrepentant about his actions on February 17, 2005. It was his bullet that had permanently maimed, and nearly killed, Aldrete-Davila, but Ramos felt that any prison time for him and his fellow agent was unwarranted. "If anything, Compean and I should have gotten an administrative punishment—if that," he told me. "As for Aldrete-Davila, you know what? He got what he deserved."

THIRTY-TWO MILES southeast of El Paso, Fabens hardly looks like the kind of place that could inspire a national media storm. The Wrangler jeans factory, once its biggest employer, moved to Costa Rica nearly two years ago, and now Fabens is just another fading West Texas town. Roosters crow in the heat of the afternoon; dust devils twist down Main Street. The train rattles by every now and then, on its way elsewhere. At lunchtime, farmers rest their white straw hats beside them at Margarita's Café, trading news over warm bowls of *caldo*. Otherwise, the town is quiet. South of the blinking red stoplight, Fabens reverts to farmland, and cotton fields and pecan orchards stretch out for miles toward the Rio Grande. The jagged blue contours of mountains rise in the distance, across the river in Chihuahua—a constant reminder, from any vantage point in town, that Mexico is always near.

Ignacio Ramos arrived in Fabens as a recruit in 1995, when the local Border Patrol station was staffed by just twelve agents. (By the time Aldrete-Davila was shot a decade later, the number of agents had grown to more than eighty.) Fabens was transitioning from a quiet spot on the river into a busy crossing point, an unintended consequence of an initiative that the Border Patrol had launched two years earlier. Operation Hold the Line had succeeded in stemming the flow of illegal immigrants into El Paso, but it had not ended the problem. Human traffic had only shifted away from the city, moving southeastward to border towns like Socorro, San Elizario, and Fabens. As the tide of people and narcotics moved in, Ramos—and later Jose Alonso Compean, who was assigned to the Fabens station as a recruit in 2000—"worked the line," patrolling the river for illegals and dope. Ramos would sometimes conduct surveillance for hours, concealed behind brush or in fields that had grown high with cotton. "I would have guys drop me off and leave me out there, and I would hide in the bushes or trees or canals," he wrote to me from prison. "Sometimes it paid off, sometimes it wouldn't, but it's what kept the job interesting and a thinking game, as well. You were always trying to be a step ahead, or at least even with the dopers."

Ramos, who is 38, and Compean, who is 7 years his junior, had followed nearly identical paths into the Border Patrol. Growing up in working-class neighborhoods on the east side of El Paso, they had each been the first in their families to graduate from high school. Both had dabbled in college and then joined the military. Both had eloped with their longtime girlfriends and had three children. Ramos coached Little League; Compean, T-ball. But for all that they had in common, they could not have been less alike. Ramos, who was tall and well built, was a seasoned agent who liked to do things his way, shrugging off paperwork and butting heads with his supervisors over Border Patrol policies that he felt reined him in. Compean, who was five feet four and heavyset, was quiet and reserved. Working the line—which required him and Ramos to keep a high profile on the river to "push back" would-be immigrants—could be tedious, but catching dope smugglers was exhilarating and earned them bragging rights around the station. (Compean's wife, Patty, had filled a photo album with Polaroids of him posing beside narcotics loads that he had helped intercept.) According to one colleague, Ramos and Compean focused on finding narcotics to the exclusion of illegals and called themselves "the drug shift."

One such shift fell on February 17, 2005, and for Compean, it had started off slowly. Local smugglers usually moved dope the same way: Backpackers would carry sacks of marijuana across the river—in

Fabens, the water is shallow enough to walk across—and load them into empty vehicles that traffickers had left on the U.S. side. Drug mules would then cross over from Mexico and drive the loads to nearby stash houses. Though marijuana was smuggled through the area nearly every day, that morning had passed without any unusual activity. According to trial transcripts and Department of Homeland Security investigative reports, a break in the monotony came early that afternoon: Sensors were tripped at a location known for drug trafficking that the Border Patrol called Area 76. Squinting into his binoculars from his post on the Rio Grande, Compean observed a van speeding away. "Did you guys copy?" he called over the radio. "There is a blue van leaving at 76, going pretty quick."

A rookie agent named Oscar Juarez was patrolling the levee by the river when he heard Compean's radio transmission. Though he was busy pushing back a large group that had gathered on the opposite side of the river, he was eager to get a drug bust under his belt, and he drove off to look for the van. He caught up with the Ford Econoline just as it reached town and fell in behind it, switching on his overhead lights. But instead of pulling over, the van suddenly turned around and headed south. Ramos, who had interrupted his lunch at the station to join the pursuit, took the lead. "It's close," Juarez radioed as they moved in, speeding down farm roads to the river. "We've got this baby."

As they approached the Rio Grande, the pavement yielded to dirt, dead-ending at a drainage canal that agents affectionately call Shit Ditch. The driver, Osvaldo Aldrete-Davila, jumped out of his van as Ramos and Juarez closed in on him. Compean, who had followed the progress of the chase over the radio, was waiting on the south side of the ditch, blocking Aldrete-Davila's path back to Mexico. As Aldrete-Davila dashed through the sewage water away from his pursuers, Compean pointed his shotgun at the tall, gangly 24-year-old and ordered him to stop. (According to Aldrete-Davila, the agent said, "¡Párate, mexicano de mierda!" or "Stop, you Mexican shit!") He raised his hands, which were empty.

Then Aldrete-Davila and Compean both heard another agent yell, "Hit him!" (Ramos and Juarez, the only other people at the scene, would later deny having said this.)

"Take it easy, man," Aldrete-Davila implored, hands still in the air. "Take it easy. *No me pegues*." ("Don't hit me.")

Compean would later testify that he had tried to use the butt of his shotgun to push Aldrete-Davila back. ("He put his hands up, but to me, it looked like he was coming at me," Compean said on the stand.) Whatever his intentions, he swung the butt of his shotgun at Aldrete-Davila, who dodged it. The agent lost his footing and fell face-first into the ditch, dropping his weapon.

Seeing his opening, Aldrete-Davila bolted toward the river, a little more than a hundred yards away. (Compean later claimed to have climbed out of the ditch and tackled him before he broke free again, although no other witness corroborated that account.) As Aldrete-Davila sprinted across the last stretch of American soil, Compean, who had never fired his gun in the line of duty, pulled out his .40-caliber pistol and started shooting. When he missed, he reloaded and tried again, firing a total of fourteen times. Aldrete-Davila kept running, and as he approached the river's edge, Ramos—who had crossed the ditch to come to his colleague's aid—fired his first and only shot. The force of the bullet, which entered Aldrete-Davila's left buttock, knocked him to the ground.

Aldrete-Davila lay on the riverbank, bleeding. He waited for a moment, thinking the two agents were going to arrest him. When he realized that they were not coming, he stood up and limped through the ankle-deep water back to Mexico. Ramos and Compean holstered their weapons and walked away.

Border Patrol agents had begun arriving, gathering near the abandoned Econoline. They included field operations supervisor Jonathan Richards, the most senior agent at the scene, who had grown concerned about the lack of radio communication and had left the station to check on the pursuit. Ramos eventually joined the group, breathing hard, and got ribbed by the other agents for being out of shape. They would later remember that he had seemed agitated. "Hey, Nacho, settle down," joked Richards. "You're acting like this is your first load."

"It's been a long time," Ramos said. "I'm fine. It's just the adrenaline."

Ramos knew the protocol: A Border Patrol agent who fires his weapon is required to inform a supervisor within an hour. (Border Patrol agents are trained to shoot to kill, not to maim.) Yet as he talked to Richards, he never mentioned that he and Compean had just shot at a suspect fifteen times. Ramos said only that Compean had fallen while he was trying to apprehend the van's driver and had gotten dirt thrown in his eyes. Richards called out to Compean, who was standing at a distance on the levee, and asked if he was all right. The agent assured him that he was, except for a few cuts on his hand and face, and said nothing about the shooting. Before leaving the area, Compean stooped down to pick up nine of his spent shell casings and tossed them in the ditch.

On his way to the station to write his report, Compean stopped to talk to Arturo Vasquez, a more junior agent, who asked what had happened. "That little bitch took me to the ground and threw dirt on my face," Vasquez recalled Compean saying. Providing no further explanation, Compean added: "I had to fire some rounds." He asked Vasquez, who was headed back to the levee, to look for the five remaining spent shell casings—which Compean had been unable to find—since he needed to return to the station. Vasquez knew that the scene of a shooting was supposed to be left undisturbed for the Sector Evidence Team, but in deference to his superior, he agreed.

Back at the station Compean washed up and ran into Richards as he was coming out of the restroom. He had a cut on his hand that had drawn blood. Richards asked him if he had been assaulted by the driver, and Compean denied that he had. "No, I'm okay. Nothing happened," the agent said. "I just hurt my hand when I fell down, that's all."

The van turned out to contain an impressive cache: Nine burlap sacks stacked in the back held a total of 743 pounds of marijuana, estimated by the DEA to be worth $594,400. (Loads that size were not unusual; from January of the previous year through mid-March of 2005, agents at the Fabens station made 155 narcotics seizures, netting a total of 43,703 pounds of marijuana and a small amount of cocaine.) On paper, the day had been an unmitigated success for Ramos and Compean. The seizure report, which Compean had written that afternoon, made no mention of the agents' having fired their weapons. In fact the two-page document devoted just one sentence to the entire chain of events that had transpired from the time that Aldrete-Davila had failed to pull over to the moment that he had fled home across the Rio Grande. It read, simply: "The driver was able to abscond back to Mexico."

TWO WEEKS LATER, a Border Patrol agent stationed in Willcox, Arizona, told his supervisor that he had learned of an unreported shooting outside El Paso in which agents were said to have fired at an unarmed Mexican national. He had heard about the incident from his mother-in-law, who knew the victim's mother. The Department of Homeland Security's oversight branch, the Office of Inspector General, launched a criminal investigation the next day and assigned Special Agent Christopher Sanchez to the case. The ex-Marine was given few facts to work with other than the date and general location of the shooting, but recordings of the day's radio traffic led him to Oscar Juarez. He divulged that Ramos and Compean had pursued a man to the river on the afternoon in question, though otherwise he remained tight-lipped. He never mentioned seeing the altercation by the ditch or the fact that he had witnessed the shooting while standing by the van. ("I didn't want to be the snitch," Juarez later testified.)

A break in the investigation came on March 11, when Sanchez reached Aldrete-Davila by phone and discovered that the most significant piece of evidence in the case—the bullet that had struck him—was still intact. Aldrete-Davila did not have the money to have it removed, and he had endured the previous three weeks with the bullet still lodged in his groin. His urethra had been severed, and only a crude rubber tube, which connected his bladder to a plastic bag, allowed him to urinate. Sanchez explained that the bullet itself could make the case; ballistics testing could possibly pinpoint which agent's weapon had fired it once the slug was removed and entered into evidence. But Aldrete-Davila refused to come to El Paso to have the operation performed, convinced that it was a ruse to lure him across the border so that authorities could arrest him. He would cooperate with the investigation, he said, only if he were given a written guarantee that he would not be prosecuted.

This left the U.S. attorney's office with two bad options: grant immunity to a drug smuggler, or allow Border Patrol agents who had shot at a man while he was running away and then concealed their conduct to go unpunished. Although Aldrete-Davila admitted to driving the load of marijuana, federal prosecutors did not think they had a viable case against him. No evidence tied him to the crime, and his phone conversation with Sanchez would not have been admissible at trial. Without a suspect in custody, the case had never been treated as an active investigation; the van had not initially been analyzed for fingerprints, and the marijuana had been destroyed. Any case brought against him—if he could be extradited from Mexico—would have to rely on the testimony of the two agents, who the prosecution's own evidence showed were hardly credible witnesses. So on March 16, Sanchez presented paperwork to Aldrete-Davila at the American consulate in Juárez, granting him immunity to testify about his actions on the day of the shooting. ("When you cast a play in hell, you don't get angels as witnesses," assistant U.S. attorney Debra Kanof later warned the jury.)

The bullet was removed by Army doctors at Fort Bliss, and ballistics tests showed that it had been fired from Ramos's handgun, which investigators had taken under the guise of performing a firearms audit. That night, federal agents arrested Ramos and Compean at their homes on assault charges.

Not until his arrest, a month after the shooting, did Compean claim that Aldrete-Davila had had a gun. He had never mentioned the weapon before—not when he stopped to talk to Vasquez about his missing shell casings and not when he confided in another agent, David Jacquez, that he had fired at the van's driver. Yet when he sat down to talk to investigators, he said that he had acted in self-defense. (Ramos requested a lawyer and invoked his right to remain silent.) "We tumbled and wrestled for a little bit," Compean wrote in a sworn statement. "I got some dirt in my eyes and he got up and started running back south towards Mexico. When he was running south he was pointing something shiny with his left hand. It looked like a gun. This is when I started shooting." He had suspected that the driver had been injured: "Nacho might have hit him . . . When we saw him climbing out of the river on the Mexican side, the alien looked like he was limping." But he had not reported the shooting, he wrote, because he was afraid he "was going to get in trouble." Before signing the statement, he added that he was unsure if the driver had actually been armed: "My intent was to kill the alien because I thought he had a gun, but I never really saw for certain that he had a gun."

The national media had not yet caught wind of the case when it went to trial in February 2006, and except for a few local reporters and relatives, it was sparsely attended. Around the federal courthouse in El Paso, it was jokingly referred to as "the case of *las comadres*" ("the case of the girlfriends"), since the shooting had become public knowledge only by virtue of a phone call between two female friends. Ramos and Compean were tried together; both agents would assert that Aldrete-Davila had turned and pointed a shiny object at them as he ran to the river. But from the start, the prosecution chipped away at the idea that either defendant had actually seen a gun or feared for his life. Three agents—Juarez, Vasquez, and Jacquez—accepted proffer letters, which shielded them from prosecution, in exchange for their testimony. The trial revealed that the defendants had not tried to take cover during the shooting or warned other agents who arrived at the scene afterward not to stand out in the open. Luis Barker, the former chief of the Border Patrol's El Paso sector, described a meeting with Compean in which he had protested his suspension after his arrest; the agent had given a detailed account of the shooting but never mentioned a gun. And while the defense's theory rested on the notion that Aldrete-Davila had been pointing something shiny with his left hand, as both agents claimed, prosecutors showed that he was right-handed.

On the stand, Compean tried to disavow the most damaging parts of the sworn statement he had made after his arrest. He had never thought that Ramos's bullet had struck Aldrete-Davila—"That's not what I meant to put down," he said—and he had never asked Vasquez to pick up his spent shell casings. ("It was two o'clock, one-thirty, in the morning" when he wrote his statement, he told the jury.) Even harder to explain was why he and Ramos had failed to report the shooting, if not for the simple reason that they felt they had something to hide. Both were experienced agents who were well versed in Border Patrol policy; Compean was a field training officer who had schooled Fabens's greener agents, and Ramos, a former firearms instructor, was a member of the Sector Evidence Team, which examined crime scenes so that investigators could determine whether agents had been justified in firing their weapons. Yet Ramos testified that he had not informed his superiors about the incident because he "assumed it had been reported by somebody." (He could not explain why, then, supervisors had never pressed him for further details or called the Sector Evidence Team.) Compean claimed that he had not reported the shooting because he did not think he would be believed. He had retrieved his spent shell casings for "no reason," he said, adding, "I just wasn't thinking. I just—I just saw them there, and I picked them up."

Defense attorneys argued that these were administrative violations that did not amount to criminal behavior and tried to persuade the jury that Aldrete-Davila had been armed. As they saw it, the entry point of the bullet on the left side of his buttock proved that he had been turned at an angle—as if he were extending his arm back to point a weapon—when he was shot. The orthopedic surgeon who had removed the bullet would say only that he could not rule out the possibility. The defense had less success reconciling the contradictions in the agents' testimony. Ramos claimed that he had heard gunfire while crossing the ditch and then found Compean lying on the ground as if wounded—a scenario that, if true, helped justify his shooting at the fleeing suspect. But Compean testified that he had stood up from a kneeling position after firing his gun, not fallen flat on his back. In closing arguments, Ramos's attorney, Mary Stillinger, tried to establish reasonable doubt by emphasizing that Aldrete-Davila was "the only government witness that can testify that he did not have a gun." (Oscar Juarez had not been able to see past the levee, where Aldrete-Davila was shot, to know if he had pulled a weapon.) "Everything depends on the credibility of Osvaldo Aldrete-Davila," Stillinger said. "Are you going to believe the admitted drug trafficker, or are you going to believe the agents?"

In the end, the case came down to the credibility of Ramos and Compean, whom the jury decided to convict on five out of six charges, rejecting only the most serious one: assault with intent to commit murder. On October 19, 2006, U.S. district judge Kathleen Cardone sentenced them to eleven and twelve years, respectively. Strict sentencing guidelines left her little latitude since one charge—discharge of a firearm in commission of a crime of violence—carried a mandatory ten-year term. The jury hadn't known the penalties for each charge when it rendered its verdict, and three jurors would later sign affidavits for the defense saying that they had been pressured to vote with the majority at the end of the two-and-a-half-week-long trial; they had been holdouts to acquit on the assault and civil rights charges, though not on obstruction of justice. (The U.S. attorney's office later issued a statement that read, "The jurors were polled in open court immediately after announcing their verdicts and all said without hesitation or equivocation that the verdicts were theirs.") Prosecutors had offered plea deals to the defendants before trial, including an 18-month term for Ramos and 21 months for Compean, if they would plead guilty to obstruction of justice charges. It was a package deal that both men had to take and which they had declined. "It was simply the principle of the whole thing," Ramos wrote to me. "I could have never lived that down." (Compean, as well as Aldrete-Davila, declined to be interviewed for this article.) Ramos's wife, Monica, put it more bluntly: "My husband was facing forty years, and they offered him eighteen months. Wouldn't a guilty person take that?"

A female juror, who agreed to talk to me on condition of anonymity saw things differently. "We didn't believe they had acted in self-defense," she said. "I think Compean got mad and started shooting." As for Ramos: "He was a marksman, and I think he knew he hit the alien. That's why he only fired once." During deliberations, she said, the jury had weighed the fact that the victim had been transporting a large load of marijuana. "We agreed that we weren't trying the alien for what *he* did," she recalled. "That wasn't the case we were given."

TWO MONTHS BEFORE Ramos and Compean were set to be sentenced, Lou Dobbs introduced the case to a national audience. "Tonight, two Border Patrol agents face twenty-year prison sentences," he began. "They were prosecuted after pursuing a Mexican citizen illegally in the United States who tried to smuggle hundreds of pounds of drugs into this country. The drug smuggler has been given immunity . . . and guess who's in jail?" Correspondent Casey Wian walked through the incident with Ramos, who recounted his version of events: hearing gunfire, finding his fellow agent lying on the ground, and then firing his weapon when the suspect pointed what appeared to be a gun. "[The public] entrusted me to stop a drug smuggler and I did," he said. CNN's viewers were never told that Ramos had failed to report the shooting, that Compean had tampered with key evidence, or that Aldrete-Davila had attempted to surrender—facts that were readily available to anyone who had read the indictment or newspaper coverage of the case. At the end of his report, an indignant Dobbs weighed in. "There should be an investigation of the U.S. attorney's office who would even suggest that . . . an illegal alien drug smuggler caught with the goods has rights superior to those of the agents that we depend on to enforce the law," he said. He promised his audience of nearly 900,000 viewers that "this broadcast will be following their story each and every day, and every step of the way, and we will be reporting to you on what in the world this government of ours is thinking."

Dobbs made good on his pledge, highlighting the case on no fewer than 131 broadcasts in the eleven months that followed, including an hour-long special called "Border Betrayal." Rather than delve into the specifics of the case, the show gave ample airtime to a rotation of family members, defense attorneys, lawmakers, and anti-illegal immigration activists who argued that the agents should never have been prosecuted. Dobbs injected his own nativist bent into the conversation, as when he reflected on whether the federal government had prosecuted Ramos and Compean because of "the influence of a powerful drug cartel" or was "blighting the lives of these two outstanding Border Patrol agents to appease the government of Mexico." Wian's reporting was no less melodramatic. "These two brave Border Patrol agents, who were only trying to do their job, are going to prison," he announced after they were sentenced. Viewers were given information about how to donate to the agents' defense funds and asked to respond to opinion polls whose loaded questions were foregone conclusions. ("Do you believe the Justice Department should be giving immunity to illegal alien drug smugglers in order to prosecute U.S. Border Patrol agents for breaking administrative regulations?" Dobbs asked. "Yes or no?") The results, announced at the end of each broadcast, were always the same: At least 90 percent of callers sided with the agents.

Dobbs defended his show's coverage of the case when I spoke with him this June, describing himself as an "advocacy journalist." He explained, "The role of our broadcast is to put forward the facts on a host of issues that are often disregarded by mainstream media. My role is not to be neutral. I've always said that the price of objectivity is neutrality, and when it comes to the well-being of the American people or the national interest, I am incapable of objectivity. I bring to my audience issues that are carefully researched and reported." When I asked Dobbs about specific facts that his program had omitted from its coverage, he said, "I believe the lack of accuracy and comprehensiveness is really an appropriate charge for the U.S. attorney."

That did not keep the *Wall Street Journal* from denouncing Dobbs in an editorial for "weigh[ing] in repeatedly with pseudo-reporting designed to rile up his viewers rather than inform them of the facts." ("Turning felons into political causes is the kind of stunt usually pulled by the likes of Al Sharpton," the *Journal* added.) Fox News devoted less time to the case than CNN, and for the most part, the network struck a more skeptical tone. "We are a nation of laws," Bill O'Reilly reminded Tom Tancredo, when the Colorado congressman came out in favor of presidential pardons for Ramos and Compean on *The O'Reilly Factor.* "These agents . . . shot the guy in the butt when he was running away." But online, their case became a rallying cry, championed by conservative bloggers, anti–illegal immigration networks like Grassfire.org, and news sites such as WorldNetDaily.com, which saw the agents' prosecution as further proof that the Bush administration was lax on border security and supported a "pro-amnesty" agenda. Grassfire.org, which gathered hundreds of thousands of signatures for a petition advocating that the agents be pardoned, issued a press release citing the "unbreachable chasm" between its supporters and the Bush administration over the case. "All the talk of fences and high-tech equipment is cheap," the press release read. "When it came time to stand and be counted on the side of our border agents, the President's administration chose to side with a career illegal alien drug smuggler."

As frustration with the prosecution built and was amplified on talk radio, Republican lawmakers who had staked their reputations on tough border-enforcement policies joined in, assailing the administration for not issuing the two agents a pardon. "Today is a day of infamy and disgrace," announced California congressman Dana Rohrabacher in January, after Ramos and Compean reported to federal prison. "Shame on you, President Bush. You have betrayed us and our defenders." He later threatened to call impeachment hearings if either man was killed in prison. U.S. representative Ted Poe, a former Houston judge who was famously tough on crime, argued in a series of interviews that "the government was on the wrong side" and should never have prosecuted the agents. He was not the only longtime Bush loyalist who was quick to align himself against the government's case. During televised hearings in April on the controversial firings of eight U.S. attorneys, Senator John Cornyn spent part of his allotted time pressing Attorney General Alberto Gonzales to say whether he would agree to cooperate if the Senate Judiciary Committee held hearings on the agents' prosecution. (In July the committee took up the question of whether the agents' sentences were excessive.) California congressman Duncan Hunter won an enthusiastic round of applause at the Republican presidential debate in June when he said that he would pardon the agents immediately. A bill Hunter introduced, which calls for the agents' convictions to be vacated, was signed by one hundred members of Congress.

Fueling anger over the case was a sealed government document that Ramos and Compean's supporters heralded as "exculpatory evidence": a DEA report that Judge Cardone had ruled as inadmissible at trial. The report, which was leaked to the press earlier this year, stated that on October 23, 2005—eight months after the shooting—the occupant of a stash house near Fabens claimed that a man he identified as Osvaldo Aldrete-Davila had dropped off a van containing 752 pounds of marijuana. The DEA had seized the drugload, but Aldrete-Davila has not been charged. Whether he has not been prosecuted because of a false eyewitness identification, insufficient evidence, or any other reason is unclear; since the report remains under seal and is part of an ongoing federal investigation, the U.S. attorney's office cannot comment on the case. (It did issue a statement that read, in part, "This office will pursue criminal charges where there is prosecutable criminal activity and competent evidence to prove it.") Critics pounced, charging that the government had given Aldrete-Davila a free pass so that he would not be further tarnished before trial. "It is obvious that U.S. attorney Johnny Sutton knowingly presented a false picture of the drug smuggler in order to justify his ruthless prosecution of Border Patrol agents Ramos and Compean," said Rohrabacher. Still, whether Aldrete-Davila was a veteran trafficker or a first-time drug mule on the day he was shot, the facts that had convicted Ramos and Compean remained the same.

Stirring even more outrage was the news that Aldrete-Davila had filed a $5 million claim against the federal government to cover the cost of future medical expenses. And then, after an episode of *America's Most Wanted* focused on the case in February of this year, Ramos was attacked in prison. Federal officials were quick to point out that Ramos had asked to be placed in general population and had escaped with minor cuts and bruises. But Web sites that followed the case cast the incident in a more sinister light, reporting that he had been beaten by five inmates who had shouted, "*Maten a la migra*" ("Kill the Border Patrol"). Soon the blogosphere was buzzing with proof of yet another injustice; four Texas congressmen announced that the Department of Homeland Security had misled them during a briefing the previous September, when the lawmakers had sought to determine whether the government's prosecution of the agents had been warranted. According to the congressmen, the department's Office of Inspector General had informed them that Ramos and Compean had made several damning admissions to investigators: that they had known Aldrete-Davila was unarmed and that they had "wanted to shoot a Mexican." U.S. representative John Culberson, of Houston, wondered if the agency's misrepresentations had been deliberate. "In my opinion, this false information was given to members of Congress to throw us off the scent and cover up what appears to be an unjust criminal prosecution," he said.

In the resulting furor, U.S. attorney Johnny Sutton made the rounds of talk shows to defend his office's prosecution of the two agents, offering an impassioned argument for why Ramos and Compean should be punished for their actions. As he tried to make his case to his critics, he became the target of their collective anger. "Dear Mr. President," began an open letter that Phyllis Schlafly, the founder of the Eagle Forum, wrote to Bush in April. "I am glad to see that you fired some U.S. attorneys. But you missed one: U.S. Attorney Johnny Sutton." Rohrabacher, who called for Sutton's resignation, accused him of being "a PR man for the drug lords." Photos of the prosecutor began to appear on the Internet, embellished with horns and the word "traitor" scrawled across his forehead. On talk radio and anti-illegal immigration Web sites, his detractors characterized him as "treasonous," "corrupt," "ruthless," "an agent of the Mexican government," "public enemy number one," and "pure evil." Blogs were filled with blistering attacks. "Shame on you, Sutton!" went a typical post. "Since when do illegal invaders to the USA have rights?" Or another: "Drop dead Johnny Sutton . . . This is the most wetback-loving administration this country has ever had!"

"ON THE DAY that everything happened, I was reacting to and trusting the actions of my fellow agent," Ramos told me from the medium-security penitentiary where he was being held in Yazoo

City, Mississippi, in the half-hour that the Federal Bureau of Prisons allotted us to talk by phone. "If Mr. Compean felt that his life
was in imminent danger and that he needed to pull his weapon
and fire, I had to trust him. I had to make a split-second decision
after hearing all those gunshots. I saw the smuggler turn around
and make a threatening gesture at me, and I fired. At that moment, I felt he had a gun."

I had hoped to better understand Ramos's actions that day, and
as he relayed his account of the shooting, he was persuasive. To
hear him tell it, he had faced the sort of terrifying moment that
might happen only once in a federal agent's career; he needed to
use deadly force because he had believed that his life, and Compean's, was on the line. But the same question nagged at me that
had bothered me from the very beginning: Why, with such a
compelling story, had he not simply reported the shooting? Why
keep quiet instead? His answer, which deflected the blame to his
supervisor, struck me as disingenuous. "I guess I should have gone
straight to Richards and told him, but he already knew," Ramos
said. "Everyone was standing around the van, including Richards,
talking about hearing shots fired. If I had told him to his face,
he wouldn't have any plausible deniability, like he does now."
(This contradicted the sworn testimony of Richards and the other
agents who were present.) Besides, he wondered, what good
would telling his supervisor have done? "The smuggler was
gone," he said. "There was nothing we could do about him anymore."

"If they had come forward and said, 'A dope dealer just pointed
a gun at us, and we shot at him fifteen times,' no grand jury in
America would ever have indicted them for that," Sutton observed one afternoon as we talked at the U.S. attorney's office in
Austin, overlooking the Capitol. "But we don't hear about a
'shiny object' until a month later. They knew they had shot him,
and they knew he was unarmed. So instead of reporting the
shooting, they covered it up, destroyed evidence, lied about it,

and filed a false report. A prosecutor can't say, 'That's acceptable behavior,' and look the other way."

Sutton, who served as Bush's criminal justice policy director when he was governor and worked on his transition team at the Department of Justice after the 2000 election, was an unlikely target for conservatives. He had been devastated by the letter from Schlafly, whom he described as "a conservative icon." He insisted that he was not soft on drug crimes, as his detractors had made him out to be, pointing out that his office led the nation last year in narcotics prosecutions and was second in illegal immigration cases. Yet he has received death threats for his role in the case, and his e-mail and voice mail are often filled with irate messages. "All people have heard is that two American heroes are in prison for doing their job and that a drug dealer has been set free," he said. "If those were the facts, I'd be furious too. But the evidence is overwhelming that these guys committed a very serious crime." If anyone was at fault for the fact that Aldrete-Davila was not in prison, he said, it was the agents. "They didn't put handcuffs on him when they had the chance," he explained. "They had him at gunpoint, at the bottom of a steep ditch, with his hands in the air. Instead of apprehending him, Compean tried to hit him over the head with the butt of a shotgun. Even after they shot him, they holstered their weapons and walked away."

Sitting beneath half a dozen framed photos of himself with the president over the years, Sutton marveled at how media coverage had allowed the case to take on a life of its own. Lou Dobbs and others "with big microphones," he noted, had repeatedly reminded viewers that Ramos had been nominated by his co-workers in 2005 for Border Patrol Agent of the Year. Yet they never mentioned that he had been arrested two times for domestic violence, in 1996 and 2002, and suspended from the Border Patrol, in 2003, for not reporting what had happened. (The charges were dropped, but Ramos was required to take a court-mandated anger management class.) More frustrating, he said, were the allegations that he was eager to lock up Border Patrol agents for doing their jobs. "Agents have shot their weapons at least fourteen times in the El Paso sector since I've been U.S. attorney," Sutton said. "On three occasions, they killed the suspect. Every time, the agents came forward and explained why they had used deadly force. And in every instance—except this one—it was ruled justifiable."

It was a case like *U.S. v. Ramos and Compean*, he said, where the defendants were federal agents, that tested our most basic principles. "What makes America great is the rule of law," he said, leaning forward in his chair to emphasize his point. "It applies to everyone, no matter how powerful or important they may be. We give law enforcement the benefit of the doubt because they have to make extraordinarily difficult decisions in life-or-death situations. But when they do wrong, they have to be held accountable."

His message fell on deaf ears on the last day of June, when roughly two hundred protesters amassed outside his San Antonio office to demand his resignation. Volunteers with the Minutemen and other anti-illegal immigrant organizations gathered on a grassy hill below the federal building holding handmade signs that read "Deport Johnny Sutton," "Johnny Sutton: Best Justice the Peso Can Buy!," "Free Our Heroes!," "Prosecute Invaders, Not Defenders," and "Amnesty for Ramos and Compean." American flags fluttered in the breeze beside posters that pictured Sutton wearing devil's horns. A woman walked through the crowd dragging a Mexican flag on the ground, asking people around her to step on it. A biker in an "America: Love It or Leave It" T-shirt shouted at the handful of counterprotesters across the street, who held up "Bad Cops Belong in Jail" and "No One Is Above the Law" placards. "Where are your green cards?" he yelled. "Go back to Mexico!" others screamed. A succession of speakers called for Sutton to step down, including Monica Ramos, whose husband, like Compean, is appealing his conviction.

Before the demonstration came to a close with the Pledge of

Allegiance, a protester climbed into the back of a pickup and grabbed a bullhorn. "There are four kinds of boxes—the soapbox, the jury box, the ballot box, and the cartridge box," he roared. "We have seen a misuse of the jury box. We're going to use the ballot box to get rid of you. But don't test our use of the last box."

PAMELA COLLOFF *has been a staff writer at* Texas Monthly *since 1997. She is a graduate of Brown University and was raised in New York City. In 2001, she was a finalist for a National Magazine Award in public interest for her article on school prayer. Her work has been anthologized in* Best American Crime Reporting 2007 *and* Best American Sports Writing 2006. *She lives in Austin.*

Coda

No other article during my ten years at *Texas Monthly* generated as much hate mail as this story. The mail was ugly and relentless. Wrote one reader, "I think everyone crossing the border into the United States illegally should not only be shot; they should be shot dead. That will secure our border in a hurry." Another wrote, "I don't give a damn if they shot [Aldrete-Davila] in the back, front, side, or wherever. He was here illegally." And: "The only 'dishonor' for these agents is the fact that they didn't kill the wetback drug mule." One reader suggested that I leave the country, and another wrote that my article was "as much a part of the terrorist activity in the United States as . . . Al-Qaeda."

These readers' reoccurring criticism was that I should have "done my homework" by "reading the trial transcript" and talking to people who actually understood the case, such as the lawmakers and radio talk show hosts who have taken up the agents' cause. In fact, I read the entire three-thousand-page trial transcript (which the article quotes extensively) as well as the lengthy investigative report issued by the Department of Homeland Security's Office of Inspector General. I used primary sources whenever possible: I interviewed Ramos himself and corresponded with him from prison; I reviewed the sworn testimony of the other Border Patrol agents who were on duty at the time of the shooting; and when Compean declined to talk to me, I drew on his detailed statement to investigators. I also traveled to the West Texas town of Fabens, where the shooting occurred, and conducted interviews in El Paso, San Antonio, Houston, and Austin.

Interestingly enough, the positive feedback I received about the article came from Border Patrol agents themselves. One former agent wrote, "I was involved in three shooting incidents during my career: two as a field agent, and one as a supervisor. I had to fire my weapon in only one of those incidents. It would never have occurred to me, or anyone else involved, to not report these incidents. I have to agree with Sutton that had this shooting been handled by following appropriate policies it is unlikely any indictment would have been handed down."

Three months after my story was published, the U.S. Attorney's Office for the Western District of Texas announced that a federal grand jury had indicted Osvaldo Aldrete-Davila on charges of conspiracy and possession with intent to distribute marijuana. The charges stemmed from alleged drug smuggling that took place after the shooting, in the fall of 2005. Aldrete-Davila was arrested in El Paso and is awaiting trial.

Ignacio Ramos and Jose Alonso Compean are still serving time in federal prison, and are not due to be released until 2016 and 2017, respectively.

Malcolm Gladwell

DANGEROUS MINDS

FROM *The New Yorker*

ON NOVEMBER 16, 1940, workers at the Consolidated Edison building on West Sixty-fourth Street in Manhattan found a home-made pipe bomb on a windowsill. Attached was a note: "Con Edison crooks, this is for you." In September of 1941, a second bomb was found, on Nineteenth Street, just a few blocks from Con Edison's headquarters, near Union Square. It had been left in the street, wrapped in a sock. A few months later, the New York police received a letter promising to "bring the Con Edison to justice—they will pay for their dastardly deeds." Sixteen other letters followed, between 1941 and 1946, all written in block letters, many repeating the phrase "dastardly deeds" and all signed with the initials "F.P." In March of 1950, a third bomb—larger and more powerful than the others—was found on the lower level of Grand Central Termi-nal. The next was left in a phone booth at the New York Public Library. It exploded, as did one placed in a phone booth in Grand Central. In 1954, the Mad Bomber—as he came to be known—struck four times, once in Radio City Music Hall, sending shrapnel throughout the audience. In 1955, he struck six times. The city was in an uproar. The police were getting nowhere. Late in 1956, in desperation, Inspector Howard Finney, of the New York City Police Department's crime laboratory, and two plainclothesmen paid a visit to a psychiatrist by the name of James Brussel.

Brussel was a Freudian. He lived on Twelfth Street, in the West Village, and smoked a pipe. In Mexico, early in his career, he had done counter-espionage work for the F.B.I. He wrote many books, including "Instant Shrink: How to Become an Expert Psychiatrist in Ten Easy Lessons." Finney put a stack of documents on Brussel's desk: photographs of unexploded bombs, pictures of devastation, photostats of F.P.'s neatly lettered missives. "I didn't miss the look in the two plainclothesmen's eyes," Brussel writes in his memoir, "Casebook of a Crime Psychiatrist." "I'd seen that look before, most often in the Army, on the faces of hard, old-line, field-grade officers who were sure this newfangled psychiatry business was all nonsense."

He began to leaf through the case materials. For sixteen years, F.P. had been fixated on the notion that Con Ed had done him some terrible injustice. Clearly, he was clinically paranoid. But paranoia takes some time to develop. F.P. had been bombing since 1940, which suggested that he was now middle-aged. Brussel looked closely at the precise lettering of F.P.'s notes to the police. This was an orderly man. He would be cautious. His work record would be exemplary. Further, the language suggested some degree of education. But there was a stilted quality to the word choice and the phrasing. Con Edison was often referred to as "the Con Edison." And who still used the expression "dastardly deeds"? F.P. seemed to be foreign-born. Brussel looked closer at the letters, and noticed that all the letters were perfect block capitals, except the "W"s. They were misshapen, like two "U"s. To Brussel's eye, those "W"s looked like a pair of breasts. He flipped to the crime-scene descriptions. When F.P. planted his bombs in movie theatres, he would slit the underside of the seat with a knife and stuff his explosives into the upholstery. Didn't that seem like a symbolic act of penetrating a woman, or castrating a man—or perhaps both? F.P. had probably never progressed beyond the Oedipal stage. He was unmarried, a loner. Living with a mother figure. Brussel made another leap. F.P. was a Slav. Just as the use of a garrote would have suggested someone of Mediterranean extraction, the bomb-knife combination struck him as Eastern European. Some of the letters had been posted from Westchester County, but F.P. wouldn't have mailed the letters from his home town. Still, a number of cities in southeastern Connecticut had a large Slavic population. And didn't you have to pass through Westchester to get to the city from Connecticut?

Brussel waited a moment, and then, in a scene that has become legendary among criminal profilers, he made a prediction:

"One more thing." I closed my eyes because I didn't want to see their reaction. I saw the Bomber: impeccably neat, absolutely proper. A man who would avoid the newer styles of clothing until long custom had made them conservative. I saw him clearly—much more clearly than the facts really warranted. I knew I was letting my imagination get the bet-ter of me, but I couldn't help it.

"One more thing," I said, my eyes closed tight. "When you catch him—and I have no doubt you will—he'll be wearing a double-breasted suit."

"Jesus!" one of the detectives whispered.

"And it will be buttoned," I said. I opened my eyes. Finney and his men were looking at each other.

"A double-breasted suit," said the Inspector.

"Yes."

"Buttoned."

"Yes."

He nodded. Without another word, they left.

A month later, George Metesky was arrested by police in con-nection with the New York City bombings. His name had been changed from Milauskas. He lived in Waterbury, Connecticut, with his two older sisters. He was unmarried. He was unfailingly neat. He attended Mass regularly. He had been employed by Con Edison from 1929 to 1931, and claimed to have been injured on the job. When he opened the door to the police officers, he said, "I know why you fellows are here. You think I'm the Mad Bomber." It was midnight, and he was in his pajamas. The police asked that he get dressed. When he returned, his hair was combed into a pompadour and his shoes were newly shined. He was also wearing a double-breasted suit—buttoned.

IN A NEW BOOK, "Inside the Mind of BTK," the eminent F.B.I. criminal profiler John Douglas tells the story of a serial killer who stalked the streets of Wichita, Kansas, in the nineteen-seventies and eighties. Douglas was the model for Agent Jack Crawford in "The Silence of the Lambs." He was the protégé of the pioneering F.B.I. profiler Howard Teten, who helped establish the bureau's Behavioral Science Unit, at Quantico, in 1972, and who was a protégé of Brussel—which, in the close-knit fraternity of profilers, is like being analyzed by the analyst who was analyzed by Freud. To Douglas, Brussel was the father of criminal profiling, and, in both style and logic, "Inside the Mind of BTK" pays homage to "Casebook of a Crime Psychiatrist" at every turn.

"BTK" stood for "Bind, Torture, Kill"—the three words that the killer used to identify himself in his taunting notes to the Wichita police. He had struck first in January, 1974, when he killed thirty-eight-year-old Joseph Otero in his home, along with his wife, Julie, their son, Joey, and their eleven-year-old daughter, who was found hanging from a water pipe in the basement with semen on her leg. The following April, he stabbed a twenty-four-year-old woman. In March, 1977, he bound and strangled another young woman, and over the next few years he committed at least four more murders. The city of Wichita was in an uproar. The police were getting nowhere. In 1984, in desperation, two police detectives from Wichita paid a visit to Quantico.

The meeting, Douglas writes, was held in a first-floor conference room of the F.B.I.'s forensic-science building. He was then nearly a decade into his career at the Behavioral Science Unit. His first two best-sellers, "Mindhunter: Inside the FBI's Elite Serial Crime Unit," and "Obsession: The FBI's Legendary Profiler Probes the Psyches of Killers, Rapists, and Stalkers and Their Victims and Tells How to Fight Back," were still in the future. Working a hundred and fifty cases a year, he was on the road constantly, but BTK was never far from his thoughts. "Some nights I'd lie awake asking myself, 'Who the hell is this BTK?'" he writes. "What makes a guy like this do what he does? What makes him tick?"

Roy Hazelwood sat next to Douglas. A lean chain-smoker, Hazelwood specialized in sex crimes, and went on to write the best-sellers "Dark Dreams" and "The Evil That Men Do." Beside Hazelwood was an ex-Air Force pilot named Ron Walker. Walker, Douglas writes, was "whip smart" and an "exceptionally quick study." The three bureau men and the two detectives sat around a massive oak table. "The objective of our session was to keep moving forward until we ran out of juice," Douglas writes. They would rely on the typology developed by their colleague Robert Ressler, himself the author of the true-crime best-sellers "Whoever Fights Monsters" and "I Have Lived in the Monster." The goal was to paint a picture of the killer—of what sort of man BTK was, and what he did, and where he worked, and what he was like—and with that scene "Inside the Mind of BTK" begins.

We are now so familiar with crime stories told through the eyes of the profiler that it is easy to lose sight of how audacious the genre is. The traditional detective story begins with the body and centers on the detective's search for the culprit. Leads are pursued. A net is cast, widening to encompass a bewilderingly diverse pool of suspects: the butler, the spurned lover, the embittered nephew, the shadowy European. That's a Whodunit. In the profiling genre, the net is narrowed. The crime scene doesn't initiate our search for the killer. It defines the killer for us. The profiler sifts through the case materials, looks off into the distance, and *knows*. "Generally, a psychiatrist can study a man and make a few reasonable predictions about what the man may do in the future—how he will react to such-and-such a stimulus, how he will behave in such-and-such a situation," Brussel writes. "What I have done is reverse the terms of the prophecy. By studying a man's deeds, I have deduced what kind of man he might be." Look for a middle-aged Slav in a double-breasted suit. Profiling stories aren't Whodunits; they're Hedunits.

In the Hedunit, the profiler does not catch the criminal. That's for local law enforcement. He takes the meeting. Often, he doesn't write down his predictions. It's up to the visiting police officers to take notes. He does not feel the need to involve himself in the subsequent investigation, or even, it turns out, to justify his predictions. Once, Douglas tells us, he drove down to the local police station and offered his services in the case of an elderly woman who had been savagely beaten and sexually assaulted. The detectives working the crime were regular cops, and Douglas was a bureau guy, so you can imagine him perched on the edge of a desk, the others pulling up chairs around him.

" 'Okay,' I said to the detectives. . . . 'Here's what I think,' " Douglas begins. "It's a sixteen- or seventeen-year-old high school kid. . . . He'll be disheveled-looking, he'll have scruffy hair, generally poorly groomed." He went on: a loner, kind of weird, no girlfriend, lots of bottled-up anger. He comes to the old lady's house. He knows she's alone. Maybe he's done odd jobs for her in the past. Douglas continues:

> *I pause in my narrative and tell them there's someone who meets this description out there. If they can find him, they've got their offender.*
>
> *One detective looks at another. One of them starts to smile. "Are you a psychic, Douglas?"*
>
> *"No," I say, "but my job would be a lot easier if I were."*
>
> *"Because we had a psychic, Beverly Newton, in here a couple of weeks ago, and she said just about the same things."*

You might think that Douglas would bridle at that comparison. He is, after all, an agent of the Federal Bureau of Investigation, who studied with Teten, who studied with Brussel. He is an ace profiler, part of a team that restored the F.B.I.'s reputation for crime-fighting, inspired countless movies, television shows, and best-selling thrillers, and brought the modern tools of psychology to bear on the savagery of the criminal mind—and some cop is calling him a *psychic*. But Douglas doesn't object. Instead, he begins to muse on the ineffable origins of his insights, at which point the question arises of what exactly this mysterious art called profiling is, and whether it can be trusted. Douglas writes,

> *What I try to do with a case is to take in all the evidence I have to work with . . . and then put myself mentally and emotionally in the head of the offender. I try to think as he does. Exactly how this happens, I'm not sure, any more than the novelists such as Tom Harris who've consulted me over the years can say exactly how their characters come to life. If there's a psychic component to this, I won't run from it.*

IN THE LATE NINETEEN-SEVENTIES, John Douglas and his F.B.I. colleague Robert Ressler set out to interview the most notorious serial killers in the country. They started in California, since, as Douglas says, "California has always had more than its share of weird and spectacular crimes." On weekends and days off, over the next months, they stopped by one federal prison after another, until they had interviewed thirty-six murderers.

Douglas and Ressler wanted to know whether there was a pattern that connected a killer's life and personality with the nature of his crimes. They were looking for what psychologists would call a homology, an agreement between character and action, and, after comparing what they learned from the killers with what they already knew about the characteristics of their murders, they became convinced that they'd found one.

Serial killers, they concluded, fall into one of two categories. Some crime scenes show evidence of logic and planning. The victim has been hunted and selected, in order to fulfill a specific fantasy. The recruitment of the victim might involve a ruse or a con. The perpetrator maintains control throughout the offense. He takes his time with the victim, carefully enacting his fantasies. He is adaptable and mobile. He almost never leaves a weapon behind. He meticulously conceals the body. Douglas and Ressler, in their respective books, call that kind of crime "organized."

In a "disorganized" crime, the victim isn't chosen logically. She's seemingly picked at random and "blitz-attacked," not stalked and coerced. The killer might grab a steak knife from the kitchen and leave the knife behind. The crime is so sloppily executed that the victim often has a chance to fight back. The crime might take place in a high-risk environment. "Moreover, the disorganized killer has no idea of, or interest in, the personalities of his victims," Ressler writes in "Whoever Fights Monsters." "He does not want to know who they are, and many times takes steps to obliterate their personalities by quickly knocking them unconscious or covering their faces or otherwise disfiguring them."

Each of these styles, the argument goes, corresponds to a personality type. The organized killer is intelligent and articulate. He feels superior to those around him. The disorganized killer is unattractive and has a poor self-image. He often has some kind of disability. He's too strange and withdrawn to be married or have a girlfriend. If he doesn't live alone, he lives with his parents. He has pornography stashed in his closet. If he drives at all, his car is a wreck.

"The crime scene is presumed to reflect the murderer's behavior and personality in much the same way as furnishings reveal the homeowner's character," we're told in a crime manual that Douglas and Ressler helped write. The more they learned, the more precise the associations became. If the victim was white, the killer would be white. If the victim was old, the killer would be sexually immature.

"In our research, we discovered that . . . frequently serial of-fenders had failed in their efforts to join police departments and had taken jobs in related fields, such as security guard or night watchman," Douglas writes. Given that organized rapists were preoccupied with control, it made sense that they would be fasci-nated by the social institution that symbolizes control. Out of that insight came another prediction: "One of the things we began saying in some of our profiles was that the UNSUB"—the unknown subject—"would drive a policelike vehicle, say a Ford Crown Victoria or Chevrolet Caprice."

ON THE SURFACE, the F.B.I.'s system seems extraordinarily use-ful. Consider a case study widely used in the profiling literature. The body of a twenty-six-year-old special-education teacher was found on the roof of her Bronx apartment building. She was ap-parently abducted just after she left her house for work, at six-thirty in the morning. She had been beaten beyond recognition, and tied up with her stockings and belt. The killer had mutilated her sexual organs, chopped off her nipples, covered her body with bites, written obscenities across her abdomen, masturbated, and then defecated next to the body.

Let's pretend that we're an F.B.I. profiler. First question: race. The victim is white, so let's call the offender white. Let's say he's in his mid-twenties to early thirties, which is when the thirty-six men in the F.B.I.'s sample started killing. Is the crime organized or disorganized? Disorganized, clearly. It's on a rooftop, in the Bronx, in broad daylight—high risk. So what is the killer doing in the building at six-thirty in the morning? He could be some kind of serviceman, or he could live in the neighborhood. Either way, he appears to be familiar with the building. He's disorganized, though, so he's not stable. If he is employed, it's blue-collar work, at best. He probably has a prior offense, having to do with violence or sex. His relationships with women will be either nonexistent or deeply troubled. And the mutilation and the defecation are so strange that he's probably mentally ill or has some kind of substance-abuse problem. How does that sound? As it turns out, it's spot-on. The killer was Carmine Calabro, age thirty, a single, unemployed, deeply troubled actor who, when he was not in a mental institution, lived with his widowed father on the fourth floor of the building where the murder took place.

But how useful is that profile, really? The police already had Calabro on their list of suspects: if you're looking for the person who killed and mutilated someone on the roof, you don't really need a profiler to tell you to check out the dishevelled, mentally ill guy living with his father on the fourth floor.

That's why the F.B.I.'s profilers have always tried to supplement the basic outlines of the organized/disorganized system with telling details—something that lets the police zero in on a suspect. In the early eighties, Douglas gave a presentation to a roomful of police officers and F.B.I. agents in Marin County about the Trailside Killer, who was murdering female hikers in the hills north of San Francisco. In Douglas's view, the killer was a classic "disorganized" offender—a blitz attacker, white, early to mid-thirties, blue collar, probably with "a history of bed-wetting, fire-starting, and cruelty to animals." Then he went back to how asocial the killer seemed. Why did all the killings take place in heavily wooded areas, miles from the road? Douglas reasoned that the killer required such seclusion because he had some condition that he was deeply self-conscious about. Was it something physical, like a missing limb? But then how could he hike miles into the woods and physically overpower his victims? Finally, it came to him: "'Another thing,' I added after a pregnant pause, 'the killer will have a speech impediment.'"

And so he did. Now, that's a useful detail. Or is it? Douglas then tells us that he pegged the offender's age as early thirties, and he turned out to be fifty. Detectives use profiles to narrow down the range of suspects. It doesn't do any good to get a specific detail right if you get general details wrong.

In the case of Derrick Todd Lee, the Baton Rouge serial killer, the F.B.I. profile described the offender as a white male blue-collar worker, between twenty-five and thirty-five years old, who "wants to be seen as someone who is attractive and appealing to women." The profile went on, "However, his level of sophistication in interacting with women, especially women who are above him in the social strata, is low. Any contact he has had with women he has found attractive would be described by these women as 'awkward.'" The F.B.I. was right about the killer being a blue-collar male between twenty-five and thirty-five. But Lee turned out to be charming and outgoing, the sort to put on a cowboy hat and snakeskin boots and head for the bars. He was an extrovert with a number of girlfriends and a reputation as a ladies' man. And he wasn't white. He was black.

A profile isn't a test, where you pass if you get most of the answers right. It's a portrait, and all the details have to cohere in some way if the image is to be helpful. In the mid-nineties, the British Home Office analyzed a hundred and eighty-four crimes, to see how many times profiles led to the arrest of a criminal. The profile worked in five of those cases. That's just 2.7 percent, which makes sense if you consider the position of the detective on the receiving end of a profiler's list of conjectures. Do you believe the stuttering part? Or do you believe the thirty-year-old part? Or do you throw up your hands in frustration?

THERE IS A DEEPER PROBLEM with F.B.I. profiling. Douglas and Ressler didn't interview a representative sample of serial killers to come up with their typology. They talked to whoever happened to be in the neighborhood. Nor did they interview their subjects according to a standardized protocol. They just sat down and chatted, which isn't a particularly firm foundation for a psychological system. So you might wonder whether serial killers can really be categorized by their level of organization.

Not long ago, a group of psychologists at the University of Liverpool decided to test the F.B.I.'s assumptions. First, they made a list of crime-scene characteristics generally considered to show organization: perhaps the victim was alive during the sex acts, or the body was posed in a certain way, or the murder weapon was missing, or the body was concealed, or torture and restraints were involved. Then they made a list of characteristics showing disorganization: perhaps the victim was beaten, the body was left in an isolated spot, the victim's belongings were scattered, or the murder weapon was improvised.

If the F.B.I. was right, they reasoned, the crime-scene details on each of those two lists should "co-occur"—that is, if you see one or more organized traits in a crime, there should be a reasonably high probability of seeing other organized traits. When they looked at a sample of a hundred serial crimes, however, they couldn't find any support for the F.B.I.'s distinction. Crimes don't fall into one camp or the other. It turns out that they're almost always a mixture of a few key organized traits and a random array of disorganized traits. Laurence Alison, one of the leaders of the Liverpool group and the author of "The Forensic Psychologist's Casebook," told me, "The whole business is a lot more complicated than the F.B.I. imagines."

Alison and another of his colleagues also looked at homology. If Douglas was right, then a certain kind of crime should correspond to a certain kind of criminal. So the Liverpool group selected a hundred stranger rapes in the United Kingdom, classifying them according to twenty-eight variables, such as whether a disguise was worn, whether compliments were given, whether there was binding, gagging, or blindfolding, whether there was apologizing or the theft of personal property, and so on. They then looked at whether the patterns in the crimes corresponded to attributes of the criminals—like age, type of employment, ethnicity, level of education, marital status, number of prior convictions, type of prior convictions, and drug use. Were rapists who bind, gag, and blindfold more like one another than they were like rapists who, say, compliment and apologize? The answer is no—not even slightly.

"The fact is that different offenders can exhibit the same behaviors for completely different reasons," Brent Turvey, a forensic scientist who has been highly critical of the F.B.I.'s approach, says. "You've got a rapist who attacks a woman in the park and pulls her shirt up over her face. Why? What does that mean? There are ten different things it could mean. It could mean he doesn't want to see her. It could mean he doesn't want her to see him. It could mean he wants to see her breasts, he wants to imagine someone else, he wants to incapacitate her arms—all of those are possibilities. You can't just look at one behavior in isolation."

A few years ago, Alison went back to the case of the teacher who was murdered on the roof of her building in the Bronx. He wanted to know why, if the F.B.I.'s approach to criminal profiling was based on such simplistic psychology, it continues to have such a sterling reputation. The answer, he suspected, lay in the way the profiles were written, and, sure enough, when he broke down the rooftop-killer analysis, sentence by sentence, he found that it was so full of unverifiable and contradictory and ambiguous language that it could support virtually any interpretation.

Astrologers and psychics have known these tricks for years. The magician Ian Rowland, in his classic "The Full Facts Book of Cold Reading," itemizes them one by one, in what could easily serve as a manual for the beginner profiler. First is the Rainbow Ruse—the "statement which credits the client with both a personality trait *and* its opposite." ("I would say that on the whole you can be rather a quiet, self effacing type, but when the circumstances are right, you can be quite the life and soul of the party if the mood strikes you.") The Jacques Statement, named for the character in "As You Like It" who gives the Seven Ages of Man speech, tailors the prediction to the age of the subject. To someone in his late thirties or early forties, for example, the psychic says, "If you are honest about it, you often get to wondering what happened to all those dreams you had when you were younger." There is the Barnum Statement, the assertion so general that anyone would agree, and the Fuzzy Fact, the seemingly factual statement couched in a way that "leaves plenty of scope to be developed into something more specific." ("I can see a connection with Europe, possibly Britain, or it could be the warmer, Mediterranean part?") And that's only the start: there is the Greener Grass technique, the Diverted Question, the Russian Doll, Sugar Lumps, not to mention Forking and the Good Chance Guess—all of which, when put together in skillful combination, can convince even the most skeptical observer that he or she is in the presence of real insight.

"Moving on to career matters, you don't work with children, do you?" Rowland will ask his subjects, in an example of what he dubs the "Vanishing Negative."

No, I don't.

"No, I thought not. That's not really your role."

Of course, if the subject answers differently, there's another way to play the question: "Moving on to career matters, you don't work with children, do you?"

I do, actually, part time.

"Yes, I thought so."

After Alison had analyzed the rooftop-killer profile, he decided to play a version of the cold-reading game. He gave the details of the crime, the profile prepared by the F.B.I., and a description of the offender to a group of senior police officers and forensic professionals in England. How did they find the profile? Highly accurate. Then Alison gave the same packet of case materials to another group of police officers, but this time he invented an imaginary offender, one who was altogether different from Calabro. The new killer was thirty-seven years old. He was an alcoholic. He had recently been laid off from his job with the water board, and had met the victim before on one of his rounds. What's more, Alison claimed, he had a history of violent relationships with women, and prior convictions for assault and burglary. How accurate did a group of experienced police officers find the F.B.I.'s profile when it was matched with the phony offender? Every bit as accurate as when it was matched to the real offender.

James Brussel didn't really see the Mad Bomber in that pile of pictures and photostats, then. That was an illusion. As the literary scholar Donald Foster pointed out in his 2000 book "Author Unknown," Brussel cleaned up his predictions for his memoirs. He actually told the police to look for the bomber in White Plains, sending the N.Y.P.D.'s bomb unit on a wild goose chase in Westchester County, sifting through local records. Brussel also told the police to look for a man with a facial scar, which Metesky didn't have. He told them to look for a man with a night job, and Metesky had been largely unemployed since leaving Con Edison in 1931. He told them to look for someone between forty and fifty, and Metesky was over fifty. He told them to look for someone who was an "expert in civil or military ordnance" and the closest Metesky came to that was a brief stint in a machine shop. And Brussel, despite what he wrote in his memoir, never said that the Bomber would be a Slav. He actually told the police to look for a man "born and educated in Germany," a prediction so far off the mark that the Mad Bomber himself was moved to object. At the height of the police investigation, when the New York *Journal American* offered to print any communications from the Mad Bomber, Metesky wrote in huffily to say that "the nearest to my being 'Teutonic' is that my father boarded a liner in Hamburg for passage to this country—about sixty-five years ago."

The true hero of the case wasn't Brussel; it was a woman named Alice Kelly, who had been assigned to go through Con Edison's personnel files. In January, 1957, she ran across an employee complaint from the early nineteen-thirties: a generator wiper at the Hell Gate plant had been knocked down by a backdraft of hot gases. The worker said that he was injured. The company said that he wasn't. And in the flood of angry letters from the ex-employee Kelly spotted a threat—to "take justice in my own hands"—that had appeared in one of the Mad Bomber's letters. The name on the file was George Metesky.

Brussel did not really understand the mind of the Mad Bomber. He seems to have understood only that, if you make a great number of predictions, the ones that were wrong will soon be forgotten, and the ones that turn out to be true will make you famous. The Hedunit is not a triumph of forensic analysis. It's a party trick.

"HERE'S WHERE I'M AT with this guy," Douglas said, kicking off the profiling session with which "Inside the Mind of BTK" begins. It was 1984. The killer was still at large. Douglas, Hazelwood, and Walker and the two detectives from Wichita were all seated around the oak table. Douglas took off his suit jacket and draped it over his chair. "Back when he started in 1974, he was in his mid-to-late twenties," Douglas began. "It's now ten years later, so that would put him in his mid-to-late thirties."

It was Walker's turn: BTK had never engaged in any sexual penetration. That suggested to him someone with an "inadequate, immature sexual history." He would have a "lone-wolf type of personality. But he's not alone because he's shunned by others—it's because he chooses to be alone. . . . He can function in social settings, but only on the surface. He may have women friends he can talk to, but he'd feel very inadequate with a peer-group female." Hazelwood was next. BTK would be "heavily into masturbation." He went on, "Women who have had sex with this guy would describe him as aloof, uninvolved, the type who is more interested in her servicing him than the other way around."

Douglas followed his lead. "The women he's been with are either many years younger, very naive, or much older and depend on him as their meal ticket," he ventured. What's more, the profilers determined, BTK would drive a "decent" automobile, but it would be "nondescript."

At this point, the insights began piling on. Douglas said he'd been thinking that BTK was married. But now maybe he was thinking he was divorced. He speculated that BTK was lower middle class, probably living in a rental. Walker felt BTK was in a "lower-paying white collar job, as opposed to blue collar." Hazelwood saw him as "middle class" and "articulate." The consensus was that his I.Q. was somewhere between 105 and 145. Douglas wondered whether he was connected with the military. Hazelwood called him a "now" person, who needed "instant gratification."

Walker said that those who knew him "might say they remember him, but didn't really know much about him." Douglas then had a flash—"It was a sense, almost a knowing"—and said, "I wouldn't be surprised if, in the job he's in today, that he's wearing some sort of uniform. . . . This guy isn't mental. But he is crazy like a fox."

They had been at it for almost six hours. The best minds in the F.B.I. had given the Wichita detectives a blueprint for their investigation. Look for an American male with a possible connection to the military. His I.Q. will be above 105. He will like to masturbate, and will be aloof and selfish in bed. He will drive a decent car. He will be a "now" person. He won't be comfortable with women. But he may have women friends. He will be a lone wolf. But he will be able to function in social settings. He won't be unmemorable. But he will be unknowable. He will be either never married, divorced, or married, and if he was or is married his wife will be younger or older. He may or may not live in a rental, and might be lower class, upper lower class, lower middle class or middle class. And he will be crazy like a fox, as opposed to being mental. If you're keeping score, that's a Jacques Statement, two Barnum Statements, four Rainbow Ruses, a Good Chance Guess, two predictions that aren't really predictions because they could never be verified—and nothing even close to the salient fact that BTK was a pillar of his community, the president of his church and the married father of two.

"This thing is solvable," Douglas told the detectives, as he stood up and put on his jacket. "Feel free to pick up the phone and call us if we can be of any further assistance." You can imagine him taking the time for an encouraging smile and a slap on the back. "You're gonna nail this guy."

MALCOLM GLADWELL *is a staff writer for* The New Yorker. *He is the author of* The Tipping Point *and* Blink.

Coda

Not long after I published this piece in *The New Yorker*, I was interviewed by National Public Radio. When I arrived at the NPR studio, I was told that I would not be the only guest on the show. John Douglas had been invited as well, to defend himself. You can imagine my apprehension. Writers are writers because we prefer to handle confrontations through the typewriter. I had a moment of anxiety. Much of my critique of FBI profiling was based on the work of the University of Liverpool group, led by Laurence Alison. Surely Douglas would have come up with some devastating critique of Alison's work?

I shouldn't have worried. The interview began, and I began to realize that Douglas knew nothing about the academic critiques of the Behavioral Science Unit. In fact, Douglas didn't really have a defense of the bureau's techniques at all, except to insist, over and over again, that they worked. Think about it. America's premier law enforcement agency develops a complex methodology for solving heinous crimes. The methodology is debunked by a group of leading academics—and the bureau is apparently oblivious. All I could think, on my way home, was that these are the people who are supposed to protect us from terrorists.

Tad Friend

DEAN OF DEATH ROW

FROM *The New Yorker*

THOUGH LIEUTENANT VERNELL CRITTENDON had been reading Michael Morales's mail and listening to his telephone calls for four months, he hadn't formed much of an opinion of him by the evening of Morales's scheduled execution. Crittendon, who had for sixteen years served as San Quentin State Prison's spokesman—though his role at the prison was actually far more complicated—felt confident only of what he had set out to learn: that Morales had no wish to escape, assault his guards, or kill himself. After twenty-two quiet years on death row, the inmate with the startled brown eyes bore little apparent relation to the twenty-one-year-old thug, high on PCP, who had taken a car ride with a seventeen-year-old named Terri Winchell, bludgeoned her head twenty-three times with a claw hammer, raped her, stabbed her four times in the chest, and then took eleven dollars from her purse to buy beer and cigarettes.

At 10 P.M. on February 20, 2006, two hours before Morales was to receive a lethal injection, Crittendon, who has been the prison's public face for all thirteen executions since capital punishment resumed in California, in 1992, made an unexpected appearance at the deathwatch cell. As Crittendon remembers it, the condemned man sat slumped on his mattress, awaiting what must come: the moment when he'd be told to put on fresh denims and a Chux incontinence pad, then marched into the death chamber and strapped to the gurneylike green chair. The spokesman, wearing a Livestrong bracelet and the black suit that he changed into for executions, gazed down at him without expression.

Ordinarily, Crittendon, an athletic man of fifty-three, is a model of affability. When he lopes through the prison, he teasingly greets passing guards and inmates—"Look out, now!" and "He ain't playin'!"—then, when they stop him to register what are sometimes esoteric grievances, he responds with vigorous nods and says "Sheez!" and "Oh, my!" and usually promises a fix, proud of his ability to bend the most rigid of bureaucracies. As a frequent guest on talk shows like "Larry King Live," Crittendon holds forth with relish on such topics as the crimes of death-row residents whose company the wife-killer Scott Peterson, recently arrived at San Quentin, might enjoy.

During an execution, though, his demeanor turns profoundly neutral. "Vernell has the hardest role," the veteran guard John Gladson says. "He has to keep the victims' families from being pissed off by not appearing too sympathetic to the condemned, but he also has to go back the next day and deal with the inmates on death row, who've all had their TVs tuned to Channel 5"—San Francisco's CBS affiliate—"watching him like they're reviewing a play."

As Morales knew, his attorneys had convinced a U.S. District Court judge, Jeremy Fogel, that two of the three poisons he would receive could cause excruciating pain if the first one to enter his bloodstream, the barbiturate sodium thiopental, didn't put him under. San Quentin's execution logs indicate that, during six of the prison's eleven lethal injections, the condemned may have been partly conscious; similar findings have led eight states to suspend use of the chemical mixture—sometimes called Texas Tea—employed in most of the death-penalty states, including California. To meet Judge Fogel's concerns, the prison had brought in two anesthesiologists to monitor the procedure. But that night, when the anesthesiologists realized that if Morales regained consciousness they were expected to sedate him again, they told the warden that it would be medically unethical to do so.

Crittendon had just informed Terri Winchell's family, who were in seclusion two hundred yards away, that the warden had postponed the execution for a few hours. He tried to radiate what he called "a veil of confidence: 'Everything is moving forward, justice will be served.'" Then, projecting an attitude he terms "professional but sympathetic," he says he told Morales of the delay, without explaining further. Morales dropped his face into his hands and said, "Oh, this is going to kill her family. They were prepared for it."

"I was speechless," Crittendon recalls. "I was just *moved*, for once. I'd never heard a statement of caring about the victim's survivors from a death-row inmate." After a slight pause, he told Morales, "I will make sure I keep you informed as this develops."

At least, that's how Crittendon related the event in conversations with me. But the execution team's log shows that Crittendon never made a 10 P.M. visit, and that Morales didn't learn of the delay until just after midnight. Crittendon acknowledged that his timetable must be off, but could provide no evidence to support his memory of the vivid exchange.

When Crittendon went to brief the press on the delay, he shifted his demeanor to appear "professional but indifferent to the eventual outcome." Believing that the press would try to blame the Judge or the anesthesiologists for the setback, he blandly announced that the warden was going over "some additional training with some of the newer members that have just been added to our team." Later, he returned to explain that "the warden has reached that level of comfort with all of the members on the execution team," and they were just awaiting a ruling from the district court on a motion for a stay. Still later, he read a statement of withdrawal from the anesthesiologists, adding—rather at variance with the facts—that "this is a new problem." Crittendon eventually announced that the prison would carry out the execution the following evening, using only sodium thiopental.

A single-drug injection had never been attempted, but Crittendon made the improvisation appear fitting and seemly, just as he had done with "citizens that were involved with civil disobedience" who had been arrested outside the East Gate; inmates "restricted to their assigned sleeping areas"—that is, locked down; and the condemned man expecting to partake of "the lethal cocktail." (In the early nineties, when California used hydrocyanic gas, Crittendon spoke of a "team approach" that would "eventually end in a lethal environment.") He excels at dispensing just enough information to satisfy reporters, and his sonorous locutions and forbearing gravity discourage further inquiry. Earlier, he had declared that Morales "was interacting with our staff in a very positive way," and that the condemned man was suggesting that "this is not necessarily a sad affair."

"To hear it from Vernell," Kevin Fagan, a San Francisco *Chronicle* reporter who has covered seven executions, says, "everyone goes to his maker the same way: 'calm, happily fed, and at peace with his fate.'"

CRITTENDON, WHO RETIRED IN DECEMBER, always sought to navigate a clean line through the acrimonious confusion surrounding the death penalty. The public broadly endorses the penalty—by about sixty-five per cent in most polls—but many capital cases are beset by doubt, mitigating circumstances, or evidence of the condemned's remorse or redemption. California has a particularly thorough appellate process, and the result, on death row at San Quentin, is agonizing stasis: six hundred and twenty-nine men, the nation's largest assembly of the condemned, now sit for an average of more than twenty-two years before their sentence is carried out.

Vernell Crittendon would seem to have been the ideal proxy for a citizenry that wished to see justice done but did not want to look too closely at its slow, and then suddenly swift, final workings. Yet Crittendon's studied professionalism about executions that occur (or, mysteriously, don't) behind stone walls late at night was greatly complicated by his role—largely unknown to the media or to inmates—in actually carrying them out. Though Crittendon was a mere lieutenant, he essentially ran the show—"the conductor of the orchestra" for executions, as one of the wardens he served under put it. Another warden says, "He trained everyone, he did everything, he choreographed it all." Crittendon would often answer reporters' procedural inquiries by saying, "I'll have to check with the warden"—although he knew exactly what was going on because he had arranged it so, and was, in effect, serving as the spokesman for himself. "As long as you keep enough fire and smoke going," he told me, "they don't pay attention to the man behind the curtain."

Crittendon wrote much of the prison's lethal-injection manual, known as Procedure 770. At the weekly "special event" meetings in the warden's office, he set the schedule for practice sessions by the execution team, for the inmate's psychological evaluations, even for the tracing of the inmate's veins to establish where the two I.V.s should go. The execution team itself was not in his purview, but he helped coördinate the prison's Tactical and Investigative Services units, and selected and supervised a thirty-five-person Internal Security team who worked the night of an execution, evaluating them afterward for post-traumatic stress (a fairly common problem). Together with the prison's litigation coördinator, he dealt with the state attorney general's office about the progress of last-minute appeals. And he solicitously escorted the victims' families to and from the prison—even as the officers he'd stationed outside the chamber were prepared to remove them if they caused a disturbance.

Crittendon would visit the condemned man at least once a week in the final months, studying him, under cover of bringing his mail and inquiring about his needs. As the prisoner was transferred from death row to a secluded cell under twenty-four-hour observation and, finally, to the deathwatch cell, he was weaned from the custody of officers he knew well to those he got to know briefly, to those, on the final evening, he didn't know and never would. Crittendon took pains to insure that the emotional atmosphere around the condemned was gradually muffled as well, as if an institutional rheostat were being dimmed. "I tell everyone to keep your voice low, don't laugh, and avoid all confrontation," he said, adding that the soothing tone was "directed to the deserved outcome of getting the inmate to walk into the chamber without a struggle, hop up on the chair, lie still, and take the ultimate punishment." Yet, he observed, "If they tell you pretty blondes in short miniskirts are going to put you to death, you're still going to feel stress when you hear those keys jingling. When I'd take the condemned to the death-watch cell that evening, I'd see it hit them. All of a sudden, they'd walk with little steps, like when you tell a child, 'Go to your room.'"

CRITTENDON LEARNED THE fate of Michael Morales the next day at 5:30 P.M., two hours before the rescheduled execution was to occur, when the warden told him that the prison would not be able, by the midnight deadline, to find a court-approved medical practitioner willing to inject Morales with an overdose of barbiturates. (Since that day, there has been a statewide stay of executions; in May, the California Department of Corrections and Rehabilitation, or C.D.C.R., announced that it would build a new lethal-injection chamber at San Quentin, and that it would overhaul staff training and tweak the chemical mixture to address

Judge Fogel's concerns.) After Crittendon told his staff, he went to the visiting room, where Morales was meeting with three of his lawyers. Crittendon approached their Plexiglas booth, turned to face Morales, and said, "I have been instructed to inform you that the warden is standing down from the execution."

The lawyers stood in confusion. "What does that mean?" one lawyer asked, three times.

"He knows what that means," Crittendon finally replied, indicating Morales with his chin. Then he turned away.

David Senior, one of the lawyers, recalls that Crittendon faced him rather than Morales, and says, "Vernell delivered the information in such a way—hands behind him, nose to a crack in the Plexiglas—that you could read zero personal feelings in it."

When I told Crittendon that Senior had been struck by his detachment at the moment of reprieve, he said, sharply, "The moment I showed emotion, his attorneys would use it for their agenda, and my staff, who were also watching, would interpret that and they would allow their emotions to be seen, and then we are an embarrassment to the State of California."

Every conversation between a guard and an inmate is circumscribed by tactical concerns. (You never give an inmate bad news when he's not secured in his cell, or on a weekend, when fewer staff are on duty, and you never confide anything intimate; to be guilty of "overfamiliarity"—of a sympathy or engagement that prevents you from enforcing the rules—is an unforgivable lapse.) Still, Crittendon couldn't help revisiting that exchange. Had Morales understood from the angling of the spokesman's body that he was trying to speak only to him, to convey a kind of solidarity? Did he grasp the constraints the spokesman was under? "I was not able to have the kind of interaction with a human being I'd like," Crittendon said. "I'd have wanted to sit down next to him, with no barrier between us."

The morning after an execution, Crittendon was always at his desk by nine—right back at it, when some on the execution team would take a permitted five-day leave. Crittendon was such a "tower of strength," as a former warden, Jeanne Woodford, puts it, that his colleagues were convinced that he both approved of capital punishment and shrugged off its impact. Yet immediately after an execution he would always linger until everyone had left and then sit in his truck in the deserted parking lot, thinking.

On the morning after the reprieve of Michael Morales, the prisoner was held in a stainless-steel shower stall on death row while guards returned his belongings to his regular cell. He was visited by Eric Messick, Crittendon's deputy, who knew that he would have to answer questions about Morales's state of mind. Messick, who is as direct and artless as Crittendon is strategic, asked Morales how he was doing.

"A lot better than yesterday," Morales said.

"So now you're just like the rest of us," Messick said. Morales looked up quizzically, and Messick said, "Now you don't know when you're going to die, either."

Morales thought that over, smiling a little, then said, "Yeah, but this is not finished." Still, he was touched by the visit, saying later, "They're usually very concerned that you're doing fine before they kill you—not after they don't kill you."

WHEN YOU PASS through the sally port at San Quentin, you feel as if you'd walked into an old Warner Bros. prison movie, the kind where Jimmy Cagney rattles his cage. Built in 1852, during the Gold Rush, this barrow of crumbling granite on the former Bay of Skulls has held Black Bart, Caryl Chessman, Sirhan Sirhan, Charles Manson, and Richard (the Night Stalker) Ramirez, among many others, and the ferocity of their hatreds seems to linger in the air.

Steven Ornoski, who was warden during the Morales matter, calls it "the worst prison in the California system: it's old, filthy, noisy, poorly laid out, and understaffed. I told people I'd been dropped on the Titanic—after it had hit the iceberg." When a federal health-care receiver visited San Quentin last spring, he found that its emergency room had lacked gauze and sutures for four months.

From 2004 to 2006, San Quentin was run by a bewildering procession of nine wardens and might well have been closed, had there been somewhere for its occupants to go. California's thirty-three prisons hold a hundred and seventy-three thousand inmates, twice as many as they were built for. Nineteen thousand inmates now sleep in hallways and gyms, and Governor Arnold Schwarzenegger recently classified the prisons as being in a state of emergency. The system's faulty health care has been blamed for one inmate death per week, and a state law requiring that prisoners be brought to a ninth-grade reading level by the time they're paroled is basically ignored. Sixty-six percent of California's released inmates return to prison within three years, twice the national average, but rehabilitation programs are nearly nonexistent: most prisoners are never introduced to anything more remedial than a barbell.

On this conveyor belt to nowhere, San Quentin is the only California prison with both accredited high-school and college programs; four hundred and fifty pass-holding volunteers from the Bay Area regularly instruct its inmates in everything from Hooked on Phonics to yoga. In a deeply conservative environment—the vast majority of the thousand guards who work in the prison grumble about "Camp San Quentin" and "hug a thug" mollycoddling—the flourishing of these programs is almost unaccountable.

They owe their survival, in large part, to Vernell Crittendon. As wardens cycled through, Crittendon became the institution's memory, conscience, and consigliere; the duties he took on included everything from organizing inmate walkathons for charity to running the prison museum. "Vernell seemed to know everyone in the whole United States," Jill Brown, a recent warden, said, "and which exact person to go to to help the prison—from who to call at the Mexican consulate to who to contact among Louis Farrakhan's people if there was an issue in our Muslim community. He was Mr. San Quentin."

Crittendon led many lives at the prison. Early in his career, he became widely known and feared as a member of the prison's "goon squad"—a buccaneering unit that beat down prisoners to gain compliance. But in the years after he was promoted to the administrative staff, in 1988, he began to trade upon that reputation in order to rehabilitate the men whose heads he had so often pummelled. It was a delicate balancing act; nearly every time he made a decision, either the guards or the inmates would complain that he was favoring the other side. Even as he publicly lauded the prison's punitive strictures, he privately began to encourage a multiracial group of inmate leaders to quit "the game": he'd ask about their families, allow them to make off-hours phone calls to their children, introduce them to reporters as "our success stories," even organize memorial services for their cellmates. Felix Lucero, a lifer, said, "You always want to feel you can be rehabilitated, that you're not an animal, and Crittendon makes you feel that way. He treated me like we were sort of . . . friends."

Crittendon helped oversee inmate self-help programs like No More Tears and the Vietnam Veterans Group, and was an adviser to many others. Every other Friday, as the centerpiece of a program called Real Choices, which tries to set wayward urban kids on responsible paths, he would escort a group of ten-to-eighteen-year-olds into the prison to meet lifers, who tried to talk—or shout—some sense into them. Crittendon, who is married to a nurse and has a fifteen-year-old son, inaugurated Real Choices in 2001, but, characteristically, he encouraged the inmates to speak of the program as their own creation. Once, he had hoped to become warden himself, but as warden after warden fell to internal politics within the C.D.C.R. he came to understand the uses of stealth. When he publicly declared that the Crips gang co-founder Stanley Tookie Williams—one of the prison's most famous inmates—was a con man whose later good works were intended solely to avoid execution, he lost the trust of many inmates he'd so carefully cultivated. The Williams matter nags at Crittendon still.

Crittendon's approval, on the other hand, can open doors. Of the fifteen lifers he originally used in Real Choices, four have been paroled, an unusually high percentage. Crittendon had written to the Board of Parole Hearings on those inmates' behalf because each met his five criteria: being responsible while at San Quentin; pursuing an education; serving as a volunteer; having a solid support system on the outside; and believing in God or a higher power. He asked Jerry Dean Stipe, a bearded Vietnam veteran known as Wolf, to be a co-founder of Real Choices—yet he didn't write a letter for Stipe, he told me, "because he was an atheist." Crittendon said, "Without a belief in something larger than yourself, you backslide. I don't help the men to be a nice guy or to make them into nice guys. The inmate's going to benefit from being rehabilitated, but it's really about protecting the decent people out in society who he'd victimize."

I SPOKE TO CRITTENDON over a number of months. Whenever I joined him at one of the Denny's or Chevy's restaurants where he suggested we meet, he always sat in the back, facing the door. Before venturing an observation, he invariably paused, making rapid calculations about message, diction, tone of voice, and the likelihood of being misinterpreted. It was of a piece with how he never attended guards' barbecues, never let anyone get in back of him or see him off duty. "I can't be effective with each camp in the prison if they know everything about me," he said. "Vernell's world is a lot neater and more controlled that way."

Crittendon's ability to shift among lingoes and affects is a common prison adaptation. But his speed is astonishing: he's like an actor who glides offstage in a tuxedo, pops his head out in an Indian headdress, and then shambles from the wings in a bear suit. When he was accompanying two clergymen out of the prison last year, Crittendon mentioned that a middle-aged lifer they'd met had been the first juvenile in San Francisco to be sentenced as an adult. "He has not even had the luxury of—the privilege of—knowing a woman," Crittendon told them. While amending his word choice, he deepened his timbre, so that what began as a salacious aside sounded, by "knowing a woman," almost Biblical. Yet Crittendon's ingratiating reserve helped prevent him from becoming just another guard. "Our training is not designed to broaden an officer's mind," Mike Jimenez, the president of the state's correctional officers' union, says, with regret. "Everyone wants to be seen as the meanest, craziest officer, because then no one screws with you. It's dog psychology."

One of Crittendon's many duties was conducting on-the-job training on such topics as "Gangs," "Drugs," and "Application of Restraint Gear." One morning last summer, Crittendon was giving a "Use of Force" class for twenty officers in a trailer behind the prison. "O.K., you're in reception and an arriving criminal refuses to give you a DNA sample," he said. He hopped to the side and played the inmate, strutting and pimp-rolling: "You ain't stickin' nothin' in *this* mouth, nohow." Then he shifted back. "You say, 'O.K., Jack, you can either give us a DNA sample from your mouth or we'll collect it as it leaks out of your nose.'" There were appreciative chuckles. "What gives you the right to say that? Because you are *gaining compliance with a lawful order*. But if some knucklehead says"—side step—"'I ain't gettin' out the shower yet, dawg, I gots soap on me,' can you use force? No, because you do not have a *lawful order* requiring you to effect the removal." He smiled, slowly. "When I came here, in the seventies, that inmate would have been touching every fixed position, every wall, post, and floor, all the way to Ad Seg"—Administrative Segregation, more commonly known as the Hole.

Crittendon arrived at San Quentin in 1977, at age twenty-three, having worked previously as a police cadet and a security guard in San Francisco. San Quentin at the time was a maximum-security prison, housing the most violent criminals. (It's now a medium-security facility.) In the early eighties, the prison reported three felonies a day, bloody incidents with spears and match bombs and blow darts and zip guns, not to mention routine "gassings"—cups of fermented urine and feces hurled in a guard's face. San Quentin recruited Crittendon as part of a belated effort to integrate a heavily white officer corps that gave the prison the feel of a plantation. Crittendon saw a prison run by "the Europeans"—"white guys who were not going to give the others a piece of the pie." Though his own father had deserted his family when Crittendon was twelve, and though he would eventually come to see himself as a role model for black inmates who had grown up in similar circumstances, he soon found himself reluctantly beating up black prisoners—and only black prisoners—on white lieutenants' orders. Even today, the prison both reflects and accentuates the broader racial divide: blacks are six times more likely to be incarcerated than whites, and once at San Quentin (and most prisons) they are housed with other blacks, on the theory that segregation reduces racial tension. The golden rule at the prison, according to an officer named Jeff Evans, is "You hang with your own."

In his class, Crittendon, who while on duty shot more than twenty men, none fatally, began explaining the complex algorithm that permits the use of deadly force: essentially, an imminent threat of death or severe injury. "Now, this is the scary part—God willing it doesn't happen," he said. "Say this C.O."—correctional officer—"comes back on the block and his son just got killed by some criminal and he pulls out a nine-millimetre and starts firing into the cells—*boom! boom! boom!*—taking the inmates out." Crittendon was pointing an imaginary pistol at the officers, mowing them down. "What do you do?"

"Wait till he runs out of bullets," someone said, and everyone cracked up.

Crittendon threw his head back to guffaw, but instantly stopped. "That was a joke," he said. "You do have to shoot him, because otherwise the inmates' families will sue you. You have that responsibility."

ONE AFTERNOON, a female San Quentin employee approached Crittendon as he was guiding some visitors around the prison museum and asked him to show her the execution chamber. In 1967, the chamber was shut down at the beginning of a series of constitutional challenges to the death penalty; since 1992, when it reopened, it has been in regular use, starting with the death by gas of Robert Alton Harris, who had shot and killed two teenage boys and then eaten their Jack in the Box hamburgers.

"Sure," Crittendon said to the woman. "Let's go."

"Oh, neato! What's it like?"

"It's a gas!" Cackling, he led her just south of the prison's main entrance and unlocked an iron gateway to a narrow courtyard. It was here, early on April 21, 1992, that witnesses assembled to observe the Harris execution. Crittendon, who had been placed in charge of the prison's programs by Warden Daniel Vasquez four years earlier, was by then the prison's spokesman, and Vasquez had told him how to publicize the event: "Don't personalize it, don't dramatize it, don't embarrass the Department of Corrections, don't embarrass me, don't embarrass yourself."

Crittendon also had significant responsibility for discharging the execution, and he recalls having "a whole sense of anticipation as the plan I had helped to create was unfolding." That final evening, he oversaw Harris's last meal: "He'd asked for pizza, and I directed that it be Tombstone Pizza—"

Tombstone? "I have a sick side of me, I guess—my own little personality thing," Crittendon said. "He put a whole piece in his mouth and he says, 'Critter, you want some?' But it wouldn't have been appropriate."

Crittendon had created a meticulous timetable, but it fell apart as the courts issued four separate stays, the last called in when Harris was already strapped in the chair. As the Supreme Court was preparing to vacate the final stay, Vasquez, under heavy pressure from the attorney general's office, told Crittendon to get the witnesses back as soon as he gave the word. "He gave the word at 6 A.M., and by 6:05 all the witnesses were entering the chamber," Crittendon says. Vasquez recalls, "There was a haste, an urgency to get it all done that to this day is a source of shame to me."

As the final witnesses passed through the courtyard Crittendon made a gesture that two witnesses remember as an excited fist pump. One describes Crittendon's gesture as "distinctly celebratory"; another, Michael Kroll, says, "Crittendon raised his fist in the air three times, as if his team had just scored a touchdown. To win, for him, was to get this done."

Crittendon said he doesn't recall making any gesture of overt triumph and that he could have been giving a "move 'em on up" signal to a driver who had witnesses waiting in a van. When I reminded him that the witnesses had already assembled in the courtyard, he said that he might have been beckoning to the "extraction team" to stand ready to remove Harris's brother if he caused a disturbance, as Crittendon had heard he might. In the event, Harris's brother watched in silence as the condemned man gasped and convulsed and turned blue before being pronounced dead, ten minutes later. (In 1994, U.S. District Court Judge Marilyn Patel banned gas as the state's preferred method of capital punishment, declaring it cruel and unusual. After some notorious executions, including two in Florida in the nineteen-nineties in which the electrocuted man's head burst into flames, thirty-seven of the thirty-eight death-penalty states use lethal injection as the primary method; only Nebraska still relies on electrocution.)

Now, after unlocking a door in the prison wall, Crittendon gave a ringmaster's flourish: "The *execution* chamber." We stepped into an airless room dominated by a squat green apparatus that resembled a bathysphere. The woman employee circled it, peering at the iron doors, the thick windows, and the flat green chair within. As Crittendon watched her, his face took on a stoical, almost sorrowful cast. "The inmate who did that welding, in 1937, Alfred Wells," he remarked, "was back inside six years later for three murders, and he died right here in the chamber he built. 'I fought the law and the law won'—*bada bing, bada bam.*"

"When's the next one?" the woman asked. Crittendon explained the stay, and when she asked his opinion of the death penalty he parried coolly, "There are those who raise the argument—as is their absolute right—that you should not have state-sanctioned killing, even though the public supports it. One will see how it all plays out."

Executioners seek to maintain their detachment, but they often begin to feel empathy or depression. John Robert Radclive said that visions of the prisoners he hanged between 1892 and 1910 "haunt me and taunt me until I am nearly crazy," and Amos Squire, the doctor at Sing Sing who between 1914 and 1925 sat beside the condemned during a hundred and thirty-eight electrocutions, wrote that he finally quit when, after signalling for the procedure to commence, he began to feel "a sudden, terrifying urge to rush forward and take hold of the man in the chair, while the current was on."

Crittendon's mother, Louise, always scrutinized him after an execution; she felt that each killing hardened her son a bit, but, she told me, "it didn't take root in him." Yet Crittendon told me that he has come to believe that lethal injection is inhumane—to the executioner. "You are eye to eye with the inmate as you have skin-to-skin touch, smelling his body odor, feeling his breath, and this is someone who has been in your care at the institution, usually without being violent, for at least fifteen years," he said. "So transference occurs. I'm the only person who was there for all eleven of the lethal injections, and every single one of them I cannot forget—I close my eyes and I can see and hear it."

On December 12, 2005, the night of Stanley Tookie Williams's scheduled execution, a crowd began gathering early outside San Quentin's East Gate and soon numbered about a thousand. Williams, widely known for building one of the country's most notorious street gangs, had become even more famous for his prison transformation: he was the most prominent cause célèbre for death-penalty abolitionists since Caryl Chessman, the charming serial rapist and author who, after twelve years in San Quentin, went to the gas chamber in 1960. Williams had been visited by such celebrities as Snoop Dogg and Jamie Foxx (who played Williams in a television movie, "Redemption"), and the crowd outside that night included Jesse Jackson and Joan Baez, who sang "Swing Low, Sweet Chariot."

At 7:20 P.M., Vernell Crittendon approached the deathwatch cell with mail and a pitcher of water. Williams, a barrel-chested man with gray cornrows, was seated on his mattress as if it were a throne. He had declined a last meal, a sedative, and the chance to vouchsafe his last words to the warden. The two men, born just days apart to absconding fathers and stern, religious mothers, stared at each other through the bars. Even then, Williams believed that the courts or the governor would intervene. "I brought the mail," Crittendon said at last.

"Fine. Send it to Barbara," Williams said, referring to Barbara Becnel, a community-services activist and his most loyal supporter. He would not take the water or speak again. A week earlier, Williams had told Crittendon, "I don't even want to talk to you—you're one of the people trying to get me executed." He had asked a captain to stop Crittendon from bringing his mail, and told the warden that he didn't want the spokesman present during discussions about the schedule.

In the years after Williams came to San Quentin, in 1981, convicted of four murders, Crittendon said that he would chat with him about black pride. "I'd play the race card," he recalls, "saying, 'How come that white officer can go down to talk to that skinhead, and you see me as an enemy—and yet we're brothers, and your whole thing is black pride?'" The talks can't have been very convivial, as Williams not only hated cops, whites, and almost everyone—as he demonstrated by repeatedly attacking other prisoners—but had no use for Crittendon, whom he referred to as an "Uncle Tom" and "Mr. Lickspittle."

But beginning in 1993, after what he described as a gradual spiritual awakening, Williams stopped fighting and began to apologize for his past. An autodidact with a fondness for words such as "braggadocio" and "anent," he went on to co-write, with Barbara Becnel, nine children's books decrying the gangster life style. Becnel says, "Vernell was very helpful at first. Stan was in the Hole and couldn't get phone calls, and Vernell would maneuver and break the rules and allow us to speak on the phone."

Crittendon says he secretly hoped that Becnel would help him to persuade Williams to renounce the Crips and name his accomplices in the murders—crimes that Williams insisted he didn't commit—and to do it on television. (Becnel and Crittendon agree that he never broached any of those topics with her.) As Crittendon recalls it, in the mid-nineties Williams finally responded to the last of a series of invitations Crittendon made to him to unburden himself on Larry King's program: "A man don't rat," Williams said. "And I'm a man." Crittendon says that he realized then that Williams was just a hustler who would never quit the game. "If I could have got *him,* that would have been great! Not for Vernell," he quickly clarified, "but for public safety."

However, in notes that Williams typed before meeting one of his lawyers in 2005, he scorned the idea that he and Crittendon had once had a promising relationship, noting that in twenty-four years in San Quentin "there was *never* a reason for him and I to speak at length." Becnel believes the turning point for Crittendon occurred in 2000, when Williams, who had helped broker a gang truce in Los Angeles over the telephone (and would later broker another truce in Newark), was nominated for the Nobel Peace Prize. Peter Fleming, Jr., one of Williams's lawyers, told me, "The clear sense I had with Vernell was 'This convicted murderer's getting all this attention—why am I not getting it?'"

Certainly Crittendon took the case personally. Beginning in 2004, after Williams's appeals had been exhausted, Crittendon waged a largely clandestine media campaign against the inmate. (He first sought and received approval for his efforts to "correct public misimpressions" from the state attorney general's office and the C.D.C.R. spokesman in Sacramento, who himself acted as liaison to the governor's office, which would have to rule on Williams's petition for clemency.) Crittendon's démarche was usually accomplished through quiet suggestion: Rita Cosby, who conducted the last television interview with Williams on her MSNBC talk show, says, "Vernell's appraisal caused me to be more skeptical, and gave me some questions to ask Tookie: was he still involved in organizing gang activity behind bars?"

A month before Williams's scheduled execution, Crittendon gave an interview to the Associated Press in which he said of Williams, "I just don't know that his heart is changed," and suggested that Williams was still orchestrating gangland activities. This was an unprecedented attack for a prison spokesman to make. "To turn public opinion in favor of executing Tookie

Williams was not just weird—Tookie simply minded his own business—it was wrong," the former warden Daniel Vasquez told me. "Vernell may have gotten addicted to his own image of what he could do."

Crittendon's observations carried weight because he repre-sented a government authority and because reporters liked and trusted him. But those observations seem to have derived more from the spokesman's animus than from the inmate's miscon-duct. Crittendon had told the A.P. that Williams's prison bank account was suspiciously large, but there was only sixteen hun-dred and eighty-two dollars in it. Crittendon had found it trou-bling that Williams was not counselling his son, Stanley IV, a former gang member in prison for murder, but he acknowl-edged to me that he checked Williams's mail only in the final month or so—and hadn't read Williams's autobiography, in which he details his extensive correspondence with and coun-selling of his son—"so I can't say for sure he wasn't writing his son." When asked whether he now considered his campaign unusual or unwarranted, Crittendon said it "was approved through the department" and "an appropriate response to the questions that were asked by the media." Yet he also eventually acknowl-edged that Williams hadn't actually been orchestrating gang-land crimes. The spokesman's problem, then, was that Williams's ongoing defiance of Crittendon—and the system that Critten-don had come to embody—made him a living symbol of the Crip life style.

At eight-thirty that night, Crittendon slipped off to the staff rest room in the prison's abandoned schoolhouse, as he always did on the eve of an execution, to change into his black suit and then sit and think about the condemned man. Crittendon often began to empathize—but not this time. "I was thinking how the gang Stanley created had destroyed the African-American commu-nity," he recalls, "how you can shoot someone on the corner in broad daylight and no one who sees it will say anything, because they fear the Crips."

At midnight, Crittendon took up his customary post in the death chamber, facing the window at the foot of the green chair, "directly across from Williams's head, so that I could look right up his nostrils. It was part of my duties to watch, because if we have a blowout and a vein starts spurting blood I have to escort the witnesses out." As thirty-nine witnesses looked on in increasingly tense silence, a nurse repeatedly tried to establish the standard backup I.V. in the convict's left arm as Williams seethed and finally made an impatient remark. When the nurse exited, after twelve minutes, the second I.V. still wasn't in, but Warden Ornoski, not realizing this and having found the delay excruciating, said, "Proceed." The chemicals began to flow into Williams's right arm.

"I always wanted to be able to see the moment when the life had left the person," Crittendon said. "Stanley went motionless pretty quickly, consistent with what you'd expect. Whereas with Manny Babbitt"—a murderer executed in 1999—"you could see a tightening in his throat, little shivers and twitches when he felt it coming on." Crittendon demonstrated, jerking his head rapidly to the side and grimacing. "Stephen Wayne Anderson"—a prison escapee and murderer who was executed in 2002—"was looking around and saying 'I love you! I love you!' to his loved ones, then he laid his head back and to the side, and I could see, Oh, he's gone. But you're under such scrutiny there's not time for emotions. The sniper, when he fires off that shot, there's not time to think, I just took a human life. No, he's got to sight on another target before someone fires at him."

Barbara Becnel, who felt that she had just seen a prolonged "torture-murder," whispered a suggestion to two of the other witnesses, and as they left the chamber they cried, in unison, "The State of California just killed an innocent man!" Shirley

Neal, a Williams supporter, happened to look at Crittendon at that moment, and she recalls that "he looked shocked and frightened." Crittendon says that he was merely surprised by the outburst, and that no personal reflections entered into it. Indeed, he says that his efforts to discredit the condemned man were unrelated to the failure of their relationship: "My goal was never to reach and change *Stanley*. He was just a tool for me to have an impact. If you pick up a cup and it's all dirty, do you worry about why it's all dirty, or do you pick up another cup and quench your thirst? I put the dirty cup down and quenched my thirst."

ONE MORNING IN JUNE OF 2006, Crittendon introduced me to Lonnie Morris, a lean black lifer he has known for more than a quarter century. It was the day before Morris and a handful of other star inmates would be the subjects of a two-part series on "Larry King Live," taped in the prison's courtyard. "You've got to educate tomorrow, man," Crittendon told Morris. "The public lives in generalities and paranoia, where you're the bogeyman."

Just before the taping, Crittendon gathered the inmates in the chapel for a briefing. He predicted, accurately, the topics that King would raise—including drugs and violence—and explained that the inmates didn't have to address them. "This is not about you," Crittendon said. "It's about the millions of incarcerated men you represent—speak for them." The inmates stayed tenaciously on message. When King asked "What about rape dangers, male to male?" Morris said, "Honestly, you're going to find in prison the same thing you find in society," and then began talking about the Real Choices program.

Many of the guards were upset that Crittendon had given murderers a national platform, and that the inmates were being taped in front of a memorial to eleven San Quentin employees killed in the line of duty. The next day, as it happened, Crittendon was the master of ceremonies at the rededication of the memorial, and he made sure he was seen scolding Morris for shaking my hand "on the day for honoring our dead." "Vernell wears a lot of hats," Morris told me, wryly. "If he's walking through with the warden, wearing his 'safety and security of the institution' hat, I'll just keep stepping by."

That same month, a new warden, Robert Ayers, Jr., took over at San Quentin, and his prison policy emphasized safety and order rather than rehabilitation. Crittendon decided to retire in December, four months short of thirty years; his deputy, Eric Messick, replaced him as the prison's spokesman, but the innumerable other duties that Crittendon had assumed over the years were absorbed—or sloughed off—by the system. His role in executions will be divided among a number of officers, who will be guided not by a protean expert in avoiding embarrassment but by written procedures. Two weeks after Crittendon retired, Ayers banned visitors from the cellblocks, long a staple of Crittendon's tours; he has since won praise from officers—and aroused concern in inmates—by putting an end to all Crittendon-style shortcuts and unilateralism. Ayers declined to talk about Crittendon or his legacy, but observed, "If you just pick which rules you want to follow, the prison is a very capricious place."

In March, Vernell Crittendon visited San Francisco's Tenderloin Community School to give a Real Choices briefing to a group of fourth and fifth graders, many of whom he would soon take on a tour of the prison. Crittendon, who by then was three months retired and contemplating an eventual run for the Contra Costa County Board of Supervisors, was wearing a black San Quentin polo shirt, a black San Quentin warmup jacket, and a ring with a tiny image of San Quentin that an inmate had made for him in metal shop. But the twenty kids he met with in a basement classroom were not intimidated by the visible tokens of incarceration. And when Crittendon tried to impress them with the importance of choosing their friends wisely, catcalls filled the air. "We'll wait for these gentlemen to finish," he said evenly.

Crittendon had brought two ex-cons with him. One of them, Michael Tomlinson, a drug dealer turned pastor who was wearing a jogging suit that covered white-supremacist tattoos, took the floor and said, "There's no tough guys in the room—you're not tough."

"*You* ain't tough," a boy named Tyrell, who had long cornrows and was slouched in his chair, replied.

"There's no one so tough the Man can't beat him down," Tomlinson said, and the bleak authority in his voice silenced the room.

Afterward, heading out, Crittendon found himself in the school's vestibule, and remarked, "Just like a prison—the sally port." We went across the street to a Peet's coffeehouse, where he said that the kids wouldn't listen to him, a policeman, and that his real role was to introduce the ex-cons. "The principal would never say, 'Come on in, Michael T., drug taker and drug dealer, killer of blacks, and talk to our kids.' I vouch for Michael, now that he's a pastor—but I never want to forget that he's a bad guy." Crittendon likes to say that he doesn't judge someone by a single bad deed, but neither does he judge someone by ten years of good deeds. "The best analogy I can think of—and this is definitely the way I thought about Stanley Williams—is the circus," he said. "You know how you see a five-foot-eight balding man with a potbelly walk into the lion's cage and snap his whip, and the lion rolls over and grovels in the dirt? You put that lion back in the jungle, and if that same man walks down a bushy path he becomes lion lunch. I will always be *friendly* to former inmates, but I won't be *friends*."

The conversation turned again to the executions. He'd been thinking about Manny Babbitt's, in 1999. "That always stood out in my mind," he said. "A war hero who saved a guy's life in Vietnam by diving on a grenade, an African-American, and it appeared that his crime centered on post-traumatic-stress syndrome—he sexually assaulted and murdered this woman, then tied a toe tag on her body, like they did in Vietnam. When I spoke with Manny in the deathwatch cell, he stood at attention three inches from the bars and always said, 'Sir, yes sir!' His brother had turned him in with the caveat that the detectives would help him and not seek the death penalty, and here I was standing with his brother, watching him be executed." Crittendon stirred his espresso. "My dad's brother was in Vietnam, and he came back with a lot of psychological problems, and he—he ended his life early by his own hand. It connected with my life experience. I didn't go around saying, 'Poor Manny,' but it was what I was thinking. You've got to make sense of this thing."

Did he ever?

"I left it in God's hands. There must be a purpose in the Lord putting me where He did, even though I would never have chosen for my legacy 'He put to death people who grew up in terrible, deprived circumstances and didn't have much chance.' When I move in black communities, the very first thing people say to me is 'You really handled your business well up there on TV—you were impartial.' So I've shown we can do it. I was the face and the voice of a major organization. I broke down Europeans' stereotypes—the articulate black man. Maybe," he said, slowly, "maybe it's not that these lives were just sacrificed but that there was a greater good to my being able to serve as a role model on those very public occasions. But there's all these layers on top of layers," he continued. "Because if they were to tell me tomorrow, 'Vernell, there will be no more executions in the state of California,' Vernell would not be sad."

TAD FRIEND *is a staff writer at* The New Yorker, *where he writes the magazine's "Letter from California." He is at work on a family memoir.*

Coda

This story held my attention because I like sorting through ambiguity, and Vernell Crittendon is extremely complicated. So are the people he dealt with. During my reporting I attended some of the college classes taught inside the prison, and one evening, during a break, I spoke with Louis Branch, Jr., a courtly-seeming black man. Branch had a history of sex crimes and was serving a life sentence, but he was a diligent student. When I asked him about Crittendon—who, concerned about Branch being near young, trusting female volunteers, had unsuccessfully sought to persuade the program's director to bar him from the classroom—the inmate picked up his pen. "Vernell Crittendon is very active in giving us a plethora of chances to improve ourselves," he said, as he wrote on a piece of foolscap. "That's the success side. The failure side is the philosophy of *revenge*. Why not challenge Tookie's compassion, challenge him to live up to Vernell's philosophy of restorative justice, of giving back? What would we have to lose? Our hate, our violence. That's all." He showed me the sentence he'd written: "Vernell Crittendon is a prisoner of the penal system, as we all are." Several months later, Branch was committed to the prison's Adjustment Center for allegedly trying to overpower a nurse. He subsequently earned more time in solitary for trying to seize a guard through the slot in his cell door.

Charles Graeber

THE TAINTED KIDNEY

FROM *New York* MAGAZINE

THE ANGEL OF DEATH LOOKS SLEEPY. His face shows nothing. His eyes are closed. Charles Cullen sits motionless in the wooden defendant's chair of the Somerset County Courthouse as, hour after hour, his victims' families take the stand. They read poems and show photographs, they weep and yell. If Cullen hears them, he doesn't say; he never does. During his three years in custody, Cullen has never apologized or made excuses. He has never issued a statement, offered a public word, never faced the families of his victims. In fact, the only reason he's in court today is because he wants to give away one of his kidneys.

To that end, he has cut a deal with prosecutors, agreeing to appear at his sentencing on the condition that he be allowed to donate an organ to the dying relative of a former girlfriend. To many of the families of his victims, this deal is a personal insult—the man in shackles still calling the shots, the serial-killer nurse wanting to control the fate of yet another human life. But for the families of his New Jersey victims, this is the first and last chance to confront Charles Cullen. So they are here, and they are angry.

"My only consolation is that you will die a thousand deaths in the arms of Satan," yells the daughter of a man Cullen spiked with insulin. "I hope, with all my heart, that you are someone's bitch in prison."

"You are a pathetic little man," says the woman whose mother-in-law Cullen killed with digoxin. "In prison, perhaps someone will choose to play God with Mr. Cullen, as he has played God with so many others."

"Charles!" cries a round woman in a lime-green pantsuit. Her body shakes in rage and grief; her hands grip a photograph of her 38-year-old son, a picture taken before Charles Cullen stopped his heart. She is screaming. "Charles, why don't you look up at me, huh? What are you, asleep?"

In fact, Charles Cullen is very much awake. His shackled hands, which look from a distance as pale and still as sleeping doves, twitch slightly in his lap, counting off silent prayers, *Jesus Christ, son of God, have mercy on me*, as if on invisible rosary beads; the expressionless shield of his cheek still tics when "burn in hell" hits his ear. His eyes open slightly, like a child pretending to be asleep, Cullen can see only a twilight view of the table, the cups, the stenographer with her leg crossed over the other, light shining hard off her shoes.

"The state asks for thirteen life sentences," says the assistant prosecutor, and there is a wrinkle on Charles Cullen's brow, a flexed cheek enunciating "thirteen," then the blankness returns, and there is again just what Cullen can see in front of him: the wooden table, the stack of pastel Dixie cups, a black plastic pitcher, and beyond, lit by her own little spotlight of halogen, the stenographer, her hands bouncing like puppets. And then Judge Armstrong is asking if the defendant has anything to say on his own behalf, anything at all about these horrendous crimes against man and nature, and the stenographer's hands stop and wait. Cullen has no comment. With a rap of the gavel and screeching of chairs, it is over. Charles Cullen is hustled into a back room with men in riot gear holding automatic weapons, then he is gone, leaving behind a courtroom full of questions.

AS FAR AS THE LAW IS CONCERNED, there isn't much left for Cullen to say. On December 12, 2003, Cullen was brought in for one first-degree murder and one attempted murder as a critical-care nurse at Somerset Medical Center in Somerville. The next day, he shocked Somerville detectives by confessing to many more murders. Cullen told detectives that he killed the sick in order to end their suffering, but at some point, as Cullen spiked bags of IV saline in supply closets and killed patients who were not terminal, his compassion became compulsion, and when his personal life became stressful, killing became his outlet.

Exactly how many patients he murdered, we will never know: His memory of his crimes, he says, "is foggy," and he drank heavily to make it foggier. He worked graveyard shifts in intensive-care units, largely unsupervised in a dark punctuated only by the beeps and breaths of medical machines. Many of the medical charts are missing or incomplete; the dead are now dust. His method was to overdose with drugs so common that sorting Cullen's private death toll from the general cadence of hospital mortality is nearly impossible.

Cullen guessed that he had killed 40 people. So far, investigators have positively identified 29 victims (confirmation of a 30th victim is currently pending). It's unlikely that the tally will ever be complete; even Cullen's lawyer, Johnnie Mask, told prosecutors they weren't finished. Some investigators with an intimate knowledge of the case are convinced that the real number is over 300. By that reckoning, Charles Cullen would be the biggest serial killer in American history.

After Cullen was arrested, New Jersey prosecutors agreed to

take the death penalty off the table in exchange for his full cooperation. Cullen would help identify his dead, then spend the rest
of his life in prison. He was 44 years old.

Months turned to years at the Somerville jail, and Charles
Cullen's life assumed a regularity he had rarely known as a free
man. He had his cell, his spy novels, time to exercise or shower.
Uniformed men turned the light off and on, governing day from
night. Once a week, he met with his Catholic deacon or the head
chaplain, the Reverend Kathleen Roney, and every so often, he
never knew when, the guards would escort him across the lawn
to the prosecutor's office, to pull through the case files.

Cullen studied the scrawled medical charts, the arrhythmic
EKGs, the final flatlines, and the blood work afterward—the primary investigator in the search for his own victims. There were
new charts nearly every week, boxes of them, covering sixteen
years of death at nine hospitals. Winter became spring and winter
again, but Cullen just kept squirreling through the files with a cup
of black coffee, getting thinner, getting it done; eventually, when
the investigations were closed and the shouting echoed out, he
could take his life sentences into a cell and disappear completely.

Then in August 2005, an envelope arrived at the Somerville
jail. By now, Cullen was inured to the interview requests and the
hate mail, even the odd "fan letter." He never answered any of
them, of course, but this was something new—a story about a man
named Ernie Peckham, clipped with kitchen scissors from a local
newspaper on Long Island. In the margin was a note in a girlish
cursive: "Can you help?"

Cullen knew about Ernie—a guy about ten years younger than
Cullen, with four kids and a wife at home and a job shaping metal in
Farmingdale. Ernie was the brother of Cullen's estranged ex-
girlfriend, who was the mother of Cullen's youngest child—a
little girl he had never seen. Maybe he and Ernie had said hi once
at a wedding years ago; Cullen couldn't recall, but they weren't

friends, they weren't even acquaintances, they certainly weren't close enough to share organs. But an organ is what Ernie Peckham needed.

DOCTORS DON'T KNOW exactly how or when, but at some point in 2002, Ernie contracted strep. Probably it was just a little scratch that got infected, the sort of thing that either swells up and goes away or takes you out for a week with a sore throat that can be treated with a dose of antibiotics. But Ernie didn't notice the infection, and it spread, overloading the microscopic filters in both of his kidneys.

Normally, these filters would have been removing toxins from Ernie's blood; now they were like a sink clogged with hair. Ernie's body began to bloat with its own poisons, swelling his hands and face and turning his urine the color of cocoa. By the time he saw a doctor, his kidneys were dead. Untreated, he'd be next. Doctors could filter Ernie's blood three times a week with dialysis, but this was a stopgap measure; what Ernie really needed was a new kidney. Unfortunately, so did 60,000 other Americans. As Ernie's health deteriorated, the seven-year waiting list for a cadaver donor would become a death sentence.

His only other option was to receive a kidney from a living donor (although most everyone has two kidneys, you only need one). The best way to match kidney with recipient is through a blood relative—but nobody in Ernie's family, nor any of his friends, was medically eligible to donate. His only chance was to find the perfect stranger. But how many people are willing to donate an organ to someone they don't know? Worse, the odds that Peckham would be a perfect six-for-six tissue-typed match with any one random donor were incalculably small. Ernie Peckham actually had a better chance of being struck by lightning.

Ernie's mother, Pat Peckham, contacted the local paper to run a public-interest item with Ernie's blood type above the hospital's donation-hotline number. No miracle donor called.

Pat was running out of options for saving her son. And what would it take except a stamp? So, without telling Ernie, she clipped the article out of the paper, stuck it in an envelope to the Somerville prison, and waited for her miracle.

The thing about miracles, you can't really predict what form they might take. They might come from anyone, even the serial killer who had knocked up her daughter.

THE REVEREND KATHLEEN RONEY wears rock-collection-size birthstone rings on her fingers and Celtic charms around her clerical collar and paint-on eyebrows that flick like conductor's batons as she talks. Roney started ministering to Cullen soon after his arrest. She figured the meditation techniques of the Desert Fathers would be appropriate for a man spending life in prison: The "Jesus Prayer" Cullen recited through his Somerset sentencing came from one of Roney's tutorials.

Over the course of nearly three years, Roney had gotten to know Cullen, but that didn't mean she understood him. She didn't, for instance, understand why Cullen had killed so many people—but her job wasn't to comprehend the serial killer, only to minister to the man. And she couldn't quite understand why, suddenly, he was so desperate for her help to donate a kidney; 22 years as a jail chaplain, and nobody had ever asked for anything like it. "So that night I went to the jail and questioned him," she says. "To make sure I wasn't being used."

Roney isn't a big woman, but she's blessed with the bullhorn voice and big-girl swagger that jail work requires, and she can turn it on when she has to. She called for Cullen, who was reading in his cell, and she asked him: "Why this? Why now? Do you want it for fame, or to rehabilitate your public image? Do you think you're making some deal with God, to save a life to wipe out the lives you took?" Or did he hope that he might die on the operating table in some sort of passive suicide attempt?

"The questions seemed to really hurt his feelings," Reverend Roney says. "But that was okay. I needed to know his heart."

Roney said she'd think about it, and drove through the dark to pray in front of her icons. Charles had told her he was serious, that he wanted to see if he was a match. He wanted to donate because he was asked, and it was good. But should she believe him? The more she examined the question, the simpler it became. She was a minister, a Christian, and there was a life at stake, a guy on Long Island named Ernie. Cullen could never orchestrate a donation alone from behind bars. He needed her help—they needed her help. How could a compatibility test be a moral dilemma?

The hospital sent color-coded tubes for Cullen to bleed into. She would be the blood mule; Stony Brook hospital on Long Island would test his antigens against Ernie's. From what she read on the Internet, a match was an incredible long shot. But at least everybody could say they tried.

When she asked her friends to pray with her that weekend, she didn't tell them what they were praying for or for whom. "We needed to keep it secret," she says. "And besides, could you ask every person to pray for a serial killer?"

EVERY EQUINOX, REVEREND RONEY and like-minded Celtic Christians spend a week at a Druid spiritual retreat in Pennsylvania. It's a profound time for her, a time of dancing around bonfires and meditating before icons and spirit-voyaging through unbounded acres of blond American farmland. Every morning, she'd walk the hard earth between the corn stubble, reciting her prayers, feeling the ancient wisdom, looking for a sign. It was then that she felt the vibration.

That was her cell phone—they encourage silence at these things, so she had it on vibrate—and right away, she knew what had happened. And her prayer group knew, too. In fact, the whole spiritual retreat knew what had happened; they just felt it and started to cry, because they knew. And she thought, *This is it, it's meant to be.*

She's crying now, retelling the story over an iced tea, ruining her mascara, remembering how Cullen was a perfect six-for-six antigen match, a match like winning the Publisher's Clearing House sweepstakes, and she wipes the tears away with a Starbucks napkin. "Honestly, we thought it was a miracle," she says. There would be more tests, X-rays, CAT scans, tests with machines you couldn't send to the jail by mail. But these were trivial compared with this spotlight in the darkness, a sign of God's larger plan.

In that halcyon moment, Reverend Roney couldn't imagine the lost friendships of her fellow Christians; she thought it was as easy as helping Charles donate to save a dying man. It was September; if she acted fast, the kidney would be like an early Christmas present.

When Roney called Pat Peckham, Pat didn't believe her. "Are you sure?" she asked. It was so improbable, it was so—then Pat started to scream. "Then I'm screaming, then she's crying, then I'm crying," Roney remembers.

Roney would have loved to have seen the look on Ernie Peckham's face when Pat told him the news. But Pat wasn't going to tell her son, not for a while, and she certainly wouldn't tell him the name of the donor. As sick as Ernie was, Pat was sure Ernie wouldn't accept a kidney if he learned it came from Charles Cullen.

THE SOMERSET COUNTY JAIL is a redbrick building conveniently catty-corner to the Somerville courthouse. On the other side of the metal detector is a wall of two-way mirrored plate glass backlit by video surveillance. Beyond that is the nine-by-five-foot cell where Charles Cullen had spent the past two and a half years of his life.

The sergeant buzzes me through a series of doors into a hall-way partitioned into stainless-steel booths. Guards escort Charles Cullen onto the opposite stool. We nod mutely to each other across the bulletproof divide, and take a phone.

"Hello? Hello?"

"Hello?" I say. "Can you hear me?"

"Yeah," he says. "I can make you out." His voice is flat and quiet. I press the plastic phone hard to my ear, and Cullen notices. "Did you get in all right?" he says, louder.

"It took two hours," I say.

Cullen glances up, reading my expression before retreating to the corners of the glass. "That happens," he says. He nods once. "It changes in here, week to week."

In pictures taken soon after his arrest, Cullen looks a little like Kevin Costner or a hollowed-out George Clooney—perhaps a bit colder, yet still a handsome guy with a bad haircut. But now, in the mercury vapor lights of the Somerset jail visiting room, Cullen looks chapped and anemic. Never an eater, he has become skeletal in jail. His face seems to hang from his cheekbones like a wet sail. A crucifix dangles from a chain over his collarbone, mixing with the sprigs of graying chest hairs where his shaven neck meets his prison togs—essentially mustard-yellow versions of hospital scrubs, insulated with a layer of white flannel under-wear. His eyes dart and flash like a man holding his breath, wait-ing to talk.

He tells me about the afternoon when Reverend Roney came to his cell, excited to tell him that he was an "excellent match" for Ernie Peckham. Cullen was happy, but his years in jail had taught him that nothing would ever be simple. "The match means the donation will happen—it's meant to happen," Roney told him. "Yeah," Cullen responded. "Well, I hope the courts think that."

Cullen knew that if word ever got out that he was trying to donate a kidney, the whole thing would probably be over right there. He needed to keep it secret; nobody could know. "I mean, it's not like I'd want the publicity," Cullen says. "But mostly I thought that if it got out, it would be bad for the donation. The way people think of me, they would think I was trying to do something. But someone leaked it—I think it was the D.A., but I don't really know. And now . . ." he rolls his eyes. The press was having a field day.

"I know people see me as trying to control things; they think I'm trying to get something out of it. But the idea that I was trading my appearance at sentencing for the donation are out-and-out lies," he says. "I was told by my lawyer, Mr. Mask, that I didn't have to appear." He shakes his head, and almost smiles. "I mean, you know, who would want to go? All those people that you—but the donation was important. The detectives suggested that I offer to go, to speed the donation along. They said I needed to give them something. But that's not me holding a gun to the prosecution. It's the other way around!

"I grant that I certainly have done some very bad things—I've taken lives," he says quickly. "But does that prevent me from doing something positive?" Cullen folds a pale arm tightly across his chest and studies the counter. "That's the funny thing," he says. "People think you're crazy for doing something for someone else if you don't know them personally."

THE NEW JERSEY OFFICE of the Public Defender is two stories of red brick with handicapped spaces and shrub landscaping and 300-pound women in nightgown-size Tweety Bird T-shirts smoking menthols by the double glass doors. In the offices upstairs, there are families in sweatpants waiting under fluorescent lights and a hole in the Plexiglas where you can announce yourself by sticking your mouth in and yelling politely.

Johnnie Mask's office is in the back. The deputy public defender looks something like an Old Testament James Earl Jones—a big man with broad leonine features and a gray Ishmael beard gone grayer over three years defending the biggest serial killer in New Jersey history.

It was a nice idea, giving a kidney, but Mask wasn't in it for the karma. "My motives were purely selfish," Mask says. "Charlie was absolutely intent on making this donation happen. I was worried that if he didn't get his way, he'd mess up my case, and all my hard work would go down the drain. More work for me, more expenses for the state—there was no way I was going to let that happen."

But right from the beginning, Mask saw signs that this thing might not go through. "Judge Armstrong signed the order for the blood test, but I don't think anybody really expected he'd actually be a match for Ernie," Mask says. "When he was, and it got into the papers, suddenly there are all these problems. The judge and the prosecutor and the victims' families got up in arms about Cullen going into a hospital again—they figured he'd kill somebody, or probably himself. Then everyone would be cheated out of their ability to yell and scream at him."

Mask was told that the donation was possible only after Cullen was sentenced. That was supposed to happen by December 2005, but a month later, two counties still hadn't even finished their investigations. "That's why on January 10, Charlie stopped cooperating with the prosecution, saying 'Sentence me now.'" By breaking his plea agreement, Cullen seemed to be risking the death penalty for the donation, but really it was a tactical move by Mask. "It forced their hand. We realized that by the time they finished, Ernie might be dead." (As of this printing, investigations in Essex and Morris counties are still open.)

They were months behind schedule, but, in theory, Cullen was about to be transported to Stony Brook Medical Center and donate his kidney side by side with Peckham. "But when [Attorney General Peter] Harvey wanted Cullen to cooperate, he was saying, you know, 'We'll work out the details later, but it will happen,'" Mask recalls. "We were counting on those promises, but he just wanted to wrap up the case before he took on his new job in the private sector."

A few weeks later, weeks when Ernie Peckham's condition continued to deteriorate, Mask walked by the desk of Vaughn McCoy, who was then the director of New Jersey's Division of Criminal Justice. "I asked him what the status was. He pulled up some e-mails and said, 'Well, apparently Stony Brook doesn't want Mr. Cullen in their hospital.' I tried to lean over and read it off his monitor, but he sort of blocked me." Mask smiles joylessly. "Said it was confidential."

By now it was February. "So what can you do? Then the old A.G. leaves, and the new attorney general's office tells us Cullen can't travel to New York anyway—it's not legally feasible!" Mask shakes his head at what's become an old joke.

"I don't know what's true now. We thought it would happen in January. Stony Brook keeps giving us new dates—they're saying April now; before, it was March. And Charlie's getting more aggravated every day. I think [allowing the] donation was always just a big dangling carrot to get Charlie to jump." It was the only reason Cullen agreed to appear at the sentencing in New Jersey. Mask was still working toward the donation, but he'd bet Roney a dinner it would never happen.

It was a good bet, especially considering what was about to happen at Cullen's next court appearance.

THE NEW JERSEY COURTS were done with Charles Cullen, but Pennsylvania still had unfinished business, and so as Ernie Peckham's condition worsened even more, Cullen was transported west to stand trial for the six murders and three attempted murders he committed in Lehigh County, while working at the hospitals surrounding Allentown.

Allentown is a poor steel town living in the ruins of a rich one, and the downtown is a grand, ceremonial public space of imported stone and soaring columns and busted crazies rooting for cans, joined now by a small parade of families in dark, formal clothes with little blue stickers from OfficeMax gummed to their lapels to show they're families of the victims of the Angel of Death.

In a legal sense, sentencing Cullen for his Pennsylvania crimes is perfunctory—he won't be finished serving his New Jersey sentence until the year 2347—but for the families of patients Cullen killed here, today's sentencing is their only chance to confront the Angel of Death with their memories and their anger. It's also an opportunity for Cullen, a final shot at showing the world that he is, as he claims, a killer with compassion. A public demonstration of that compassion would go a long way toward saving Ernie Peckham's life. In Pennsylvania, Cullen could do what he hadn't done in New Jersey.

Just like the victims' families at Cullen's New Jersey trial, the families who fill the Allentown jury box have brought poems and speeches and photographs of the dead and are prepared to exercise their right to confront the killer. But this time, Cullen rises to speak—reciting, from memory, statements Cullen believes have been hostile to him that the judge has made to the press.

"And for this reason, your honor," Cullen says, "you need to step down."

Judge William Platt is not amused. "Your motion to recuse is denied," he says.

"No, no, your honor," Cullen insists. "You need—you need to step down. Your honor, you need to step down."

"If you continue this, I will gag and manacle you," the judge warns.

Cullen shouts over him. "Your honor, you need to step down!" he says. "Your honor, you need to step down! Your honor . . ."

The high marble walls make this court a beautiful room but a terrible courtroom, amplifying and distorting all sound. Cullen fills this room. The families wait as Cullen gets to speed-shouting his statement ten times, 30, 40. He's not going to stop, and now the court officers are on him.

They pull a spit mask over his head—a mesh veil that keeps a prisoner from hawking loogies on his captors—but the noise continues. They wrap the spit mask with a towel and screw it behind his head and now Cullen sounds like a man screaming into a pillow. The families of the victims try to read. "You are a total waste of a human body." "You are the worst kind of monster, a son of the devil." But soon the sergeant's hands begin to cramp, and chorus by chorus, Cullen's voice gets clearer. Judge Platt nods, and the sergeant produces a roll of duct tape the size of a dinner plate, and tapes a big cartoonish X over Cullen's lips, which does nothing. And so the victims read their personal statements, and Cullen screams his, like a nightmarish version of "Row, Row, Row Your Boat."

"If my grandmother was alive right now, she's say to you, 'I hope you rot in hell, you sick son of a bitch.'"

"Your honor, you must step down. Your honor, you must step down."

"Six more life sentences, served concurrently with those already handed down."

"Must step down. Your honor, you must . . ."

And with a final "Such that you will remain in prison for the rest of your natural life," the court officers frog-march Cullen—bound, gagged, duct-taped—into a waiting elevator. He is still chanting when the doors close. The silence that follows is terrible, too.

Afterward, the families huddle in the hallway, shaken and unsatisfied. "I think he intentionally meant disrespect to everyone in that courtroom," says Julie Sanders, a friend of one of Cullen's victims. Sanders stabs her finger toward the hole in the air where Cullen had been. "He says he is a compassionate man, that he wants to donate a kidney to save someone's life. I needed to say something to him: Where's the compassion now? Does he know what he's done to our lives?"

NOW WHAT MASK AND RONEY had wasn't a legal problem— they had a court order authorizing the donation from Judge Armstrong—it was bigger. "Basically, there's not a lot of goodwill toward Charlie Cullen among the citizens of New Jersey," Mask says. "Nobody wants to seem to be kowtowing to a serial killer's requests. Some of the families see his donation request as a slap in the face. It's like he's asking them for a favor."

After the scene at Allentown, Cullen's kidney was simply too hot to handle. Roney would call the D.A.'s office, which told her to call the New Jersey Department of Corrections, who'd tell her to call the hospital. Months passed with no answers, no schedule, no deadline. If the donation was going to proceed, there were state and private institutions to coordinate, insurances to inter-face. The Corrections Department would need to guard Cullen in the hospital, against escape and vigilantes and, because he had already attempted suicide multiple times, Cullen himself. The only ones with real deadlines were Cullen and Ernie. Cullen's donor test was valid for only a year; Ernie might not even survive that long.

And then there was the kidney, which would need to travel 125 miles from Cullen's hospital in New Jersey to Peckham's hos-pital on Long Island fast enough to keep it viable. Depending on traffic, that could be a bitch of a drive. A construction snarl or a fender bender or even a Hamptons rush hour could imperil Er-nie's life, but who was going to pay for a helicopter?

Ironing out the details would require a lot of hard, unpaid work by a great number of people, but at this point, Cullen was the last guy anyone wanted to do a favor for. That's how they saw it, a favor to Cullen, not a way to save another man's life. "It's his choice, he's a grown man, but realistically, the stuff he does in front of the victims' families isn't winning him any points either," Mask says.

"And Charlie doesn't really feel bad about any of this. He's concerned how it affects his kids, but he doesn't feel bad. And Charlie's not the kind of guy to fake it," says Mask. "It makes some people feel like he's getting away with something." Prison was supposed to take away his options. And yet there he was, still making demands.

AFTER ALLENTOWN, HIS FINAL SENTENCING, Cullen was shackled in the back of a windowless van. He was met at the Trenton prison by guards in riot gear. They strip-searched him, gave him prison clothes, and led him to the psych ward, where they took the clothes away and strip-searched him for a second time. He was handed a disposable gown like medical patients wear, but it was made from the stuff they wrap around new TV sets, and he was put into a padded room for a 72-hour observation period. The gown shredded after the first day. He tried not to listen to the "time for your insulin" comments from the guards, focusing instead on Psalm 25: "My enemies are many, they hate me. Deliver me, let me not be ashamed." Then he was given clothes again and moved into DD Block, where he was to serve his now eighteen life sentences, and where I visit him again.

From the Trenton River Line train, the prison appears as a block of brick and razor wire across the highway from a McDonald's. Another minute's walk past the front gate gets you to a security check-in with a metal detector and a uniformed guard. After a pat-down, you're buzzed through three bolted steel doors and into a guarded hallway partitioned into steel booths. I find Cullen waiting in the third one, waving a little hello. We nod mutely across the bulletproof divide, and plug in our phones. There is static, then breath.

Cullen and I had been communicating through letters for nearly a year, and I had learned a lot about the man—his accidental entry into nursing school and his first job scrubbing dead skin from burn victims, the depressions and suicide attempts and marital problems, his drinking and his hospitals and his sixteen-year murder spree. But even knowing the facts, I was still unable to fully connect the mild man across the glass with the serial killer and his monstrous crimes.

I tell him that some of the families of his victims are against the kidney donation, that they see it as special treatment for a serial killer, and nothing more. "I'm trying to get something? I'm in prison, I can't control—there's nothing to bargain for—no island off the coast of New Jersey that they send you to torture you, no Guantánamo Bay. All I can do is sit in a cell. And I know that New Jersey doesn't make license plates anymore, so what would the families rather I did, just sit and watch TV?"

Cullen is indignant at a system that he said was willing to sacrifice an Ernie Peckham to punish a Charles Cullen. Saving a relative stranger's life is undoubtedly heroic—would *you* give up a kidney?

Of course, heroic compassion is easier to talk about than mass murder. I can admire Cullen for the one and hate him for the other, but I have no idea how to connect the two—they seemed to be the actions of two very different men. And so I ask him: Is it any wonder people question your motives? You're in prison for having taken dozens of lives, and yet now you're fighting to save one. It seems . . . inconsistent.

Cullen is only a foot away, on the other side of the glass, but I cannot decipher his expression. Then he glances to the side of the glass, as if reading there, and slowly begins to speak.

"If you're asking if I knew what I was doing was wrong," he says, "I saw that I was stopping pain, removing pain. I saw it as shortening the duration of the pain, ending pain. Sometimes the pain was patients who were suffering and terminal; sometimes it was the pain of families being ripped apart; sometimes it was the lives of patients that would only be tied up in an endless series of procedures and complications and pain.

"But if you're asking—well, I knew that it was illegal," Cullen says. "And that it wasn't my choice to make. But it's how I thought about it. I felt compelled to do what I did. I didn't see it as bad. I did know it was illegal."

Cullen is looking at the table but not looking at it. I don't know what he sees. "But, if you're asking, when I was asked to donate a kidney, I felt that I did what I would normally do, in any circumstance. To be helpful. It was something that I could do. It was something that was needed. I was asked to do it, and it's possible. And I felt compelled to, because I could do it and I was asked to."

I don't know what I expected from his answer. Ultimately, the only answer to the question of "why" is, simply, "because." Cullen did what he felt he needed to, or wanted to, or could; at some point, they had become the same thing. In such a tyranny, bad and good don't figure. It's a simple answer, but it's the only one that makes sense.

Cullen fixes me with a look, then takes his glance away, as if to study my response in private. "I know a lot of people find it surprising that someone like me would want to do this, donate. But for me, it's totally consistent. For me, as a nurse, it's what I would do, what I would have always done. It's who I am. But if you need to wonder why I should, or why someone like me would, well, it really depends on how you think of people. And what you think people are capable of."

AS IT HAPPENS, it was a Tuesday when the waiting ended. They came for Cullen in the night, guards with keys and handcuffs. He was going to the prison's medical center at St. Francis hospital. If they knew why, they wouldn't say. They gave him the paper gown again, drew his blood, cuffed him to the bed. The television in the corner was always on, local news, *Oprah*. A day passed, and he thought, *Here we go again.* He had only fourteen more days before his donor tests expired, but this wasn't the donation. It was something else.

The guards came again in the morning. They were taking him downstairs; they didn't say why. He was instructed to respond only to direct questions. He was told that Charles Cullen was not his name. His name was now Jonny Quest. The doctor called him Mr. Quest. It was a security measure, but also someone's idea of a joke. Cullen thought it was funny. "It could have been worse," he said later. "Saddam Hussein or something."

They gave him something to relax him, Valium, he thinks; they wouldn't say. It made him woozy. They gave him forms to sign. He held the pen, unsure of which name to use. "Use the one you're supposed to," the doctor said. He'd watched the cartoons as a kid, he remembered the handsome blond boy and his adventures, a helpful boy with skills, full of potential. He signed the paper "Jonny Quest." It wasn't legally binding, of course, so they gave him another form that he was to sign "Charles Cullen, a.k.a. Jonny Quest." The nurse looked away when he did this. It was supposed to be a secret. Then they gave him another shot, and now he was feeling kinda gone.

An hour later, Jonny Quest's kidney was tucked into a cooler and readied for its journey. It would have been crazy to risk traffic, so it likely flew via a Life Star helicopter, northeast from Trenton, keeping Manhattan on its left, banking up Long Island. That day the traffic far below was heavy with Hamptons weekenders, a line of lights leading past the massive Stony Brook medical complex, lit on the dark hillside like Bilbao under construction.

I parked in the C lot. On weekend nights, hospitals are usually busy only after the bars close and usually only in the emergency room. At 8 P.M., the main lobby was as quiet as a dead department store. A guard read yesterday's newspaper again; the gift shop was just Mylar balloons in darkness. Surgery is on the fourth floor, with the burn unit and radiology. The kidney took the back elevator; I took the front.

In the surgical waiting room, the TV is always on, approximating normality for the families camped there, the children and their mothers holding each other, the men clutching Dunkin' Donuts cups. This TV played the movie *Freaky Friday*, two people switching bodies and identities and, it being Hollywood and Disney at that, coming closer together as a result. But that was just a movie. For transplants, parts are parts. You take what you can get to survive.

And so, while Jamie Lee Curtis and Lindsay Lohan had their first mother-daughter argument about whose life was more difficult, Ernie Peckham lay face up on a table, anesthetized and encircled by masked strangers in disposable blue clothes. Some traced a curved incision through the fat of his abdomen, others parted the draped muscles of his belly wall with cool steel clamps. Jonny Quest's kidney was about the size of a surgeon's hand, a quivering bean shape mottled in yellowish fat that nested neatly into the half-shell of Peckham's pelvis. A stump of renal artery, pruned only hours before from its owner's aortal stalk, was patched into Ernie's blood supply with 5-0 suture wire; vein was stitched to vein. And later, as Jamie Lee and Lindsay, back in their own bodies again, smiled knowingly at each other across a climactic concert scene, a surgical clamp was removed from an external iliac artery, and Jonny Quest's kidney swelled pink with oxygenated blood, alive again—Ernie Peckham's kidney now.

Underneath the xenon lamps, this medical miracle didn't look like much more than cauterized gristle in a blue paper hole. It showed nothing of the millions of tiny tubules stacked inside its medulla, or the arterial branches, as infinite as crystals in frost, that would filter his blood as a brain filters choices, sorting bad from good as well as humanly possible.

CHARLES GRAEBER *is a National Magazine Award–nominated contributing editor at* Wired *and* National Geographic Adventure *magazines. A former medical student, breakfast chef, and bar columnist for the* Budapest Sun, The Cambodia Daily, *and the* Phnom Penh Post, *Graeber has also written for* The New Yorker, GQ, New York *magazine, the* New York Times Magazine, Ha'aretz, Men's Journal, *and numerous others. Born in Iowa, he now moves between a Brooklyn apartment and a Corten steel icebreaker anchored off Nantucket Island.*

Coda

Apparently it's common wisdom that we are the sum of our actions, or the sum of our parts, or both. In this story, the actions included both murder and cure, and the parts were actual body parts moved man-to-man, Frankenstein-style. And all of this in a series of hospitals, the buildings where so many of life's mundane mysteries unfold. From the first moment it was obvious that this story would beg bigger questions than it answered—as good a reason for writing as I could imagine. It started with the morning paper and a two-inch column about a killer nurse who wanted to save a life. The weirdness of that one stayed with me for days. Cullen had never spoken to anyone, but I wrote him anyway. His response pushed me into a crossroads.

Twenty-first-century writers chronicling their relationship with a convicted killer do so in the shadow of both the genre and its ethical hangover; not only are you trespassing through the creaking mansion of *In Cold Blood*, but you're also haunted by the cautions of Capote. And so while one (thankfully former) editor high-fived me for "tricking" a famous killer into delivering a mother lode of salacious material, my mother mourned the sure-blackening of her son's pure Iowan soul. I tried hard to keep them both wrong—and myself sane—by playing it straight with Charlie Cullen. The fact was, I was invested in his kidney donation attempt—I have a family history with medicine that ranges from Revolutionary War surgeon great-grandpappies to a passionate nephrologist father to my own aborted stints in med school and kidney medical research. Also, I'm not a heartless dick. But it was also true that I was only writing about this kidney donation because the donor had murdered dozens, if not hundreds, of people. Realistically, my ability to tell Cullen's kidney story at proper length, in a popular magazine, was dependent on access to his dirty details. So I told him: I believed the donation was a good thing, the murders were bad, and that I was a writer, not an accountant. I wouldn't average his life into a simple sum. Cullen didn't like hearing this calculus and I didn't enjoy explaining it. The truth helped my sleep but not my reportage. To Charlie Cullen, public interest in his murders is no different than that of motorists slowing to ogle a grisly accident. And Charlie's right; part of the "true crime" appeal is the pornography of horror presented as news. But that's not all of it. Because of his (true) crimes, Charles Cullen is commonly referred to as the "Angel of Death," or more simply, a "monster." Personally, I don't believe in either—or rather, I believe that we are all potential angels or monsters, depending on the directions we walk from various crossroads. Cullen's crimes are terrible, but not inhuman—comprehensible if only in the context of his own life and mind. In my first meeting with Cullen, the bulletproof Plexiglas seemed to me like a smudged mirror. There are no monsters, there's only ourselves through the lens of another life. There are a few questions I always get about this story, the first of which is, of course: Why did Charlie kill all those people? But forget that one. What answer would suffice? The second regards the story's final scene, my access, and all the dovetailing details. This one is easier. At the time I'd been on the story for about a year. Cullen's donation appeal seemed dead. Months passed with no news, and Cullen had been sentenced to eternity. Nobody official would talk to me, so I started cold-calling the hospital desks. One night I found an E. Peckham checked in, surgical ward—the recipient. It was happening, maybe. The drive from Brooklyn took an hour, and the whole time I wondered what the hell I was going to do when I got there. The place was dead. I felt like a tabloid creep just for showing up. I decided to shadow the operation, but not intrude—following the route of the kidney, lurking the halls, eyeballing the too-appropriate Disney movie. After six hours I was on friendly terms with the janitors and the shattered families in the waiting room—complications from birth, a baby born with intestines outside his body and a hole in his heart—and why was I there? Waiting on a friend. I tried to be present for this family, talking when they wanted to talk, reciting the oblique reassurances of waiting and hope, and wondering why I had chosen writing over medicine, watching over doing. Like nurse Cullen, I was in the gritty backstage of the purportedly grand human pageant, where we are born and will die among OfficeMax furniture and a muted TV. When Ernie was wheeled into recovery through the saloon-style doors I could see where the family was hovering, big women with big purses, the nurses in sanitary blue, the anesthetized guy in industrial pajamas. Ambition threw an elbow in my ribs, my moment to be the great writer from the mold of the Capotes and Mailers, whose need for truth and access required jumping every hurdle. I ignored that moment and drove home in silence, knowing it was done and thinking about a newborn, the sum of broken parts, lying on a table with a hole in his heart.

Mark Bowden

THE PLOY

FROM *The Atlantic Monthly*

IT WAS A MACABRE MOMENT OF TRIUMPH. At a closed compound within Balad Air Base in Iraq, behind Jersey barriers 30 feet high, the men and women of the interrogation mill crowded around a stark display: two freshly dead men, bare and supine on the floor.

The audience members were expert interrogators, most of them young, some of them military, others civilian contract workers. They called themselves "gators," and they were the intelligence arm of Task Force 145, the clandestine unit of Delta Force operators and Navy SEALs who hunt down America's most-wanted terrorists. For years, their primary target had been Abu Musab al-Zarqawi, the Jordanian leader of the grandly named Al Qaeda in Mesopotamia, the gloating, murderous author of assassinations, roadside bombings, and suicide attacks. Together, living and working inside this "Battlefield Interrogation Facility," the gators had produced leads for the Task Force to chase. They had put in thousands of hours probing, threatening, flattering, browbeating, wheedling, conning, and questioning, doing what

Major General William B. Caldwell IV, in his press conference the next day, would call "painstaking intelligence gathering from local sources and from within Zarqawi's network." It was, as Caldwell would put it, "the slow, deliberate exploitation of leads and opportunities, person to person," all striving to answer just one critical question: Where is Zarqawi right now?

This day, June 7, 2006, had finally produced the answer.

And so here he was, stretched out on the floor, stiff, pale, gray, and swollen in death, his "spiritual adviser," Sheikh al-Rahman, lying alongside him. The men had been killed, along with two women and two small children, when an American F-16 had steered first one and then another 500-pound bomb into the house they occupied in a palm grove in the village of Hibhib. Task Force operators had recovered the men's bodies and carried them as trophies to Balad. Both now had swaths of white cloth draped across their midsections, but were otherwise naked. Zarqawi's face— wide, round, and bearded, his big eyes closed, a smear of blood still lurid across his left cheek—was unmistakable from his frequent videotaped boasts and pronouncements. He had been more sought-after than Osama bin Laden, and in recent years was considered the greater threat.

No more. The mood was one of subdued celebration. President Bush would call that day to congratulate the Task Force's boss, the Joint Special Operations Commander Lieutenant General Stanley McChrystal. For many, the satisfaction was tempered by photos of the dead children. They were hard to look at.

The unit's female J2, or chief intelligence officer, embraced a young woman in a T-shirt and khaki cargo pants who was part of the two-person gator team that had produced what is known in the trade as "lethal information."

"I am so glad I chose you for this," she said.

McChrystal himself came by. A tall, slender, very soldierly-looking man, he was an Army briefer during the Persian Gulf War, but has been infrequently seen or photographed in recent years because of his clandestine post. He and his top commanders stared down at Zarqawi with evident satisfaction. Everyone leaned in to listen.

"Yep," said one of the colonels, "that's one dead son of a bitch."

EARLY THE NEXT MORNING, the terrorist's demise was revealed to the rest of the world at the Combined Press Information Center, in Baghdad.

"Today is a great day in Iraq," said General Caldwell, the spokesman for the Multi-National Force in Iraq. "Abu Musab al-Zarqawi is dead, no longer able to terrorize innocent Iraqi civilians . . . Today, Iraq takes a giant step forward—closer to peace within, closer to unity throughout, and closer to a world without terror."

Perhaps. Like so much else about the Iraq War, it was a feel-good moment that amounted to little more than a bump on a road to further mayhem. Today, Iraq seems no closer to peace, unity, and a terror-free existence than it did last June. If anything, the brutal attacks on civilian targets that Zarqawi pioneered have worsened.

Still, the hit was without question a clear success in an effort that has produced few. Since so much of the "war on terror" consists of hunting down men like Zarqawi, the process is instructive. In the official version of how it happened, which is classified, the woman embraced by McChrystal's J2, and her two male interrogation partners, received primary credit for the breakthrough. All three were duly decorated. But like the whole war in Iraq, the real story is more complicated, and more interesting.

The truth is known to those interrogators involved, to their immediate chain of command, to a military historian who interviewed the principals, and to a small circle of officials who have been briefed about it. There are detailed accounts of the interrogation sessions that describe the tactics and motivations of the gators. So there are those who know the story well who were not directly involved in it. In deference to the secret nature of the work, I have not used the real names of the interrogators involved, but the aliases they assumed in Iraq. Their story affords a unique glimpse of the kinds of people employed in this secret effort and how they work, and it limns the hidden culture of interrogation that has grown up in the last six years.

"The Customer"

Most of the gators directly involved in this breakthrough were recruited in 2005. They were young men and women who had accumulated valuable experience conducting hostile interrogation. Some were on active duty, a good number from military-police units. Some were veterans of Afghanistan and Iraq, where they had so distinguished themselves that the Special Operations Command had sought them out. Some were working for private contractors such as L-3 Communications; some were civilian employees of the Defense Intelligence Agency. Some had experience in civilian law enforcement or criminal law, and had volunteered to do such work for the military. Some were lawyers. Some had advanced degrees. Some called themselves "reserve bums," because they signed on for tours of duty in various parts of the world for six months to a year, and then took long, exotic vacations before accepting another job. One raced cars when between jobs; another was an avid surfer who between assignments lived on the best beaches in the world; another had earned a law degree while working as a city cop in Arlington, Texas; another worked as an investigator for the U.S. Attorney's Office in Montgomery, Alabama. They all loved the work and signed up for the most dangerous and important assignments.

This one had come with an irresistible job description, with phrases like *high priority* and *top secret* and *for an unidentified military client*. Enlistees were sent to the Army's interrogation school at Fort Huachuca, in southeastern Arizona, for a few weeks of brush-up training. They all received a dazzling two-hour Power-Point presentation about Iraqi history and culture. They had all surmised right away that the job meant working with "special operators"—the military's elite, secret soldiers, who handle only top-priority jobs—but they did not know for sure until after the training, when they were flown from Arizona to Fort Bragg, in North Carolina, headquarters for the Special Operations Command. At Bragg, no one speaks directly of Task Force 145, but it was abundantly clear that was the outfit they would be working with. They were told, "There is no such thing as rank where you are going; everyone is focused on the mission. No one will get any credit for anything that happens."

Before being sent to Iraq, the gators underwent a final interview designed to weed out anyone emotionally ill-suited for the work. During the interview, the eager recruit would usually be insulted. "You must be kidding," the questioner would say. "You don't have anywhere near enough experience to do a job like this." Any recruits who got angry, flustered, or upset—and some did—were sent home. Those selected to proceed were instructed to adopt aliases by which they would be known "in theater."

Only then were they told that the "customer" would be Zarqawi.

The Team

Balad Air Base is a sun-blasted 15-square-mile expanse of concrete, crushed stone, and sand about an hour's drive north of Baghdad. It is one of the largest and busiest bases in Iraq, complete with a Green Beans coffee shop, Pizza Hut, and Burger King open around the clock. It is also known as Camp Anaconda, or, informally, as "Mortaritaville," for the frequency of mortar attacks on the 25,000 personnel stationed there. Few of that number ever set foot behind the towering concrete barriers in the far north corner, known to one and all as "The Compound," home to the estimated 1,000 American and British special-operations soldiers of Task Force 145, and to the most urgent special-ops campaign in the world.

Because of the exigency of the fight in Iraq, according to groundbreaking reports by Sean Naylor of *Army Times*, Zarqawi had been assigned a higher priority than even Osama bin Laden and his second-in-command, Ayman al-Zawahiri. The Task Force's soldier elite, its "shooters," includes Delta operators, SEALs, members of the Air Force's 24th Special Tactics Squadron, and selected soldiers from the Army's 75th Ranger Regiment. Transportation is provided by helicopter crews and pilots from the Nightstalkers, the Army's 160th Special Operations Aviation Regiment. The tempo is rapid; the unit conducts an average of a mission a day, with four strike forces stationed around Iraq. The intel operation that guides the Task Force hums around the clock, seven days a week. Its mission is to unravel Al Qaeda in Mesopotamia and other insurgent groups from the inside out, by squeezing each new arrest for details about the chain of command. Newly arrested detainees are constantly delivered to the facility, blindfolded, bound, wearing blue jumpsuits.

Inside the Compound are a number of small buildings that have been recently erected as well as two large ones left over from when Saddam Hussein's air force owned Balad—one a large dome-shaped airplane hangar, the other a flat-roofed structure of about the same size. Both were painted tan to blend with the desert landscape. The flat-roofed building houses the holding cells, each of which has stone walls, a concrete slab, a pillow, and a blanket. Detainees are kept one to a cell. The interior of the hangar is divided into 10 interrogation rooms, separated by plywood walls and usually furnished with white plastic chairs and a small table. Each room has a video camera so that a senior interrogator in a separate control room with two rows of TV monitors can observe the questioning.

During the hunt for Zarqawi, interrogations took place in two shifts, morning and night, with interpreters, or "terps," providing translation. The gators wore civilian clothes for their sessions, and were allowed to grow out their hair or beards. The less the detainees knew about their rank or role in the military, the better. There was virtually no downtime. When the gators were not questioning detainees, they were writing up reports or conferring with each other and their commanders, brainstorming strategy, eating, or sleeping in their air-conditioned "hooches," small metal rectangular containers flown in by contractors. Alcohol was forbidden. Their rec center had a gym, a television set that got the Armed Forces Network, and a small Internet café. But recreation was not especially encouraged. One gator described the atmosphere as "spare and intense, in a good way." They were doing their country's most vital work.

The hunt for Zarqawi had begun shortly after the invasion of Iraq, in the summer of 2003, when the U.S. military took two Special Forces units (one was in Iraq looking for Saddam Hussein; the other had been in Afghanistan hunting for bin Laden and other al-Qaeda leaders) and joined them together into what was then called Task Force 6-26. The Special Forces had come maddeningly close to getting Zarqawi on several occasions. In late 2004, Iraqi security forces actually captured Zarqawi near Falluja but, supposedly ignorant of his identity, released him. In February 2005, Task Force members had learned that he would be traveling on a stretch of road along the Tigris River, but their timing was off, and after the elusive terrorist crashed through their roadblock, he was gone.

The interrogation methods employed by the Task Force were initially notorious. When the hunt started, in 2003, the unit was based at Camp Nama, at Baghdad International Airport, where abuse of detainees quickly became common. According to later press reports in *The New York Times, The Washington Post,* and other news outlets, tactics at Nama ranged from cruel and unusual to simply juvenile—one account described Task Force soldiers shooting detainees with paintballs. In early 2004, both the CIA and the FBI complained to military authorities about such practices. The spy agency then banned its personnel from working at Camp Nama. Interrogators at the facility were reportedly stripping prisoners naked and hosing them down in the cold, beating them, employing "stress positions," and keeping them awake for long hours. But after the prisoner-abuse scandal at Abu Ghraib came to light in April 2004, the military cracked down on such practices. By March of last year, 34 Task Force members had been disciplined, and 11 were removed from the unit for mistreating detainees. Later last year, five Army Rangers working at the facility were convicted of punching and kicking prisoners.

The unit was renamed Task Force 145 in the summer of 2004 and was moved to Balad, where the new batch of gators began arriving the following year. According to those interviewed for this story, harsh treatment of detainees had ended. Physical abuse was outlawed, as were sensory deprivation and the withholding or altering of food as punishment. The backlash from Abu Ghraib had produced so many restrictions that gators were no longer permitted to work even a standard good cop/bad cop routine. The interrogation-room cameras were faithfully monitored, and gators who crossed the line would be interrupted in mid-session.

The quest for fresh intel came to rely on subtler methods. Gators worked with the battery of techniques outlined in an Army manual and taught at Fort Huachuca, such as "ego up," which involved flattery; "ego down," which meant denigrating a detainee; and various simple con games—tricking a detainee into believing you already knew something you did not, feeding him misinformation about friends or family members, and so forth. Deciding how to approach a detainee was more art than science. Talented gators wrote their own scripts for questioning, adopting whatever roles seemed most appropriate, and adjusting on the fly. They carefully avoided making offers they could not keep, but often dangled "promises" that were subtly incomplete—instead of offering to move a prisoner to a better cell, for instance, a gator might promise to "see the boss" about doing so. Sometimes the promise was kept. Fear, the most useful interrogation tool, was always present. The well-publicized abuses at Abu Ghraib and elsewhere put all detainees on edge, and assurances that the U.S. command had cracked down were not readily believed. The prospect of being shipped to the larger prison—notorious during the American occupation, and even more so during the Saddam era—was enough to persuade many subjects to talk. This was, perhaps, the only constructive thing to result from the Abu Ghraib scandal, which otherwise remains one of the biggest setbacks of the war.

It was an exciting, challenging job, filled with a sense of urgent purpose. Most of the gators had a military background, and they found the lack of protocol liberating. As the gators had been told, rank inside the Compound was eschewed entirely. People referred to each other by their nicknames. The key players in the final push for Zarqawi were known as:

- "Mary." The young woman congratulated by the J2, Mary was a stocky woman in her early 20s, with Asian features and straight dark hair; her intelligence and tenacity had earned her the reputation of being the most skilled interrogator in the unit.

- "Lenny." A Navy reservist from the Philadelphia area, Lenny had a background in the computer industry and had done a previous tour at Guantánamo Bay's Camp X-Ray. A wiry man in his mid-30s, he smoked a lot, shaved his head, and wore a goatee. He had a tough-guy, street-kid manner, and was usually teamed with Mary.

- "Dr. Matthew," aka "Doc." A tightly wound, precise man in his 30s, with short, thin blond hair, Doc had worked as a military-police investigator before becoming a reservist. A senior interrogator at Balad, he was considered an intellectual, though his honorific was an exaggeration: He had earned two master's degrees, one in international relations and another in management. Between jobs, he surfed.

- "Matt." A slender, dark-haired active-duty Air Force technical sergeant in his early 30s, Matt liked to present himself as a simple country boy, but was not one. He was from the Midwest and liked to race cars.

- "Mike." A commercial pilot from Nebraska in his early 30s, he had joined the Army because he wanted to be involved in the war effort. Extremely energetic and gung-ho, Mike had less experience than most of his colleagues, but was quickly regarded as a natural.

- "Nathan." Tall, wiry, and dark-haired, Nathan was one of the few gators who could speak some Arabic. A civilian contractor, he once got in trouble with the unit commander for stretching even the Task Force's loose apparel standards by wearing a bright Hawaiian print shirt to the mess area.

- "Tom." A veteran of Bosnia in his late 40s, Tom was unlike most of the others in that he was married and had children. He was short and round and balding, and was always slightly unkempt.

This was the team that would locate Zarqawi.

The Interrogation Begins

The first major clue on the trail that led to Zarqawi came in February 2006, from a detainee Mike was questioning. The man had admitted his association with the "Anger Brigades," a Sunni group loosely aligned with al-Qaeda. In a series of intense sessions that the other gators regarded as brilliant, Mike learned of residences in Yusufiya that the insurgent leadership sometimes used as safe houses. They were placed under heavy surveillance, and through a mid-April series of raids during which a number of suicide bombers were killed, a new crop of suspected mid-level al-Qaeda operatives was captured and delivered to Balad. It was on one of these raids that Task Force operatives found a videotape with outtakes from a recent Zarqawi press release, the one showing him wearing a black do-rag, a black shirt, and a suicide belt, and carrying an automatic rifle. The outtakes showed this fearsome terrorist fumbling awkwardly with the weapon and being instructed in its use by another man. The military released the new images in hopes of diminishing Zarqawi's stature. What the Task Force didn't realize when they discovered the tape was that Zarqawi himself was only one block away.

Five of the men captured during these raids were assigned to teams of interrogators at Balad. Two of them would prove to be the most valuable. The first, whom we will call Abu Raja, was assigned to Matt and Nathan. The second, an older and more imposing figure, we will call Abu Haydr. He was assigned to Mary and Lenny.

Abu Raja was a sophisticated man in his mid-30s, a professional who spoke fluent English. Round, soft, and balding, he wore the regulation Saddam-era Sunni moustache. He came from a family that had been well-connected during the tyrant's reign; before the American invasion, he'd had a thriving business. A relative of his had been killed in the long war Iraq fought with Iran in the 1980s, and Abu Raja hated all Iranians. He saw the

American invasion as a conspiracy between the Iranian mullahs and the United States to wipe out Iraq's minority Sunnis. Though Abu Raja was initially defiant, Matt and Nathan sized him up as a timid man, neither ideologically committed nor loyal. They battered him with rapid-fire questions, never giving him time to think, and they broke him—or so they thought—in two days. He agreed to talk about anyone in al-Qaeda who outranked him, but not about those who held less important positions. Since the Task Force's method was to work its way up the chain, this suited the gators perfectly.

Abu Haydr was more difficult. He was a big, genial man who nearly buckled the white plastic chairs in the interrogation rooms. He was 43 years old, with a wide, big-featured face, big ears, a well-trimmed beard, and fair skin. He was married and had four children. He also spoke fluent English. Before the American invasion, he'd had an important government job and had made a good living. He had hated Saddam, he said, but when the tyrant fell, he had lost everything. He looked tough and boasted that he had a black belt in karate, but his manner was gentle and his hands were smooth and delicate. He spoke in a deliberate, professorial way. He had studied the Koran and, while not overtly pious, knew a great deal about his faith. He admitted his sympathy for the insurgency. He had been arrested once before and had served time in Abu Ghraib, he said, and did not wish to return. He said Abu Raja had asked him to attend the meeting where they had both been captured, and that he was there only because the people at the house needed him to operate a video camera. This was the same story told by Abu Raja.

"I don't even know why we were there," he told Mary and Lenny.

FOR THREE WEEKS, from mid-April to early May, Abu Haydr was questioned twice daily, and gave up nothing. Three weeks is a long time for interrogators to hold on to someone. Mary was forceful and thorough. Lenny's approach was consistent; he tended to hammer at the man relentlessly, taking him over the same ground again and again, trying to shake his confidence or just wear him out. It wasn't sophisticated, but it often got results, especially when combined with Lenny's imposing tough-guy demeanor. Abu Haydr took it all in stride, stubbornly unruffled. Before every response, he would lean his bulk back in the groaning chair, fold his graceful hands, and meditate like a scholar.

Doc, who was observing both interrogations in his role as a supervisor, saw that Mary and Lenny were getting nowhere, so he asked the Army captain supervising the process to replace them. This was not an unusual request from a senior gator; detainees were often placed with different teams when someone felt that an alternate approach might work, and Doc had asked to shift detainees before. But this request was denied. Given the circumstances of Abu Haydr's arrest—and his age and sophistication—the Task Force was highly suspicious of him, and there were those high up the chain, Doc was told, who wanted Mary on his case.

It was easy to dismiss Doc's concern for several reasons. He was known to be overbearing, and some of the gators felt he supervised their work a little *too* closely. That may have been particularly galling to Mary, who had been at Balad longer than Doc and was regarded as the best in the Task Force. Their colleagues knew that there was something of an ego clash between those two. Doc was older and more experienced, and could not always disguise his resentment at the organization's higher regard for his younger colleague. To orient him when he first arrived at Balad, Task Force officers had assigned Doc to observe Mary. After a few days, he had told his commander that he was unimpressed and had asked to be placed with someone else. When he was assigned the supervisory role, he reprimanded Mary directly and complained to others that she seemed to spend an inordinate amount of time on the Internet chatting with her boyfriend, who was also serving in Iraq. She sometimes skipped staff meetings, and while some of the gators were doing three and four interrogation sessions a day, she stuck resolutely to two. Doc argued that she seemed inexcusably out of step with the fervid pace. Others had also expressed concern about the way she dressed. Mary usually wore khaki cargo pants and two layers of T-shirts, which they suggested were cut too low at the top, exposing cleavage, or too high at the bottom, showing her midriff—displays offensive to religious Muslim detainees. But neither Mary's status nor her habits had changed in response to Doc's complaints. The tension between them was observed by all. For whatever combination of reasons, Doc's attempt to move her aside failed.

ABU RAJA, MEANWHILE, WAS A WRECK. After weeks of grilling, he had given up all that he could give, he complained, but the gators kept after him day and night. One day, Doc sat in on his questioning. Watching an earlier interrogation, he had noticed that Abu Raja had slipped. Going over a story he had told many times before, Abu Raja mentioned for the first time that Abu Haydr had sometimes met alone with Abu Raja's boss.

This was different, and odd. Why, Doc now asked, would Abu Haydr, Abu Raja's subordinate, a man who had been called in just to operate a video camera, be meeting separately with Abu Raja's boss? The detainee had no convincing explanation for it, and it left Doc with a hunch: What if Abu Raja had been lying about the other man's status all along? Why would he do that? Was he frightened of Abu Haydr? Protecting him? It forced a fresh look at the older prisoner, who was more impressive than Abu Raja anyway. What if he had been Abu Raja's superior in the organization? That would mean Abu Haydr was even more important than they had suspected. The problem was that Mary and Lenny were stymied, and the team had all but given up on getting information from Abu Haydr. He had made a final statement, been issued new clothes, and was on the list for transport back to Abu Ghraib.

With Abu Haydr just hours away from being shipped out, Doc asked for and received permission to speak to him one more time. He knew Abu Haydr dreaded going back to Abu Ghraib, and he had an idea for how to get him talking.

Breaking Abu Haydr

The two men—the big Iraqi and the intense blond-haired gator—talked for five hours in the interrogation room; because Doc was a supervisor himself, their conversation was not monitored. They talked about children and football and wrestling.

"I was a great wrestler," Abu Haydr announced.

"You look like one," Doc told him.

In his weeks of watching, the American had noted Abu Haydr's chronic braggadocio. The Iraqi constantly trumpeted his skills—the black belt in karate, advanced knowledge of the Koran, expertise in logic and persuasion—like a man determined to prove his importance and worth. He spoke little about his family, his wife and children. He seemed completely preoccupied with himself, and he presented his frequent opinions forcefully, as the simple truth. The two men discussed the historical basis for the rift between the Sunnis and the Shia, something Doc had studied. And when the Iraqi lectured Doc on child-rearing, the younger man nodded with appreciation. When Abu Haydr again proclaimed his talents in the arts of logic and persuasion, Doc announced himself out-argued and persuaded.

Their conversation turned to politics. Like many other detainees, Abu Haydr was fond of conspiracy theories. He complained that the United States was making a big mistake allowing the Shia, the majority in Iraq, to share power with the Sunnis. He lectured Doc on the history of his region, and pointed out that

Iraqi Sunnis and the United States shared a very dangerous enemy: Iran. He saw his Shia countrymen not just as natural allies with Iran but as more loyal to Iranian mullahs than to any idea of a greater Iraq. As he saw it—and he presented it as simple fact—the ongoing struggle would determine whether Iraq would survive as a Sunni state or simply become part of a greater Shia Iran. America, Abu Haydr said, would eventually need help from the Sunnis to keep this Shia dynasty from dominating the region.

Doc had heard all this before, but he told Abu Haydr that it was a penetrating insight, that the detainee had come remarkably close to divining America's true purpose in Iraq. The real reason for the U.S. presence in the region, the gator explained, was to get American forces into position for an attack on Iran. They were building air bases and massing troops. In the coming war, Sunnis and Americans would be allies. Only those capable of looking past the obvious could see it. The detainee warmed to this. All men enjoy having their genius recognized.

"The others are ignorant," Abu Haydr said, referring to Mary and Lenny. "They know nothing of Iraq or the Koran. I have never felt comfortable talking with them."

It was not a surprising comment. Detainees often tried to play one team of gators off another. But Doc saw it as an opening, and hit upon a ploy. He told the prisoner that he now understood his full importance. He said he was not surprised that Abu Haydr had been able to lead his questioners around by their noses. Then he took a more mendacious leap. He told Abu Haydr that he, Doc, wasn't just another gator; that he was, in fact, in charge of the Compound's entire interrogation mill. He was the Boss; that was why he had waited until the last minute to step in.

"I believe you are a very important man," he told Abu Haydr. "I think you have a position of power in the insurgency, and I think I am in a position to help you."

Abu Haydr was listening with interest.

"We both know what I want," Doc said. "You have information you could trade. It is your only source of leverage right now. You don't want to go to Abu Ghraib, and I can help you, but you have to give me something in trade. A guy as smart as you—you are the type of Sunni we can use to shape the future of Iraq." If Abu Haydr would betray his organization, Doc implied, the Americans would make him a very big man indeed.

There was no sign that the detainee knew he was being played. He nodded sagely. This was the kind of moment gators live for. Interrogation, at its most artful, is a contest of wits. The gator has the upper hand, of course. In a situation like the one at Balad, the Task Force had tremendous leverage over any detainee, including his reasonable fear of beating, torture, lengthy imprisonment, or death. While gators at that point were not permitted even to threaten such things, the powerless are slow to surrender suspicion. Still, a prisoner generally has compelling reasons to resist. He might be deeply committed to his cause, or fear the consequences of cooperation, if word of it were to reach his violent comrades.

The gator's job is to somehow find a way through this tangle of conflicting emotions by intimidation or bluff. The height of the art is to completely turn the detainee, to con him into being helpful to the very cause he has fought against. There comes a moment in every successful interrogation when the detainee's defenses begin to give way. Doc had come to that moment with Abu Haydr. He had worked at the detainee's ego as if it were a loose screw. All of his ruses dovetailed. If Doc was an important, powerful man—better still, if he was secretly in charge—his respect for Abu Haydr meant all the more. After all, wouldn't it take the most capable of the Americans, the man in charge, to fully comprehend and appreciate Abu Haydr's significance?

Doc pressed his advantage.

"You and I know the name of a person in your organization who you are very close to," Doc said. "I need you to tell me that name so that I know I can trust you. Then we can begin negotiating."

In fact, the American had no particular person in mind. His best hope was that Abu Haydr might name a heretofore unknown mid-level insurrectionist.

Ever circumspect, Abu Haydr pondered his response even longer than usual.

At last he said, "Abu Ayyub al-Masri."

Doc was flabbergasted. Masri was the senior adviser to Zarqawi, the second-in-command of Al Qaeda in Mesopotamia. The gator hid his surprise and excitement. He thanked the prisoner, pretending that this was the name he had expected.

"Now we can begin negotiating, but I have to leave now."

"I only will talk to you," said Abu Haydr.

"I can't promise you that," the American said. "You should talk and be friendly to whoever comes in to question you. I will be watching."

He promised—avoiding the usual hedge—to get Abu Haydr an extra blanket and extra food, and did. And he got the detainee off the list for transport to Abu Ghraib.

The Feud that Felled Zarqawi

"Why did he decide to talk?" asked Doc's commander.

The gator explained that he had promised Abu Haydr "an important role in the future of Iraq." He also reported that he had represented himself to the detainee as the man in charge. That infuriated Lenny, who was already annoyed that Doc had been questioning "his" prisoner behind his back. Lenny complained that the lie undermined his position in future interrogations.

"He was scheduled to leave," Doc reminded him.

Despite Abu Haydr's insistence that he speak only to "Dr. Matthew," his interrogation resumed with the regular team of gators. Lenny promptly told him that their colleague had lied when he said he was in charge.

Doc was infuriated, and he took his outrage to his commander. Lenny was more concerned about protecting his turf than the mission, Doc complained, and demanded that he be reassigned, but this request, too, was denied. Concerned that his break-through would be squandered, Doc decided to go behind his commander's back. He paid the first of many unauthorized visits to Abu Haydr's cell in the holding block, away from the cameras monitoring the interrogation rooms. He told Abu Haydr that his colleagues were not allowed to reveal that he was in charge.

"I'm still around, and I'm still watching," Doc told him. "Talk to them as if you were talking to me."

Abu Haydr asked how much information he would have to give to earn Doc's assistance.

"Right now, you are at about 40 percent," he was told, "but you must never mention our deal to anyone." Doc swore him to secrecy about their informal talks.

And, curiously, the feud between the gators began to help the interrogation. Abu Haydr seemed to enjoy the subterfuge. Doc's visits with him were unauthorized; if his fellow gators found out about them, they would be furious, as would his commander. So Doc, unable to deliver the captive's information himself, had to persuade Abu Haydr to talk, not to him but to Mary and Lenny. He stayed vague about what information he wanted and kept us-ing the percentage scale to push the detainee. Sure enough, Abu Haydr responded. In his sessions with the others, he confirmed his status above Abu Raja's and began talking about significant al-Qaeda figures. He was still cagey. He wanted to buy himself Doc's help, but he didn't want to pay any more for it than neces-sary.

Doc would regularly slip into Abu Haydr's cell to grade his progress.

"What percent am I at now?" the detainee would ask.

"Fifty percent," Doc would say.

This went on for three weeks, and soon the Task Force was

mapping Zarqawi's organization with greater and greater detail.
During a series of raids on May 13 and 14, shooters killed one of
Zarqawi's lieutenants, Abu Mustafa, and 15 others in his network.
Eight suspects were detained. Intel gleaned from them sent the
shooters back out to arrest more men, who delivered still more
information. The eventual result was what the Task Force called
an "unblinking eye" over the network. On May 17, two of
Zarqawi's associates were killed, one of them his manager of foreign fighters. Punishing raids went on throughout that month.

Still, even though he clearly relished his "secret" sessions with
Doc, Abu Haydr protected the men at the very top of the organization. The ploy played upon his belief that he was operating in a
multilayered reality, and at a deeper level than those around him;
the secrecy just reinforced the ruse that Doc was a high-level connection. In the middle of this process, Mary started questioning
Abu Haydr with the older gator they called Tom, and Lenny continued on in separate shifts by himself.

In early June, after Doc told the prisoner he was at "90 percent," Abu Haydr promised to give up a vital piece of information
at his next session. And he did.

"My friend is Sheikh al-Rahman," he told Mary and Tom.

He explained that Rahman, a figure well-known to the Task
Force, met regularly with Zarqawi. He said that whenever they
met, Rahman observed a security ritual that involved changing
cars a number of times. Only when he got into a small blue car,
Abu Haydr said, would he be taken directly to Zarqawi.

Days later, with the Task Force watching from a drone high over
Baghdad, Rahman got into a small blue car, but the surveillance
team promptly lost him in traffic. There was tremendous disappointment and frustration at the Compound. Another precious
chance had been lost. But after just a few more days, late in the afternoon of June 7, Rahman got into the blue car again. This time
the Task Force observed him all the way to the little concrete house
in the palm grove at Hibhib. Electronic intercepts may have helped

confirm that Rahman was meeting with Zarqawi in the house (the terrorist leader never used cell phones, which are relatively easy to track, but he did use satellite phones, which are harder to pinpoint, but not—as he apparently assumed—impossible). Convinced they had their man, the Task Force leaders decided not to wait for their shooters to get into position. Waiting seemed ill-advised, and besides, storming the house would likely result in a firefight; in the confusion, Zarqawi might find another chance to slip away. A faster, more certain, and more deadly strike was ordered.

High over Iraq, the U.S. Air Force maintains a constant patrol of strike aircraft that can be called upon immediately. The mission was tasked to two F-16 pilots, who had spent the day looking for roadside bombs from the sky. The pilots were told only that the target was "high value." At 6:12 p.m., one of the jets dropped the first laser-guided bomb; minutes later, it dropped the second. Both hit their target, reducing the house to rubble. Villagers said the earth shook with each blast.

According to General Caldwell, Iraqi forces were on the scene first, having heard the explosion from nearby. They found Zarqawi badly wounded but still alive, the only one to survive the strike. About half an hour after the second bomb hit, he was being carried out on a stretcher when the first American soldiers arrived, an 11-man military training team embedded with a local Iraqi army unit. The Americans took Zarqawi from the Iraqis, and a medic began treating him, securing his airway. Zarqawi spat blood and drifted in and out of consciousness. Caldwell said that the terrorist tried to get off the stretcher, but the soldiers resecured him. His breathing was labored, and his lungs soon failed him. Then his pulse gave out. It was pleasing to his pursuers that Zarqawi's last sight was of an American soldier.

Caldwell initially said that a child was killed in the bombing, but altered his statement the next day to say that no children had been killed. In the Compound, pictures from the blast site showed two dead children, both under age 5.

The Fight Goes On

A tape of the air strike was played at Caldwell's press conference. A black-and-white video shot from one of the bomber jets shows the long shadows of late afternoon on a dense patch of palm trees, and a large house before a narrow road. The first blast sends dark billows of gray smoke in four directions, in the shape of a cross. About two minutes later, when the smoke has blown off, the second blast produces a smaller, more contained plume of white smoke. Those inside would have had no warning. They would not have heard the jets, nor the bombs hurtling toward them.

Four of the gators involved were decorated for their service. Mary, Lenny, Tom and Doc were called to the general's office. Doc and Lenny, the Navy reservist, were awarded Bronze Stars; Mary and Tom received civilian medals. Two other civilian analysts were also recognized.

Several of those who had worked on the case for months felt the recognition was appropriate but somewhat misallocated. Mike, after all, had developed the information that had led to the arrests of Abu Raja and Abu Haydr; Matt and Nathan had broken Abu Raja; and Doc had invented the ploy that ultimately enabled the killing blow. His deep knowledge of Iraqi history and religion, and of Abu Haydr's distinctly Arab outlook, went well beyond the two-hour PowerPoint lecture on Iraqi culture the gators got at Fort Huachuca.

IN THE LONG RUN, the successful hunt for Zarqawi may not amount to much, but it offers lessons in how to use American power in subtler and more effective ways.

"The elimination of Zarwaqi is neither the beginning nor is it the end, but it is a stride in the direction of law and order, to an Iraq that is primed for the future, by a government that respects the rights of all Iraqi citizens," said General Caldwell at his triumphant press conference. He later added, "For the first time in three years, the Iraqi people really do have a chance here."

Some of the members of Task Force 145 were less sanguine. "Zarqawi's death was an achievement, but it was only symbolic," said one of them. "Zarqawi had hoped to incite a sectarian war, according to his letters, and he accomplished that. His strategy worked: Target the Shia so they will retaliate. When we killed Zarqawi, there were 10 just like him to take his place. As I see it, there is no incentive right now for the Sunnis *not* to join the insurgency. We haven't offered them anything—no economic, ideological, nor personal incentives. We tell them, 'You will have a voice in the government,' but they know that will not happen. They don't believe the Shias will give them a say. They hate the United States for creating this nightmare that destroyed their lives, and which clouds their future, but they need us as a buffer. I've talked to a lot of Sunnis, and most are not motivated by religion or ideology. They are just trying to make it."

"This is the story of the whole war," said another. "'Kill this one guy, and it will make things all better.' I still don't understand where this notion comes from. It's like we are still fighting a conventional war. This one doesn't work that way."

Seventeen other raids were conducted in and around Baghdad soon after Zarqawi's death. The shooters found suicide vests, passports, Iraqi army uniforms, and license plates hidden under floorboards. Another 25 Iraqis were issued blue jumpsuits and led to the interrogation rooms. Task Force 145's primary focus shifted to Zarqawi's successor, Abu Ayyub al-Masri. The insurgents' bombings continued. The fight went on.

As for Abu Raja and Abu Haydr, they were processed and shipped out. "Probably to Camp Cropper," said one of the gators, referring to a detention facility near Baghdad International Airport.

Mary and Lenny felt that Abu Haydr deserved a reward of some kind, but they were reminded that he had been an important mid-level figure in the deadly insurgency, a man who had on his hands, at least indirectly, the blood of many civilians and American soldiers. The idea of a reward was quickly dropped.

And what of Doc's pledge to Abu Haydr?

"Doc promised him an important role in the future of Iraq," said one gator. "And, by God, Abu Haydr got it. He was the man who led us to Zarqawi."

MARK BOWDEN *is a bestselling author, screenwriter, and journalist. He is a national correspondent for* The Atlantic Monthly, *and writes a column for The* Philadelphia Inquirer. *His book* Black Hawk Down *was a finalist for the National Book Award, won the Overseas Press Club's 1997 Hal Boyle Award, and was the basis of the film of the same name, which won two Academy Awards. His book* Killing Pablo *won the Overseas Press Club's 2001 Cornelius Ryan Award, and has been optioned for motion picture, as has his book,* Guests of the Ayatollah. *His latest book is* The Best Game Ever: Giants vs. Colts, 1958, and the Birth of the Modern NFL. *Mark teaches journalism and creative writing at his alma mater, Loyola College of Maryland. He lives on a small horse farm in Oxford, Pennsylvania. He is married and has five children.*

Coda

This is one of the most tightly-focused stories I ever wrote. It was intimate, and involved only a handful of people. Indeed, you can count the number of *possible* sources for it on one hand. Part of my challenge in writing it was to obscure the identities of those who helped me the most.

I had written about interrogation on a theoretical level for *The Atlantic Monthly* several years earlier, an article called "The Dark Art of Interrogation," which predated the revelations of abuses at Abu Ghraib and elsewhere. In the years since, the subject matter had become politically-charged and highly controversial, with liberals viewing harsher tactics as a sign of moral and legal degeneration, and conservatives regarding attitudes toward coercion as a litmus test of one's seriousness in a war on "terror."

This was a chance to revisit the topic with a real case, and one of the more successful ones since the United States went to war against Islamo-fascists in Afghanistan, Iraq, and around the world. I was surprised (although I should not have been) to discover that a culture of professional interrogation had taken root in the military, and that in the years since the September 11, 2001, attacks, a cadre of seasoned "gators" had been developed. One of the most interesting aspects of the story for me was these characters, most of them very young, male and female, military and civilian, who had distinguished themselves at this esoteric, important, and often troubling discipline. It is interesting to see how clever questioners can manipulate prisoners to provide vitally important information to their enemy, without resorting to unsavory tactics. The better the "gators" are at their work, the fewer the occasions when more severe methods may need to be employed. Our society is engaged in a necessary and important debate over interrogation methods, precisely because the stakes are high and the need for actionable intelligence is vital to prevent murderous attacks. I'd like to think that "The Ploy" has made a contribution to the discussion.

D. T. Max
_____

DAY OF THE DEAD

FROM *The New Yorker*

MALCOLM LOWRY DIED in his cottage in the village of Ripe, in Sussex, late at night on June 26, 1957, or early the next morning. He was forty-seven years old. His wife, Margerie, found his body upstairs, on the floor of their bedroom. An autopsy revealed that Lowry, an alcoholic, had been drunk, and the doctor who examined the body found that he had swallowed a large number of barbiturates and had inhaled some half-digested food from his stomach. An inquest was held, at which a police officer, the Lowrys' landlady, and Margerie testified. The coroner ruled the fatality a "misadventure"—that is, an accident. Lowry had choked to death on his own vomit.

Lowry is known for his 1947 novel, "Under the Volcano," which chronicles the final hours of Geoffrey Firmin, an alcoholic Englishman living in Mexico, in the shadow of the Ixtacihuatl and Popocatepetl volcanoes. On November 1st, the Day of the Dead, Firmin, the former British consul, finds that his estranged wife, Yvonne, has come back to town. Paralyzed by his alcoholism, he drifts from cantina to cantina, considering ways to reclaim her, but he never acts. By nightfall, Firmin is dead in a ditch, shot by Mexican paramilitaries. "Volcano" fuses modernist and romantic sensibilities: the story is told from shifting points of view, and Firmin's daylong odyssey is borrowed from "Ulysses"; at the same time, Lowry's prose is fervent, laid down in unstable, looping sentences. Shortly before his death, the consul sees on a house an inscription that reads *"No se puede vivir sin amar"*—"One cannot live without love." Lowry, in a 1946 letter to Margerie's family, wrote, " 'Volcano''s theme: 'only against death does man cry out in vain.' " Dawn Powell wrote soon after the book's publication, "In 'Under the Volcano' you love the author for the pain of his overwhelming understanding."

Lowry began writing "Volcano" in his late twenties. The writing took four drafts and almost a decade. In his early attempts, he was more interested in seeing how many images and symbols he could embed in the text than in creating lifelike characters. It was only in 1939, when Lowry met Margerie, who was herself an aspiring writer, that the novel began assuming a coherent shape. Margerie suggested characters and plot turns, added sentences, and cut back Lowry's wordiness. She was a good editor, and the only person who could manage her husband's reckless temperament.

"Volcano" was published to broad acclaim. The critic Mark Schorer, reviewing the book in the New York *Herald Tribune*, wrote that few novels "convey so feelingly the agony of alienation, the infernal suffering of disintegration." Lowry was hailed as a successor to Joyce, who had died six years earlier. "Volcano" was a popular success, too—for a time, Lowry bragged, the book outsold "Forever Amber."

He soon fell apart. "Success," he wrote to Margerie's mother, "may be the worst possible thing that could happen to any serious author." According to Lowry's biographers—there have been six—his drinking, always prodigious, became incapacitating. He had persecution fantasies. At times, his delirium tremens was so

severe that he could not hold a pencil. Lowry worked on many
books in these years—he had in mind a multipart novel called
"The Voyage That Never Ends," which would parallel the Divine
Comedy, with "Volcano" in the position of the Inferno—but the
manuscript that he cared most about was "October Ferry to Gabriola," a novel about the happiest phase of his marriage, in the
nineteen-forties, when he and Margerie lived in a squatter's shack
on an inlet north of Vancouver. Lowry could not make the novel
come together; Margerie edited and suggested, Malcolm rewrote
and rewrote, and the book slid sideways. They began fighting, in
part because of their failure to tell the story of their happiness.
They countered their frustrations with heavy doses of alcohol,
prescription sedatives, tranquillizers, and stimulants—sodium
amytal, phenobarbital, Benzedrine, Allonal, Nembutal, Soneryl.
(Lowry joked that he and his wife should be known as "Alcohol-
ics Synonymous.") But they could not inure themselves to the
pain of their creative failure. Twice, during a trip to Europe,
Lowry tried to strangle Margerie. Though she was a fraction of
his size, she attacked him, too. Shortly before Lowry died, he told
a psychiatrist whom he was seeing that either Margerie was going
to kill him or he was going to kill her.

Margerie, who died in a Los Angeles nursing home in 1988, at
the age of eighty-three, did not like to talk about the details of
Lowry's death, but when she did she said that Lowry committed
suicide. To most of their friends, that explanation seemed more
likely than the official one, that he had accidentally swallowed too
many pills. A lot had been going on in Lowry's life at the time.
There was the agony of "October Ferry," which in its various
drafts amounted to more than four thousand pages. In the months
before his death, he had largely stopped drinking, under the care
of his psychiatrist, who was encouraging him to be more independent from Margerie; for years, she had been lighting his cigarettes and even tying his shoelaces. He began to do things that he
hadn't done in a long time, from taking the bus by himself to

carrying his own money. These changes may or may not have destabilized him: it is not easy to make surmises about a man as grandly dysfunctional as Lowry. Fifty years ago, on July 3rd, he was buried in a corner of Ripe's thirteenth-century churchyard, which overlooks the South Downs. About a dozen mourners accompanied his wife. Margerie hoped to be buried by his side, but by the time she died the spot next to him had long since been taken; her body was interred forty yards away, at the other end of the churchyard.

IN JUNE, 1939, Clarence Malcolm Lowry met, by his own description, "a grand gal named Margerie" on Hollywood Boulevard, in Los Angeles. A friend of his had set them up. He took the bus; she drove. Lowry was twenty-nine years old, and separated from his first wife, Jan Gabrial—the inspiration for Yvonne in "Volcano." He and Gabrial had lived in Mexico for a year, trying to hold together their volatile marriage. Lowry, an Englishman with a Cambridge degree and a handsome allowance—his father was a wealthy cotton broker in Liverpool—believed his destiny was to be a great writer. But he had published only one book, six years earlier: "Ultramarine," a minor novel whose overexcited style owed a great deal to other writers, especially Conrad Aiken, his mentor. Many of Lowry's friends saw him as a figure of entertainment rather than as a serious artist—they enjoyed him most when he serenaded them with his ukulele. He had been working for nearly three years on "Volcano," which was based on his troubles in Mexico with Gabrial. The project clearly exceeded his skills, or at least his limited focus. Lowry was such a heavy drinker that, in a letter to Aiken, he described himself as a "Lear of the Sierras, dying by the glass in the Brown Derby."

Margerie Bonner had tried her hand at murder mysteries but had not published any work. In the meantime, she had bit parts in several silent Westerns, and worked as the personal assistant to

Penny Singleton, who played Blondie in movies based on the comic strip. Margerie's rapport with Lowry was immediate. Several years older, she had a toughness that he lacked; she wore furs and high heels and exuded glamour. (According to Gordon Bowker, the author of "Pursued by Furies," an incisive 1993 biography of Lowry, she had already been married, but she apparently did not tell Lowry.) Margerie saw Lowry as an exotic aristocrat. He was insecure sexually—he had an unusually small penis—but Margerie gave him confidence. He started calling himself El Leon ("the Lion") and gave her the pet name Miss Hartebeeste. Less than two months after they met, he wrote to declare his love: "The sensation of underground bleeding, of being torn up by the roots like a tree by a big wind—do you feel that? God, I do!"

Lowry was impractical in most ways, but he never met a woman without sizing her up as a typist and as an editor. In Margerie, he found both. Six weeks after they met, Lowry moved to Canada—his American visa had expired—and he asked her to follow him. She agreed. Margerie wanted Lowry to be a great writer almost as much as he did, and even in what he described as a "freezing bison-smelling attic in Vancouver" she got him to work. Lowry's sordid habits did not daunt her; she could drink nearly as much gin as he could. She told another Lowry biographer, Douglas Day, that she had once found him passed out in a Vancouver whorehouse, having sold all his clothes for liquor except his underwear. She demanded that the proprietor give Lowry something to wear; after he got dressed, she stood by him as he begged on the street for money to buy beer.

In 1940, Lowry and Margerie married, and she took his name. Lowry began working more intensely on "Volcano." His original manuscript, a short draft, had emerged from an incident that Lowry and Jan Gabrial had seen in Mexico. On a bus trip, they had come upon an Indian peasant lying by the road, apparently dying; the bus driver stopped, and one of the passengers got out and robbed the Indian. Lowry began to expand the story with Margerie's guidance. He wrote to Aiken, "We work together on it day and night." After Lowry wrote fresh material in longhand, Margerie typed it and offered criticism, a document they called the "margerieversion"; he then made revisions, and the cycle began again. Within six months, Lowry had produced a second draft.

The new version of the novel was his most sustained and inventive fiction to date. His portrait of an unravelling drunk was unnervingly intimate. The manuscript had better pacing, thanks to Margerie, and it had an extensive overlay of symbolism, thanks to Lowry, who was an admirer of Baudelaire. "I felt that it is the first real book I've written," Lowry wrote to Aiken at the time. He credited his relationship with Margerie for the difference: "I'm more than glad I never got a chance to finish it without her."

The manuscript remained flawed. Much of the dialogue was wooden—"Get this so you can hear it," Lowry lectured himself in the margins—and the plotting was often heavy-handed. "I wonder what's happened to that *peón* we had to leave beside the road," one character comments in the first chapter. "Gosh, that was an ugly business." When Lowry's agent, Harold Matson, submitted the new version of "Volcano" to publishers, twelve in all, not one accepted it. Lowry collapsed, but with Margerie at his side he pulled through. Together, they wrote to Matson, admitting that the manuscript still needed work. "Youth plus booze plus hysterical identifications plus vanity plus self-deception" was Lowry's explanation of what had gone wrong.

In August, 1940, they learned of a coastal village north of Vancouver, on the Burrard Inlet, called Dollarton, and rented a ramshackle cottage there. (Lowry was rich on paper, by the terms of a family trust set up in 1938, but the family gave him access only to the interest.) Built on land owned by the city, the house had no heat, electricity, or running water. Eight months later, they bought a nearby shack. After building a swimming pier with their own hands, they resumed work on "Volcano." They largely gave up drinking, and each morning, when Margerie typed Lowry's latest additions, he swam in the inlet, surrounded by seagulls and mergansers. They fetched their drinking water from a nearby stream, and local fishermen dropped buckets of crabs on their pier. Margerie was writing, too—she told Douglas Day that she had begun her first mystery novel, "The Shapes That Creep," to give Lowry something literary to assist on after "Volcano" was rejected.

According to Day, she finished the mystery in a few months, then quickly wrote another, a noirish tale called "The Last Twist of the Knife." At one point, an ingénue named Dora, who is falsely accused of murder, declares, "If you and your high-class friends think you can pin this on me because I'm poor and help-less and you're rich and important, you can just think again." Another character, Delight Dryden, braves a murder inquest, re-turning "the Coroner's benevolent gaze with artistically mingled fear and innocence." Scribners accepted both of Margerie's books for publication.

After Lowry's death, Margerie sold his papers to the University of British Columbia, in Vancouver. The "Volcano" manuscripts reveal the process of refinement that took place in Dollarton. The two rewrote many sentences over and over, as Margerie kept an eye out for Lowry's tics. On one page, she writes, " 'Terrifying'—watch this word Malc!," and crosses it out in the two places where it appears. On another page, Yvonne states, "We won't have the moon tonight." Margerie writes, "Watch this moon—you've got one in Chapter xii." In the margin of one version of the consul's last monologue, Lowry asks, "Is all this a bit muddled?" Margerie's response is not recorded, but the next draft is tighter. "A good, thorough agonizing cut," Lowry writes after Margerie has deleted a hokey moment in which a character imagines that he hears the consul lamenting his failure to reconcile with his wife: "If only

I had not been so sure I were the stronger." In a 1950 letter to a fan, Lowry said of the revising process, "After a while it began to make a noise like music."

To the novel's tremendous benefit, Margerie helped Lowry reconsider its dismissive portrait of his first wife. Originally, Yvonne was the consul's daughter, a trifling character fixated on the needs of her equally callow boyfriend. "She looked at herself in the mirror," Lowry writes, soon after she arrives in Mexico to see her father. "She was a white satin nightgown. She was a robe, but where was the person?" In subsequent manuscripts, Margerie's handwriting can be seen changing Yvonne from daughter to wife; Margerie also helps shape the character, refining Yvonne's feelings about a past lover and amplifying her background, which is similar to her own—Yvonne is an actress who has appeared in "Western pictures." In the published version, Yvonne is closer to how Margerie saw herself: more woman than girl, more giving and forgiving. She is also able to think independently—parts of the novel are written from her point of view. Significantly, she is perhaps the only Lowry character who doesn't drink to excess.

The archive also indicates that Lowry and Margerie borrowed freely from each other's work. After they agreed that Yvonne should die, Margerie later recalled to biographers, she suggested that Yvonne could be trampled by a runaway horse. She was at work on a third novel, "Horse in the Sky," which contained such a death: "The horse suddenly . . . screamed in terror. He reared, reared again, then plunged wildly, in uncontrollable panic." Lowry liked the idea; near the end of "Volcano," Yvonne now "saw, by a brilliant flash of lightning, the riderless horse. . . . She heard herself scream as the animal turned towards her and upon her." Lowry, in a letter to his friend the novelist David Markson, explained, "We swop horses and archetypes to each other all the time."

At the end of 1944, Lowry finished the novel. In February, 1946, while he and Margerie were in Mexico, revisiting some of

the locales of the book, he received acceptance letters from Jonathan Cape, a publisher in England, and from Reynal & Hitch-
cock, an American publisher, on the same day. To Jonathan Cape,
he wrote, "We are wallowing in success, feeling in fact like starving men whose eyes are being stuffed with potatoes."

IN FEBRUARY OF 1947, as "Volcano" began receiving excellent
reviews, Lowry and Margerie made a celebratory visit to New
York. ("The city buzzes with your name," a friend wrote.) But
for Lowry the trip was a horror. He had begun drinking again,
and, when literary celebrities crowded to congratulate him at a
party in his honor, he was too inebriated to respond. Dawn Powell, who was there, noted his distress in her diary. "He is the
original Consul in the book," she wrote, "a curious kind of
person—handsome, vigorous, drunk—with an aura of genius
about him and a personal electricity almost dangerous, sense of
demon-possessed." In another entry, she noted of Lowry, "Wife
Marjorie [sic] in control."

For many of Lowry's literary friends, the publication rounds
were their introduction to Margerie, and though they applauded
her effect on him, they found her pretentious and overly invested
in her association with an English genius. David Markson, one of
Lowry's last surviving friends, told me, "She had a strange manner of speech. She was always saying things like 'May I have a
little more milk in my Scotch, duckie?' Aiken came over one evening and afterward wrote me, 'Please don't invite me when she is
here.'"

Already Lowry was worrying that he might never write another book as good as "Volcano." After the New York trip, he and
Margerie briefly returned to Dollarton, where they worked on a
story about a couple looking for a new home, based on a visit they
had made in 1946 to an island in British Columbia called Gabriola. They submitted the story, "October Ferry to Gabriola," to

their agent under a double byline; it did not sell, however. In November, 1947, they began a yearlong grand tour of Europe. Margerie had wanted the trip—she craved a larger stage than Dollarton provided. Lowry knew that abandoning his austere life was not good for him. "The French have enormous vitality," he wrote to Margerie's sister after visiting Paris. "But it's a quality I don't always admire. I like things rather sleepy."

A friend, spotting him drunk in London, asked him what was next, and Lowry joked that he was writing "Under Under the Volcano." He and Margerie began to quarrel. Lowry was by turns depressed and threatening: one night in the South of France, during a fight, he grabbed her by the neck; later, she found him a sanitarium outside Rome and took an adjoining room. Sneaking past a guard, he tried to strangle her again. At one point, he boasted in a letter to his French translator, he capped off nine whiskeys—six of them doubles—with the sedative Soneryl. During their European tour, Margerie wrote a letter to Albert Erskine, Lowry's American editor, claiming that Lowry was "becoming actively dangerous: first to himself & me but now more savage towards everyone who crosses him in any way." She got into the habit of giving him phenobarbital at night, to calm him.

Her journal entries, which are also at the University of British Columbia, reveal her anger. In an entry from December, 1947, she writes, "Altho he makes a great pretense of working . . . & of exercising & tries to fool me it is too obvious he is drinking all afternoon. . . . I had thought when I adored him as tho he were a god that love could survive anything but I begin to think that there are certain insults to *human dignity* that one should not survive." She had also begun wondering about the effect of their folie à deux on her own creativity: "I have stopped thinking of myself as an artist because the last years my whole consciousness has been so completely absorbed by Malc & his immediate desires & storms." Around the same time, she asked in her journal, "Is it conceivable that a man's weakness can be so strong, that such evil can overpower me & exhaust me to the point that I become evil too?"

They came back to Dollarton in January, 1949, and Lowry sobered up. He took up several projects, including "Dark as the Grave Wherein My Friend Is Laid," a fictionalized account of his 1946 trip to Mexico with Margerie. For a time, the collaboration between Lowry and Margerie grew more harmonious. They co-wrote a screenplay of Fitzgerald's "Tender Is the Night," which M-G-M expressed interest in. It was never produced, but Christopher Isherwood wrote Lowry to praise it. "It ought to be printed as well as played," he said.

In 1950, Lowry returned to the "October Ferry" manuscript that he and Margerie had written. Around this time, the city government of Vancouver intensified an effort to evict the squatters of Dollarton, and Lowry's mood darkened. He expanded the draft of "October Ferry" into a short novel, and folded in an eviction motif. He wrote quickly, without the false starts that were typical of his writing. He thought that he had a clear vision for a novel. "I have completely rewritten it by myself and finally I'm extremely pleased with it," he wrote to Matson.

It was the last positive thing he would write about the book for seven years. In April, 1952, Erskine, who had moved to Random House, put him on retainer; but by August Lowry had become, as he wrote to Erskine, "half dead with discouragement." In the summer of 1953, in a letter to Erskine, he said that the challenge of writing the book was "a matter of life or death, or rebirth, as it were, for its author, not to say sanity or otherwise." The story kept rocking to and fro; the voyage to Gabriola went from real to metaphorical, then back again. "At my back I always hear Time's winged chariot changing gear," Lowry joked to Erskine.

Lowry and Margerie kept up their routine of swimming, eating crabs, and working on the book. They exchanged comments first in written form, then in conversation. But Lowry couldn't stop drinking, and the book's focus was changing daily—each new event in their lives was crammed into its pages. After Margerie gave him the omnibus edition of a writer named Charles Fort, whose work charted inexplicable coincidences, Lowry added to his book a chapter called "The Elements Follow You Around Sir," in which his alter ego stumbles upon Fort's book in a library. And, after they moved to a hotel in Vancouver during a cold winter, the hotel showed up in the draft. Between drafts three and seven, two time schemes emerged, and Lowry had trouble keeping them straight. The birth date of the couple's child, Tommy, fluctuates by four years. Lowry scribbled in the margin, "How old is Tommy? Check."

The collaborators began to despair. "The work has suffered," Lowry wrote to Erskine. "And so has she. And so, by God, have I. . . . This damned thing . . . has cost me more pains than all the 'Volcano' put together." As the Lowry archive reveals, his output had become a torrent of words flowing nowhere. Deletions grew more frequent. He was now rewriting sentences almost spastically. Vik Doyen, a Belgian academic who has made a definitive study of the "October Ferry" drafts, told me, "You feel sadness, the waste of possibilities and of genius."

At one point in the text of "October Ferry," the husband sees a prostitute at a newsstand. Lowry tries to capture her: "A woman seemingly out of the blue . . . with beautiful legs, eyed him, swaying her hips with aimless lust." He crosses this out, and substitutes, "A heavily painted young woman, evidently a premature noctambulist, wearing clothes & shoes so new they seemed just to have been stolen, eyed him, half humming." He crosses this out, too. Above such pages, Lowry often writes invocations, in small lettering, to the patron saint of lost causes: "St. Jude S.O.S."; "St. Jude Help me to think through this impossibility." At other times, he pleads to Turgenev, God, and "E. A. Poe."

Margerie could not be as helpful to Lowry as she had been with "Volcano." The portrayal of Jacqueline, the wife, in "October

Ferry" was two-dimensional, just as the initial conception of Yvonne in "Volcano" had been, but, this time, Margerie could not offer an outsider's perspective—Jacqueline was based on her. As Lowry grew angrier with himself, his protagonist grew angrier at his wife. In one draft, the wife complains about the "goddam shack" that is obsessing her husband, and pettily points out that, "for a woman," its primitive stove was terribly inconvenient. In the back-and-forth notes that accompany the passage, Margerie reminded Lowry that her initial response to Dollarton was more complicated. She proposes adding this nuance: "He recalled the tumble-down dirt & disorder of the 'Goddam shack' when they'd first seen it, & how under her hands it had become . . . beautiful; he recalled the vision, the enthusiasm, the love with which she had labored." Lowry ignored her; above this suggestion he writes, "phony, sentimental, bourgeois."

Around the same time, Lowry and Margerie were working on another autobiographical novel, "La Mordida." In one editorial exchange, their marital tension becomes overt. "I absolutely refuse to be made out such a fool," Margerie writes in a comment. "This is not true; why not tell the truth?" And, in a testy exchange over "October Ferry," Lowry writes to Margerie, "Try to imagine yourself *reading* the story in bed etc. etc.—occasionally at least as a reader rather than a writer." To which Margerie replies, with underscoring, "SEE MY NOTES." Lowry begins to respond to her criticisms with posturing. Of one scene from "October Ferry," in which a character dreams that he is venturing inside a dark cave, he writes, "With a little discipline, one of the high spots in English literature."

These disputes found no resolution in print or in life. Even in the relative calm of Dollarton, Margerie was worn out. She wrote to David Markson, Lowry's friend, that "October Ferry" had become a "blood sucking monster." (These words, which are in the archive, appear on a letter begun by Lowry that describes his struggle with "October Ferry," but he was apparently too drunk to finish it; Margerie did.) Soon, Dollarton would be gone, too. Bulldozers had knocked down most of the shacks. Albert Erskine had cancelled Lowry's contract with Random House, because, as he told the biographer Gordon Bowker, the draft of "October Ferry" sent to him by Lowry was "just about as tedious as anything I'd ever read." Margerie was growing tired of living twenty-five hundred miles away from New York—having published three novels, she felt that she and Lowry ought to have a more normal life, one that might help her career. (Her books had not sold especially well.) She felt that her health was also suffering in the damp and cold of Dollarton. And Lowry's drinking made him entirely dependent on her.

In 1954, Margerie persuaded Lowry that they had to leave Dollarton. They decided to move to Taormina, in Sicily—in the shadow of Mt. Etna, an idea that gave Lowry pleasure. On the way to Europe, they passed through New York and stayed with David Markson. Margerie and Markson left Lowry for a time in Markson's apartment, in Morningside Heights, with just a six-pack of beer. Upon their return, Lowry met them with what Markson remembers as a "sheepish" look: Lowry had drunk Markson's aftershave. Markson noticed that Margerie, in an attempt to take the edge off Lowry's hangovers, shoved vitamins down his throat before sending him to bed.

Margerie and Lowry sailed for Sicily. Lowry disliked Taormina and missed Dollarton. In Italy, he did not write a word of fiction; he barely wrote a letter. Margerie toured the sights, while Lowry drank and menaced her. At night, Margerie locked up the liquor in her room while Lowry begged for a drink outside. Sometimes she gave him Cognac and pentobarbital tablets to get to sleep. And she continued giving him vitamin pills when he got drunk. Their friends thought that the couple should break up—no one could understand how Margerie tolerated the relationship. Eventually, Italy proved too much even for Margerie. She complained of gallbladder problems. After eight months, they went to

London. Margerie, suffering from nervous exhaustion, checked herself in to a hospital.

Lowry, in turn, was persuaded by friends to see a doctor for his alcoholism. At a hospital in Wimbledon, in November, 1955, he met a psychiatrist named Michael Raymond, whom he grew to trust. Raymond gave Lowry a course of "aversion therapy," which consisted of an injection of apomorphine followed by heavy drinking. The goal was for the patient to associate alcohol with the nausea brought on by the medicine. Raymond wanted Lowry to be near him after he was discharged, and in 1956 Margerie rented a house, known as the White Cottage, in the village of Ripe. After a relapse—caused, in part, by Margerie's continued drinking in front of her husband—and another, more intense course of aversion therapy that summer, Lowry returned to the cottage, determined to give up liquor for good.

In Ripe, Lowry sustained himself on Cydrax, a non-alcoholic cider that Raymond had recommended. He was able to work in earnest on "October Ferry" for the first time in three years, and soon boasted to Markson that he was back in the "Sacred or Budding Groove." In a genial mood, he described his rebirth to Dr. Raymond with some doggerel:

> *When to your brothel-monastery I came*
> *I could not dress myself or open my own mail . . .*
> *When you suggested I should live at Ripe*
> *I thought it very funny, it appealed to me*
> *Recalling the initials R.I.P.*
> *Requiescat in pace if you choose*
> *Or rise if possible you challenged me.*
>
> *Well I have risen, I am high and dry.*
> *High on achievement, and as we rehearsed*
> *Dry cider's little sibling slakes my thirst.*

Its family resemblance keeps it near
Yet free from all the menaces accursed. . . .

I rise quite early and as you advised
I work to schedule and to my relief
I find Phrases will still come tumbling through my mind
Though man's predicaments engage my thoughts.

To Lowry's surprise, his improvement did not thrill Margerie. She began drinking more heavily, and spent most days sitting in the house, shaking and crying. In October of 1956, she checked herself back in to a hospital for a long course of heavy sedation meant to calm her nerves. Lowry called her therapy "her Rip Van Winkle snooze."

Before entering the hospital, Margerie had told their friend Dorothy Templeton that she'd had enough: she was putting aside all the money she could for the day she would leave Lowry. "She is absolutely callous towards ML," Templeton wrote her companion, Harvey Burt, in July, 1956. "Her idea of love is not mine or the average woman's."

During Margerie's hospital stay, Lowry wrote her letters about how happy he was in Ripe now; of working steadily again; of being the object of competition between their landlady and the vicar's housekeeper, who gave him his meals. He knew that his words did not make Margerie smile. He writes in his poem to Raymond, "As with the see-saw in the childhood rhyme/Now I am riding high poor Margerie is low." Lowry speculated to Markson that Margerie felt "robbed of the potential in-a-sense nurse-able object." He did not know what to do about the change, and as a novelist part of him wanted simply to observe it. He wrote Markson, "The trouble is it is part of the plot of the book."

THE VILLAGE OF RIPE has changed little in fifty years. A dozen houses, a roundabout, and a pub named the Lamb Inn remain its center. The narrow lanes out of the village still give way to the farmland of Sussex. At Lowry's grave, a terracotta marker bearing the last lines of "Volcano" now rests in front of his weathered headstone. The White Cottage, where Lowry died, is down a short pebble lane from the pub; a few months after the Lowrys arrived, in 1956, the proprietor banned them because Lowry was unruly.

In 2004, the *Times Literary Supplement* published a provocative article by Gordon Bowker, Lowry's most capable biographer, which revived some long-unanswered questions about Lowry's final days in Ripe. How trustworthy was the coroner's verdict of death by "misadventure," or Margerie's insistence that her husband had committed suicide? Why would Lowry, in good spirits and finally writing again, kill himself? "Volcano" was about to be reissued as a Vintage. Classics paperback. And Hollywood directors were awakening to the book's cinematic potential; José Quintero had expressed particular interest. Jan Gabrial, Lowry's first wife, told an interviewer shortly before she died, in 2001, "Malcolm's death, to me, isn't quite explained."

In England, coroners' reports are usually sealed for seventy-five years. But Bowker had persuaded the Sussex coroner to give him Lowry's. The document contained some news: after Lowry's death, Margerie could not at first find the bottle for the pills that Lowry had swallowed, and only produced it for the police several hours later. The bottle had been stashed in one of his drawers. The coroner's report also recorded Margerie's claim that she had found the bottle with its top screwed on—meticulous behavior for a man as sloppy as Lowry. Even at the time of his death, friends had wondered about the challenge that unscrewing a top would have posed for Lowry. Harvey Burt, in a letter written four months after Lowry died, expressed doubt that he could have done it: "I can't understand. . . . His powers of coördination at such times were very low."

In the article, Bowker noted Margerie's habit of dosing Lowry with vitamin pills. He then offered a speculation: Lowry would not have noticed if what she fed him that night were not vitamins but sodium amytal, the barbiturate that helped kill him. He suggested that Margerie had developed a crush on a writer friend, Peter Churchill, a viscount and a recent widower. Finally, Bowker laid out an accusation of murder: "Margerie had the motive (hankering after Churchill), the means (the pill-feeding ritual) and the opportunity (the cottage after dark)."

Bowker also reported that Margerie and Winnie Mason, the landlady, had both testified to the police that they had spent the evening chatting in Mason's cottage, next door. Later, however, they both said that Margerie had been at home with Lowry. (Margerie made this claim in a letter to Lowry's French translator, Mason in a 1966 BBC interview.) For Bowker, these statements suggested collusion.

Lowry scholars did not take offense at the murder theory when the *T.L.S.* published it. Many of them have been drawn to Lowry as much by the drama of his life as by his writing. On his birthday, they gather at Dollarton and drink gin. The possibility of foul play has only added zest to their work. Bowker's notion of a romantic motive did not strike them as convincing, though. By the fatal night, Margerie was so run-down by Lowry that she could barely get out of bed; she was in no state to take a lover. For some Lowry scholars, this became the point: the idea of murdering Lowry was not just conceivable but almost justifiable. Lowry had not only used Margerie's talent; he had taken over her life. Then, after abusing and exploiting her for eighteen years, he had grown weary of her. Recently, I asked a leading Lowry scholar, Sherrill Grace, a professor at the University of British Columbia, who edited the two-volume edition of Lowry's collected letters, if Margerie murdered Lowry. "Gordon's right," she told me, then said of Margerie, "She should have done it sooner!"

The White Cottage is now owned by a farmer and his wife. When I knocked on their door this summer, they invited me to walk around the house. The cottage is dark and oppressively small, though a previous owner had installed a skylight in the kitchen. The owners had not read "Under the Volcano," but they knew about Lowry. We walked through a room with exposed wood beams and a hearth. "This was Lowry's study," the husband told me, showing me the room in which Lowry had wrestled with "October Ferry." The murder rumor had recently reached them—some visiting Japanese academics had mentioned it.

By the time the police arrived at the White Cottage on the morning of June 27th, Lowry had likely been dead for hours. He lay on his back by the side of Margerie's bed, the rug rumpled beneath him. According to the coroner's report, a transcript of which Bowker shared with me, a "quantity of sliced cold cooked meat" was by Lowry's arm. On the other side of the bed was a broken orange-squash bottle and a broken gin bottle. There were glass splinters on Lowry's chest and blood on his left palm. Two chairs had been thrown: an easy chair lay on its side by the window; a kitchen chair had been smashed to pieces.

After Margerie found Lowry's body, a constable named William Lord, from the nearby town of Selmeston, took her statement and that of Mason, the landlady. Margerie also spoke of what happened that night to Douglas Day. Lowry, she said, had once again fallen off the wagon. With the Lamb Inn off limits, they had walked to the Yew Tree pub in Chalvington, a mile away, where they drank beer. (The bartender recalled Margerie crying.) Lowry then bought a bottle of gin, over her objections, saying that it would cheer her up—he told the bartender that she was sad over their lost Dollarton home—and they walked back to Ripe on the country lane. They were planning to listen to the radio. Lowry began drinking from the bottle, getting wilder. Margerie said that after a BBC concert—Leopold Stokowski conducting Stravinsky—Lowry began "raving." He turned up the radio. Margerie, who had been downstairs making supper, came up and turned it down, not wanting to disturb Winnie Mason next door.

According to the police report, Lowry struck Margerie. She grabbed the gin bottle and broke it to keep him from drinking it. Lowry then brandished the broken bottle and chased Margerie downstairs; she recalled to Douglas Day that her husband had "a fiendish look on his face." She took refuge in Mason's house. She told Day that she then took a sleeping pill—she did not explain how she came to have one with her—and went to sleep. (Both she and Lowry were heavy users of sleeping pills; Lowry called them his "pink things." They both had prescriptions for sodium amytal. In October, 1956, Lowry wrote Margerie of Dr. Raymond's appearing at his door in Ripe, "bearing, in hand like a malt-shovel, a half-dozen sodium amytals to tide me over.")

Lowry's death made the regional paper, the Brighton *Argus,* with the headline "SHE BROKE GIN BOTTLE—FOUND HUSBAND DEAD." All the same, the Sussex police did not press an investigation. Lowry had no connections in the area. No one knew who he was. (The *Argus* called him "Clarence Lowry," and no other British paper recorded his death.) Locals did not like him; Roy Medhurst, the last living Ripe resident who knew Lowry, told me that Lowry was a "drunken yob" and said that his death left "some people relieved."

The inquest was routine. Constable Lord told the coroner what he saw. Winnie Mason, in her deposition, recalled Margerie showing up at her door, distraught, and claimed that Margerie had not gone out after retiring to a camp bed that she had made for her. If she had, Mason insisted, "I would most certainly have heard her, being a light sleeper, and also my dog would have barked."

Margerie at first told friends that there had been a suicide note but then said that there wasn't. The lack of a note surprised them. Alcohol would hardly have stopped his pen—he wrote while drunk all the time. And he was someone for whom written words accompanied nearly every moment of life; he even scrawled observations as he sat drunk in bars. Some four hundred jotted notes to Margerie are in the British Columbia archive—messages from

El Leon to Miss Hartebeeste. "Lowry was always saying, 'Make notes,'" Markson told me. Lowry's despair was always part theatre; and, for such a person, self-destruction practically demanded documentation.

The coroner did not call Lowry's psychiatrist, Dr. Raymond, who, far from considering Lowry "incurable," as Margerie told the police, thought that he was getting better. Angry that Margerie had kept drinking in Lowry's presence, he later refused to treat her for her emotional exhaustion. He also thought that Lowry's spiritual beliefs precluded suicide. The coroner failed to call members of Lowry's family—he had three older brothers. Had he done so, they might have told him that they were suspicious of Margerie; in an unpublished reminiscence, one of the brothers called her "the very material Margerie," adding that the Lowrys, who thought she wore too much jewelry, referred to her as Bangles. Nor did the coroner speak to Dorothy Templeton and Harvey Burt, the couple who knew the Lowrys best. They had spent their summers near them in Dollarton for years; more recently, Templeton had visited them in Sicily, where Lowry had confided to her that Margerie had complained until he named her as his sole beneficiary. (In 1945, Lowry's father died, leaving a fortune that was the equivalent of ten million dollars.) In a letter, Templeton wrote of the couple, "I'm sure if she knew he would never write again she would hope for widowhood." In another letter, she recalled watching them argue one night in Taormina, when "all of a sudden Marg turned into a ferocious maniac" and beat up the enormous, cowering, and incapacitated Lowry. And on another occasion, she wrote, Margerie broke Lowry's nose in a fight in "the *corso,* with hundreds looking on." (Margerie told Douglas Day that this incident never occurred.)

"They think I murdered him," Margerie told Burt and Templeton when they came to Ripe to help her, shortly after Lowry's death. Fairly or not, Burt and Templeton began to suspect Margerie, too. Publicly, she seemed devastated, but they found her oddly energized in private. According to Bowker, to whom they spoke extensively, they thought that Margerie was playing the distraught widow.

In Ripe, I saw that Winnie Mason's cottage was so close to the Lowrys' that they almost formed one building. Margerie could easily have fled Lowry in his drunken rage, then returned home later for a pill. Perhaps, as she looked around for the sodium amytal, a decade of frustration caught up with her. Maybe she went to Lowry and told him that he'd better start preparing for his hangover with some vitamins. Her conciliatory manner would not have surprised him; their battles were often followed by more tender exchanges. Margerie, herself soothed by the barbiturate, could have returned to bed at Mason's several minutes before the pills would have knocked Lowry to the floor. The next day, Margerie would have discovered the body, just as she said she had.

Lowry's death will always remain a mystery. Even if his body were exhumed, it would offer no insight into how the barbiturates had entered his system. Maybe Margerie meant only to make Lowry sleep, as she had many times before—she had been drinking, too, and might have given too many pills by mistake. David Markson said of the murder theory, "What do I think? What I think is he was a drunk and then he died."

New York Review Books has just published a compilation of Lowry's work, including portions of the posthumous books, which have long been out of print. "The Voyage That Never Ends," as the volume is called, shows Lowry's extraordinary imagination and his ability to pull the English language in whatever direction he wanted to go. A typical aphorism: "The lightning, a good writer, did not repeat itself." And this description of a storm at sea: "One could see, as the ship lurched . . . great doctor of divinity's gowns of seas furling to leeward, the foam like lamb's wool." But the anthology does not change the impression that Lowry was a writer who brought only one significant book to fruition.

"Under the Volcano"—his "ultima thule of the spirit," as he

called it—contains a remarkable death scene, and some of the language evokes Lowry's own. The Mexican paramilitaries close in on the consul. One pulls out a pistol and shoots him, then shoots him twice more, and the world becomes a giant symbol of despair: "Suddenly he screamed, and it was as though this scream were being tossed from one tree to another, as its echo returned, then, as though the trees themselves were crowding nearer, huddled together, closing over him, pitying." This is pure Baudelaire. But, at the moment when the consul sees the gun firing, Lowry sees things more plainly: "At first the Consul felt a queer relief. Now he realized he had been shot. He fell on one knee, then, with a groan, flat on his face in the grass. 'Christ,' he remarked, puzzled, 'this is a dingy way to die.'"

AFTER LOWRY'S DEATH, Margerie never married again, and never published another of her own books. She moved back to Taormina, while Lowry's family dragged its feet over her inheritance. After she threatened to move in with them, they released a small sum. "For all they care, I can starve in Sicily," she wrote Dorothy Templeton, four months after Lowry's death. "I am dead or wish I were," she wrote in another postcard. She had already begun to look for publishable work in the trunk of manuscripts that Lowry left behind.

Soon, most of Lowry's friends and family dropped her. "I haven't heard one bloody word from anybody in England since I left," she wrote Templeton and Burt in 1959. (When I met Lowry's great-nephew Jeremy Lowry in England this summer and asked about the family's opinion of Margerie, he said, "She was never referred to.") Margerie settled in Los Angeles and dedicated herself to her husband's legacy. Her agent, Peter Matson, Harold Matson's nephew, remembers her as a small, intense, heavy-drinking woman who "seemed to live very much in the past." She wrote Burt in 1971, "Malc is hotter than ever in Paris and *Le Monde* gave two full pages to him last fall," but noted a few months later that she warded off her "grief and troubles with vodka, mixed with ice and plain water."

The reputation of "Under the Volcano" kept rising with the years. Critics extolled it as the last great modernist novel, and scholars worked to unweave its web of symbols. "The doctorates are piling up all over the U.S. and Canada," Margerie wrote to Burt and Templeton in 1965. In 1998, the board of the Modern Library ranked it No. 11 of the best hundred books of the twentieth century. Gabriel García Márquez has said that it was probably the novel that he had read the most often in his life.

Every four or five years until her death, Margerie published a novel or story collection that she had retrieved from the unpublished part of the "bolus," as Lowry called his writing. Most scholars did not think that these works were anywhere near the level of "Volcano," and wondered if Margerie was truly fulfilling Lowry's wishes in offering them to the public. "I told Margerie not to publish them," David Markson remembers. Margerie told Douglas Day that she found such criticisms ridiculous. In a letter, she said, "I certainly wrote plenty of lines, and scenes, when I was editing 'The Forest Path' and 'Through the Panama'"—stories that Lowry completed—"both of which have received high praise and people write me about them all the time." She was keeping alive her side of their collaboration—the selecting and the shaping—even though the man who sometimes rejected and improved upon her ideas was silent.

In 1970, Margerie finally published "October Ferry to Gabriola." A short afterword, titled "About the Author," claimed that Margerie had based her edit on "an almost complete revision" that Lowry had been working on just before his death. This was wishful thinking: there had been no such revision, just thousands of pages of a half-dozen versions, none close to complete. Margerie pulled sections from different drafts and gave the book the happy ending that she had been pressing for: the Lowry stand-in realizes that his nostalgia for the squatter's shack is damaging his marriage. He cuts his ties to the past and the couple moves to Gabriola to begin life again. Margerie did not include any of the material from Lowry's final burst of inspiration—the pages written in Ripe, largely without her, which might have marked a creative renewal for him.

During this time, Lowry produced fascinating additions to "October Ferry"—almost a hundred pages, written in his tiny hand, in which he began to examine what he called the "alcoholocaust" of his life, and the way that drinking had affected his art. He wrote about his aversion treatment, and clearly expected to integrate this experience into the story of Ethan Llewelyn, the protagonist of "October Ferry." His talent for imagery is apparent when he merges the nautical and the medical to describe "a psychiatric ward at noon, waiting for the doctors to pass through, with two tall nurses at anchor." He had also put wholesale into the draft various letters of apology that he had written to Margerie over the years. None of this ambitious work was finished, but it pointed to a novel very different from the ones that Lowry had written before, one that might have taken him not under "Under the Volcano" but beyond it.

When Margerie consigned these manuscripts to the University of British Columbia, she added notes in her looping script. "Rambling notes," one said. "Seems like a dissertation on alcohol." Another said, "Nothing useful here."

D. T. MAX *is the author of* The Family That Couldn't Sleep: A Medical Mystery, *the true story of an Italian family that for two hundred years has suffered from a fatal inherited insomnia. The book came out in paperback in the fall of 2007 from Random House. Max has been a book editor and a newspaper columnist. He lives outside of Washington, D.C., with his wife and two small children and a rescued beagle who came to them, fortuitously, already named Max.*

Coda

The pleasure, I think, in "Day of the Dead," is that although the particulars—the manuscripts, the correspondence, the ups and downs of publication—are distinctive to literary life, there is nothing really literary about it. It asks the question: Can we ever really know what takes place in a marriage? Marriage is the ultimate terra incognita, the last true zone of privacy in our 24-7 cable news, give us your social security number world. Did Margerie kill Malcolm? That we can almost answer. But if she did, why?—that, even after twenty-four pages, I can't pretend we'll ever know.

Nick Schou

JUST A RANDOM FEMALE

FROM *OC Weekly*

AT FIRST, THE MOTIONLESS FIGURE lying face-up on the pavement must have looked like a mannequin. There were no street lamps nearby, and perhaps the security guard thought it was a stray dummy left there by a drama student. He kept driving, but something about the shape made him curious; he turned around and drove back to Lot 12, a student parking lot on the west edge of Mission Viejo's Saddleback College. It was about 10:30 p.m. on Saturday, January 18, 1986. The lot was pitch-black and, other than a few parked cars, completely deserted.

As the guard got out of his car and approached the pale form stretched out on the asphalt next to a Chevrolet Citation, two students walking to their vehicles from the nearby fine-arts building joined him. They gasped in horror.

Lying in a crimson pool next to her car was someone they had seen minutes earlier at a party in the fine-arts building: 23-year-old communications major Robbin Brandley. She had just left the party, which followed a piano concert at which she had been a volunteer usher. Her long, flower-print dress was hiked up above her stomach, exposing bikini-style underwear and knee-high stockings. Her purse sat on the pavement a few feet away.

The blood stained the pavement on both sides of her torso. By the time Michael Stephany, a homicide investigator with the Orange County Sheriff's Department, arrived at the scene, automatic sprinklers in the parking lot had turned on and covered the body in an eerie mist. An autopsy would later reveal that Brandley had been stabbed 41 times. Most of the wounds were in her neck, chest and back, and there were several deep cuts—defensive marks, police figured—in her hands.

But besides the victim's gruesome injuries, there was nothing for police to investigate: no fingerprints; no suspect's blood, hair or DNA; no physical evidence of any kind. It was what prosecutors often call the "perfect crime."

The grisly murder would remain unsolved for 11 years. Witnesses offered inconsistent accounts of events in the hours preceding the crime; Brandley's parents became convinced that someone she knew was responsible for the killing. Then, in April 1997, a man confessed to the murder—and several others. The cop writing down his confession would note that the killer had simply wandered around Mission Viejo until he ended up at a dark parking lot, where he saw a woman walking to her car.

The victim, in the words of the confessed murderer, "could have been anybody." She "was just a random female."

ON A RECENT AFTERNOON, Jack and Genelle Reilley sit on either side of a table at the *Weekly*'s offices in downtown Santa Ana. They're taking turns answering questions about the murder of Robbin Brandley, their daughter, 21 years ago. It's a story they've told so often that it's almost become routine for them, although there's nothing routine about what they have to say—or about the pain of their loss, still visibly etched in the deep wrinkles on Jack's tanned forehead and the strained, almost helpless smile on Genelle's face. Only a few minutes into the interview, her eyes well up with tears.

Part of the routine is explaining why their daughter had a different surname at the time of her death. Robbin, they explain, was born in Long Beach—the town where Jack and Genelle grew up and became high-school sweethearts—on December 6, 1962, with the name Dana Reilley. She spent most of her youth in Huntington Beach and then St. Louis, where Jack had been transferred to work at the headquarters of Ralston Purina, the company that employed him until his retirement a few years ago.

It was in St. Louis, when Dana was 11 years old, that she changed her name to Robbin Brandley. Genelle, a New Age enthusiast who claims to have psychic visions, says the idea came from a numerological booklet that uses one's birth date to come up with a new name. "It was my idea," she adds.

Her daughter had been a hyperactive child and poor student in her younger years, but once she had a new name, Genelle insists, she blossomed into a focused, highly motivated child. "I believe in all that stuff," Genelle says. "If what you're doing isn't working, delve into it. She grew up to be a really fabulous, sensational person. I guess everyone thinks that about their child, but she just loved to make people laugh. She was very funny and very bright."

In 1983, the family returned to California, settling in Laguna Beach, where Brandley enrolled at Saddleback College to pursue a career in journalism.

She had lots of friends at Saddleback and dated a lot of young men, but, her parents say, she refused to get involved in any steady relationships because she wanted to focus on her career. Aside from her classes, she worked at KSBR, the campus radio station, and helped book performances at the college, including established musical acts such as the Thompson Twins. She loved to volunteer for campus events, like the piano concert that brought her to Saddleback College on the last day of her life.

In the hours leading up to her trip to the unlit student parking lot in Mission Viejo, Brandley spent several hours with her father at their home in Laguna Beach watching television. Jack Reilley was a big fan of Charles Dickens; he was delighted when she told him that the 1946 Hollywood adaptation of *Great Expectations* was on television. After watching the movie, they sat through several reruns of the popular 1960s black-and-white TV comedy *The Munsters*.

"It had been 15 years since we'd watched that show, and it was as funny as ever," Jack recalls.

At around 2 the following morning, Jack awoke to loud knocking at the door: Detective Stephany and another officer were standing on his porch. "He had a big grocery bag," he recalls. Stephany asked Jack if he could identify anything in the bag. Inside, Jack found Brandley's purse, and inside that, her wallet and driver's license. "The first thing that went through my mind was the drunks in [Laguna] Canyon, a car wreck or something like that," he says. "And then he said she'd been murdered, and I just couldn't believe it. It was like being hit with a hammer."

Jack woke up Genelle and told her the news. Four hours later, at sunrise, he called their son Jayeson, and several other family members and friends. They received another visit from the sheriff's department and answered interminable questions about their daughter. "They came down to figure out the sequence of events," Jack said. "Who her friends were, what type of girl she was, any [love] triangles or anything else. They were curious because her last name is different than ours and thought maybe there was an ex-husband or something."

LESS THAN A WEEK LATER, 300 mourners attended a memorial service for Brandley at a San Juan Capistrano church, an event covered by the *Los Angeles Times*. "She was a vibrant, energetic, caring person whose concern for and love of other students was the foundation of her existence," Vern Hodge, then-dean of student development at Saddleback College, told the crowd. The article noted the sheriff's department had "no significant leads" in solving the murder.

On March 7, Saddleback College hosted a series of bands, including Fishbone, the Rave-Ups and Secret Service, for a memorial concert in tribute to Brandley, an event prominent enough that *Times* music critic Randy Lewis covered the show. His story also noted that the sheriff's department had no leads. "It's very much an active case, but I'm not aware of any new information at this time," a department spokesperson told Lewis.

By this time, the Reilleys were conducting their own, unofficial murder investigation, based on statements they say were made to them by police and friends of Brandley who called them to share their suspicions. Those suspicions centered on Valerie Prehm, a student at Saddleback College who worked with Brandley at KSBR and who also had volunteered as an usher at the piano concert on the night of the murder.

According to witnesses who spoke to the Reilleys, Prehm had left the party with Brandley, making her the last person to see her alive. More disturbingly—to the Reilleys, at least—was the fact that other witnesses told them Prehm and Brandley had gotten into an argument just a few weeks before the murder when campus administrators had rejected Prehm's proposal to bring Manhattan Transfer to campus, saying they wanted Brandley to handle the project. Furthermore, the Reilleys say, Prehm disappeared for three days after the murder.

Yet police ruled out Prehm as a suspect, citing witnesses who saw Prehm leave the after-concert party alone. And Prehm hadn't disappeared for three days, they said: She was at home in San Clemente all weekend, unaware that Brandley had been murdered until she returned to campus on Monday. Police hadn't been able to interview her sooner because they didn't know her telephone number.

But to the Reilleys, particularly Genelle, Prehm clearly had a motive to harm their daughter. She became convinced Prehm had persuaded somebody to rob her daughter, to scare her into leaving campus in revenge for stealing her project. She even claims Brandley visited her in a psychic vision just three days after the murder. "She screamed. 'Mom, Valerie did it! Valerie did it!'" Genelle says. "I was stunned."

As the years passed with no progress in the case, the Reilleys say they grew increasingly frustrated with the sheriff's department, especially Stephany, who has since retired and could not be located for an interview for this story. "He said 'Don't call; don't bother me,'" Genelle claims. "He just couldn't solve the case."

The Reilleys filed a lawsuit against Saddleback College, arguing that the school was in part responsible for their daughter's murder because of the lack of streetlights at the parking lot where she died, but they dropped the suit after their lawyer quit. They also lobbied for a bill to require that all California universities and colleges provide lights at student parking lots, but the legislation, signed into law in 1990 by California's then-Governor George Deukmejian, only applied to future campus construction.

Meanwhile, they continued their private hunt for their daughter's killer, inviting a series of psychics to visit the crime scene in the late '80s and early '90s. A few years later, they also consulted with a pair of psychics on an episode of *The Jerry Springer Show*. Genelle brought a ring that belonged to her daughter to the studio and handed it to one of the psychics, who then closed her eyes and narrated what she purported to be a description of the murderer, a supernatural echo of the killer that was emanating from the ring itself.

"She was holding this ring and looked like she was going to pass out," Genelle recalls. "She said this person was in uniform, in camouflage, and Robbin knocked the knife over his left eyebrow.

She said the man works as a security guard." After the show, Genelle says the psychic's husband approached her and said his wife would offer her services free of charge in the hope of solving the crime. "I was going to do that," she says. "But then she died not long after the show. She was a big, heavy woman."

By then, the couple had hired a private detective to track down Prehm and confront her about the crime. In 1992, Genelle drove to rural Washington, where Prehm was living with a boyfriend, and convinced her to take a polygraph test in exchange for $10,000.

Wanting to clear her name, Prehm took the test and passed. Genelle believes the test was improperly administered. She provided the *Weekly* with a videotape of Prehm answering questions about Brandley's murder. In the tape, recorded on June 25, 1992, Prehm denied having any knowledge of the crime and stated that while she may have argued with Brandley a few weeks before her death, she certainly wasn't angry enough to kill anyone. She also claimed that she last saw Brandley at the party and left by herself that night.

Asked if she had seen anyone suspicious that night, however, Prehm stated that while she was working as an usher, a man with curly hair and glasses wearing an olive-drab hunting jacket had approached her and asked if Robbin Brandley were in the building. He didn't look dressed for the concert.

"I almost asked for his ticket, but I was too busy, and unfortunately, I just turned and pointed her out," Prehm said on the videotape, adding that she told police about the mysterious stranger at the concert, but that they didn't believe her because nobody else had seen anyone matching that description. It probably didn't help her case, Prehm added, that she prefaced her statement to police by mentioning that the mother of one of her friends had also told her she'd seen a similar man in a dream.

"The police saw me twice, and they never wrote it down," Prehm continued. "I don't remember his nose, but I remember his hair and glasses, and he was wearing a dark-green jacket, kind of a backwoods jacket. It was an olive green with long sleeves, like an army jacket."

THREE MONTHS LATER, on the evening of September 27, 1992, Jennifer Asbenson, a 19-year-old nursing assistant, had just bought a snack at Palm Canyon Liquor in Palm Springs. She was on her way to work at a home for handicapped children in Desert Hot Springs, several miles away. As she waited for her bus outside the liquor store, a young man in a blue car pulled up to the curb and asked her if she needed a ride.

"No, it's okay," Asbenson replied.

The man smiled. "Are you sure? I'm going to Desert Hot Springs."

Because the driver seemed friendly and didn't care if she accepted his invitation, but mostly because she did need a ride, Asbenson got in the car. For some reason, she took note of his license-plate number, and as they rode together, she kept repeating it to herself. But after several minutes, she figured she was being paranoid. " 'Why do I keep memorizing his license plate?' " she wondered. " 'This guy is totally nice.' . . . He was just a really friendly guy, and I thought I was lucky to get a ride with such a nice guy."

As the man drove through the desert, he asked Asbenson what she did for a living. She told him she wanted to be an actress. "He asked me if I was interested in pornos," Asbenson later testified. "I said, 'No, that's sick.' " She inquired as to what he did for a living and the man replied that he was a detective. She didn't believe him. She thought it was a little odd that he kept staring out at the desert. Then, halfway through the trip, she got "creeped out" when she told him to make a left turn. He seemed to be ignoring her, but he finally pulled over at the last moment and made the turn.

When the man dropped her off at her job, he asked for her telephone number and invited her to breakfast the next morning. Asbenson, who had a boyfriend, gave him a phony number, hoping to let him down easy. But when she left the building the next morning at 6, she saw the blue car idling down the block. "He just pulled over and rolled the window down and said, 'Good morning,'" she recalled. "And he was nice. I didn't feel threatened at all."

Asbenson accepted his offer for a ride back to Palm Springs. Almost immediately, the driver became angry about the phony telephone number, and Asbenson realized she was in trouble. "He was being persistent, but then all of a sudden, he just flipped out, and he had a knife, and he just held it up to my throat and started screaming at me, calling me a bitch and telling me to shut up." The man pulled over on the side of the road, pushed Asbenson's head into the dashboard and grabbed a ball of twine from under his seat.

"He pulled my hands behind my back and just started wrapping them," she said. "And it just felt like I was doomed. . . . I couldn't believe what was happening, and I couldn't even think, and I just said, 'This is a joke. Oh, my God, all this over the phone number. Oh, my God.' And he just said, 'Shut up.'"

Asbenson asked the man what he was doing, but he wouldn't answer. When she told him he wouldn't get away with anything, he placed a hat and sunglasses on her head, then locked her door and pushed her seat back so other motorists wouldn't be able to see her.

The sun was just coming up over the horizon, and from her vantage point, Asbenson would later recall, she could see nothing but an endless parade of telephone poles in the early-morning sky. She asked if he planned to rape her. "He wouldn't say anything," she said. "He had a lot of rage. I kept looking at him. I provoked no emotion. No matter what I said, he couldn't feel a thing for me. He was just really pissed off."

As he drove through the desert, one hand on the wheel and the other gripping a knife to her neck, the man forced her to perform oral sex on him. The road became bumpy, and Asbenson, who grew up in Palm Springs, knew he was taking her to a remote area. After what seemed like nearly an hour, he pulled over, cut off all her clothes and stuffed her panties in her mouth, using her bra as a gag. As he raped her, he began viciously cursing Asbenson.

"And then he just told me to tell him that I loved him," she said. He removed the gag, and Asbenson did her best to sound sincere. It didn't work. The man punched her in the face. She tried again, imagining what it would be like to say those words and truly believe them. Her second effort didn't fare much better. He called her a "bitch," and the next thing Asbenson knew, he was strangling her. The world turned white, and Asbenson passed out. When she awoke, the man was licking her neck, biting her. He pushed her out of the car and, holding a handgun to her head, forced her once again to perform oral sex. She thought about biting his penis, but she couldn't muster the courage. Instead, she asked him to shoot her.

The man then forced her into the trunk and began driving down the road, deeper into the desert. Gathering all her energy, Asbenson managed to pop the twine off her wrists. Terrified that she would be cut to pieces by her captor, she tried to strangle herself with the twine. When that failed, she began feeling around the darkness until her fingers gripped a latch. As she did so, the trunk popped open. Asbenson lifted the trunk a few inches and stuck her hand out, hoping to attract the attention of passing motorists. But her abductor immediately noticed the trunk was open and pulled over to the side of the road. He got out and slammed the trunk shut again.

"Keep it shut, bitch," he yelled. Then he ran back to the driver's seat and revved the engine. But he hit the gas so hard, his wheels spun, stuck in a sandy rut. Asbenson opened the trunk and, naked except for her sweat shirt, ran down the road. In the distance, she could see an approaching truck. She turned around and saw the man running after her, waving a machete. She kept running, eyes closed. When she opened them, the truck had screeched to a halt.

"Catch him!" she screamed. "He kidnapped me! I just got out of his trunk!"

Inside the truck were two Marines who listened in horror as she described her ordeal. "They were really mad," she recalled. "They said they were going to kick his ass. They started driving as fast as they could, trying to catch him." The blue car sped off into the distance. Asbenson was treated for her injuries and gave a statement to Riverside County Sheriff's detectives, but they were unable to locate the car or its driver.

NEARLY FIVE YEARS LATER and more than 2,000 miles away, Officer Warren Fryer of the Hammond, Indiana, Police Department received an emergency call from a security guard at the American Inn, a run-down motel in the working-class suburb 30 minutes east of Chicago. According to the guard, two guests, a man and a woman, were arguing in the motel parking lot.

It was April 1, 1997. Fryer, who was on routine patrol that evening, drove to the motel. As he got out of his car, he immediately recognized the woman mentioned by the guard: Patricia Kelly, a local prostitute Fryer had arrested in the past. Apparently, she had just stolen a personal check from her client while they were having sex in their motel room, and the john was angry, chasing her around the parking lot, demanding she return it, which she couldn't do because she had flushed it down the toilet. Fryer also recognized the john. He was a Chicago security guard and former Marine named Andrew Urdiales.

Some five months earlier, on November 14, 1996, Fryer had arrested Urdiales outside a crack house on Becker Street in

Hammond. Urdiales had been sitting in his silver-and-white Toyota pickup with a prostitute. While Fryer talked to the prostitute, his partner, Edwin Ortiz, was questioning Urdiales when he noticed a .38 caliber handgun sticking out from under his seat. They also found a gym bag in the spotless bed of the truck containing a few rolls of duct tape. Urdiales said he used the gun for his security work, but the cops arrested him for carrying a concealed weapon without a permit. They confiscated the gun, and Urdiales spent the night in jail.

At the American Inn, Urdiales was standing in the parking lot, seething. "That bitch took one of my checks," he told Fryer, who then questioned Kelly separately. She told him that Urdiales, a regular client, would routinely drive her to nearby Wolf Lake and pay her $40 to have sex with him. But that was always during the day, and tonight, she'd refused to go with him because it was dark. Not only that, but she also knew a couple of prostitutes who'd been murdered at Wolf Lake late at night.

"This guy is kind of kinky," Kelly told Fryer. "He wants to take me in the back of his pickup truck and go up by Wolf Lake, duct tape me, and fuck me in the ass."

Fryer made no arrests that night, but he typed up a report on Kelly's statement, making sure to note Urdiales' previous firearm arrest—knowing full well that it would be forwarded to other local police departments. He figured a couple of Chicago homicide detectives might be interested in what Kelly had to say.

ONE OF THOSE DETECTIVES, Don McGrath, still works nights for Chicago's Area Two Homicide Unit, which covers the southeast portion of the city. He's been with the force 31 years; so far this year, his unit has handled 135 murder investigations. But he still remembers well the night in April 1997 when he read Fryer's report because it seemed to have everything to do with three bodies that had been found in the previous year, two in Wolf

Lake and one in the Vermilion River 100 miles away near Pontiac, Illinois.

Although it was out of his jurisdiction, McGrath was familiar with the Vermilion case. On the evening of July 13, 1996, three young fishermen spotted a body floating in a remote area of the river near a footbridge. It was a nude woman who had been shot above her left eye and stabbed seven times in the chest. She had bruises all over, three broken teeth, duct-tape residue on her mouth and ankles, and strangulation marks on her neck. She also had a small, homemade tattoo on her ankle with the initials "C.C." Police later identified her as 21-year-old Cassandra Corum, a prostitute from Hammond.

As McGrath saw it, Corum's murder seemed awfully similar to the murders his unit had been investigating at Wolf Lake, a recreational park bordered on the southeast side of Chicago by a chemical plant. The first body had been discovered on April 14, 1996, when a man was driving along the shore, looking for rocks to use as decoration in his garden. From his car, he spotted what looked like a mannequin floating in the water 20 feet from shore.

Police determined the victim was Laura Uylaki, a 25-year-old Hammond prostitute, who had been stabbed 25 times and shot three times in the head. She had been raped anally, and her body was covered in bruises.

A few months later, on August 2, a Chicago city employee was coming home after an early-morning fishing trip with his son, when he spotted what he thought was a mannequin floating in the water. It turned out to be Lynn Huber, a 22-year-old homeless prostitute from Chicago who had been stabbed repeatedly in the chest, back and neck, and then finished off with close-range gunshots to the face and head. The bullets matched those which had been retrieved from the bodies of Corum and Uylaki.

When he read Fryer's report about Urdiales, McGrath immediately called the Hammond police and learned that the handgun that had been confiscated from Urdiales was scheduled to be destroyed in the next few weeks. "I asked would it be okay to pick up the gun and examine it," he recalls. "We brought it to the crime lab, and it took them about a week to analyze it. They said we had the murder weapon."

ON APRIL 22, 1997, McGrath and his partner Raymond Krakausky drove to the house on the south side of Chicago where Urdiales lived with his parents. They sat in their car from early that afternoon until 9 a.m. the following day, when Urdiales walked out the front door dressed in a security-guard uniform. "We snagged him in the alley and told him we wanted to talk to him about the handgun charge," McGrath says. "He said that the matter had already been adjudicated, but he agreed to come with us to the station. He was unremarkable. There was nothing about him that stood out, that would make you look twice, just an average-looking Joe."

McGrath began his interrogation with a casual chat about *Star Trek*. Both he and Urdiales happened to be fans of the show, and McGrath was impressed that Urdiales could quote from the series.

McGrath and Krakausky already had a suspect in mind for the murders, a man who knew all three prostitutes, who had failed a polygraph and then tried to commit suicide by slashing his wrists.

"He was an evil guy," McGrath says of their suspect. "Evil incarnate, deep-set eyes, disheveled hair, a Charlie Manson expression, and in my 32 years, I never had the sense of evil like when I talked to this guy, but we couldn't find any physical evidence to connect him. We kind of believed Urdiales acquired his gun from this guy or loaned it to the guy, and he was the guy we were looking for."

At the station, however, Urdiales insisted he had purchased the gun from a dealer, still had the receipts, kept the gun locked in a box in his basement, and nobody else had the keys. McGrath and Krakausky exchanged glances and informed Urdiales that his gun had been used to murder three prostitutes. Urdiales unpinned his security-guard badge and untied his shoelaces. "I guess I'm not going to be going to work today," he said, and then confessed to murdering Uylaki, Corum and Huber.

Urdiales described the murders in detail: how he lured them to Wolf Lake for sex but got angry each time. He shot Uylaki after she saw his gun under his seat and tried to grab it. He then removed her clothes, stabbed her and dumped her in the lake. Huber met the same fate after she acted "ditzy" in his car. He grabbed her by the hair, then shot her when she tried to leave and dumped her in the water.

Corum, according to McGrath's notes of the interview, said "something that pissed him off," so Urdiales hit her in the face, took off her clothes and used duct tape to tie her feet together. He also taped her mouth shut, but he took off the tape to let her smoke a cigarette while he drove down Interstate 55 toward the Vermilion River. He pulled off the freeway near a farmhouse, driving through cornfields to the river.

Once there, he untied Corum, marched her out of the car, shot and stabbed her, then dropped her from a footbridge into the river. "Andrew Urdiales states that he didn't feel anything for Cassie after he shot her," McGrath wrote. "That she was just a whore. And he was trained to kill in the Marine Corps."

Urdiales didn't stop there. After confessing to the three Illinois murders, he told McGrath to call the cops in California.

"There are things they'd like to talk to me about, too," he explained.

McGrath took furious notes as Urdiales recited a list of horrific murders in California. "It seemed he was glad to get it off his chest," McGrath recalls. "During the recounting of the incidents, we'd crack a couple of jokes, and he'd laugh and go on to tell us about somebody else he killed. Pretty bizarre."

In 1987, Urdiales said, he'd picked up a prostitute (later revealed to be Mary Ann Wells) in an industrial neighborhood of San Diego. He paid her $40 for sex, then shot her and took his money back. The next year, he returned to San Diego and murdered a woman police identified as Julie McGhee, a 20-year-old prostitute. In 1989, he murdered another prostitute, 19-year-old Tammie Erwin, in Palm Springs. He told McGrath he returned to Palm Springs on at least two other occasions. In 1995, he'd murdered a prostitute named Denise Maney there. And three years earlier, he'd kidnapped and raped a young woman who managed to escape his vehicle.

Within days, police throughout Southern California were matching Urdiales' description of the murders with their unsolved homicides. Urdiales had also talked about a storage locker in Twentynine Palms, where he served in the Marines after leaving Camp Pendleton. Inside the locker, Riverside County Sheriff's detectives found several guns, rolls of duct tape, assorted knives and a machete. They also tracked down Jennifer Asbenson and showed her a series of photographs. Without hesitation, she identified Urdiales as the man who had kidnapped and raped her and, after she escaped from his trunk, chased her down the road with a machete.

The last person Urdiales confessed to murdering, as he sat calmly across a desk from McGrath inside the Chicago police station, was Robbin Brandley.

A FEW DAYS LATER, then-Orange County Sheriff Brad Gates paid a surprise visit to Jack and Genelle Reilley at their home in Laguna Beach. An ex-Camp Pendleton Marine named Andrew Urdiales, who was in custody in Chicago, had confessed to murdering their daughter.

"Gates was 6-foot-6 and wore a big hat and boots with a 2-inch heel," Jack recalls. "He showed up with all these detectives and said this guy had confessed in Chicago to all these murders. It was on CNN and all over the news."

Gates told the Reilleys he was holding a press conference to announce the Brandley murder case had been solved. "He said Robbin was the first [victim], and we are going to get him here [to stand trial] first," Jack says. "And after that, it went back to nothing again."

Getting Urdiales to stand trial in California wouldn't turn out to be so easy. First, he'd go to court for the three murders in Illinois. The first case finally went to trial in April 2002, five years after Urdiales confessed. The prosecution's case understandably focused on the three Illinois murders and featured dozens of witnesses: everyone from Patricia Kelly, the prostitute who alerted Hammond police to Urdiales' sexual proclivities, to Don McGrath, who arrested Urdiales. But the star witness was Jennifer Asbenson, who recounted for the jury in gripping detail her ordeal in the desert at the hands of the accused killer.

Urdiales pleaded not guilty by reason of insanity. He didn't testify during the trial. Instead, jurors heard his voice primarily in tape recordings made on April 24, 1997, the day after his arrest, when Orange County Sheriff's detectives Bob Blackburn and Helen Moreno flew to Chicago and met with him. In his interview, Urdiales described his upbringing in Chicago, how he joined the Marine Corps in 1984, and served at Camp Pendleton before deployments in Okinawa, the Philippines, and California, where he was stationed at Twentynine Palms.

In 1988, Urdiales said, he'd re-enlisted, and the next year, he went back to Okinawa before returning once again to California, and then shipping out to Saudi Arabia for Operation Desert Shield. Urdiales served as a radio operator in the Persian Gulf War and received an honorable discharge. After leaving the Marines, he returned to Chicago, visiting California on occasion to visit family members—and, according to his previous confession, murder five women.

He told Blackburn and Moreno that his stint at Camp Pendleton in 1985 was the "best year" of his life, but that things turned sour when all of his buddies were transferred elsewhere in early 1986. Urdiales explained that he had a "rotten temper" and "just couldn't deal with the new group of people coming in" to the base.

On the night Brandley died, Urdiales claimed, he "got mad with one of the other guys" in his barracks. He just needed to "get off that fucking base." He drove north along Interstate 5, armed with what he described as a "big ol' hunting knife" with a serrated edge and hollow grip for survival gear with a compass on the end.

"I just drove around," he continued. "I notice this sign said Saddleback College, so I stopped, and I just, I parked my car, and we just, uh, uh, just walking [sic]. I had my knife with me. I don't know why. . . . So I wandered up, probably, wandered up toward the, uh, college. . . . It was dark. . . . No lights, no nothing, just darkness . . . Maybe I just wanted to just kind of have an idea of what would happen if I just, you know, maybe robbed someone or a mugging or something. Maybe just try, you know, just kinda go on the edge. See what happens. 'Cause I was always trained, always trained to kill in boot camp."

At this point, Urdiales said, he noticed a woman walking to her car. "No one else was around, just the two of us," he said. "So I just started walking to her, kinda. And she turned around and looked but didn't say anything." Urdiales kept following her. "I think that it became apparent that something was wrong, and she looked around, and then she saw the knife, and then she screamed briefly."

Urdiales covered her mouth with his hands. He told the detectives that he doesn't clearly remember what happened next. "It's just kinda like, just dark, fuzzy," he said. "It's kind of like things going on back and forth in my mind just like, yes, no. Do it now." Urdiales said he told the woman to hand over her purse. She complied, and he placed it on top of the nearest car.

The detectives then asked Urdiales to describe the purse. "I don't think the purse had nothing to do with that," he answered. "I think it was her that we wanted, and we just sat there for awhile—I don't know what happened. The next thing I know is the knife went into her back, once, twice, several times. And I don't remember, I just don't remember, just uh, you know, uh, walked away. Wiped the blood off somewhere. I don't remember where we did."

After murdering Brandley, Urdiales claimed, he cut his hand jumping a fence, then drove back to Camp Pendleton. The Marines guarding the base entrance noticed blood on his clothes, but Urdiales convinced them he'd injured himself fixing his car. "Those guys are so stupid," he told the detectives. Urdiales kept his knife for a few weeks and even brought it with him when he took a bus to Hollywood and had sex with a prostitute. "I just had sex, and then I left," he explained. "Lucky for her."

When he returned to the base that night, a security guard searched his backpack, found the knife and confiscated it. Thus, the Brandley murder weapon disappeared. Detective Blackburn testified that Orange County Sheriff's detectives contacted Camp Pendleton and verified he was treated for a hand injury and, a few weeks later, was found in possession of a large knife, which was confiscated.

Because Urdiales repeatedly used the word "we" when describing the Brandley murder, his confession to Blackburn and Moreno became the centerpiece of his defense team's attempt to convince the jury he was a crazed killer who couldn't be held responsible for his crimes. His lawyers presented evidence that Urdiales had been counseled for depression at a Veteran's Administration clinic in Chicago.

"Andrew is a paranoid schizophrenic," Kathryn Lisco, Urdiales' court-appointed public defender, told the jury during her closing arguments. "Andrew has brain damage."

Lisco then launched into a biography of Urdiales that featured repeated injuries as a child, beginning as an infant, when his sister accidentally dropped him on his head. She asserted that he'd been in a car crash when he was a year old, hit his head on a cement step two years later, and then was repeatedly molested by his sister, who in turn had been abused by a family friend. "This went on for several years," she argued. "He became confused. He became ashamed. He suffered humiliation. And as he grew, this fueled his rage tremendously."

When Urdiales was a young child, his brother Alfred died in Vietnam. As a result, Lisco argued, his mother "abandoned" him, retreating into her bedroom. Urdiales was bullied throughout high school and joined the Marines to make his family proud. At first, the Marines seemed to provide the discipline and sense of belonging Urdiales lacked at home. But after he was stationed at Camp Pendleton and promoted from private to corporal, Lisco said, he began to lose his nerve—and eventually his mind.

"Andrew begins to hear things in his mind," she told the jury. "And he doesn't know exactly what they are. He begins to hear things that he interprets as messages and says that sometimes these messages are in code. . . . And Andrew begins to go on missions."

Lisco told the jury that Urdiales' first "mission" was murdering Brandley. "When he first acted on his delusions and killed Robbin Brandley, he had gone for a drive, nowhere in particular, and at some point, he believed he was on this CIA mission," she told the jury. "The instructions came to him through his receiver, and he felt that he had a test coming on, and the test was to see if he could kill without any feeling. And this was a secret mission, therefore it's conducted at night. . . . He's looking for his CIA contact. He's looking for his target of opportunity. He sees the sign for Saddleback College. . . . That's where it all started."

ON MAY 23, 2002, after a six-week trial, the jury rejected Andrew Urdiales' claim of insanity and found him guilty of first-degree murder of Laura Uylaki and Lynn Huber. The verdict may have been influenced by the fact that despite being treated for depression for several years, Urdiales had never been medicated nor diagnosed with any mental illness or personality disorder.

"The evidence of his guilt is overwhelming, and the evidence of his sanity is even more so," lead prosecutor Jim McKay told the jury in his closing arguments. "He is angry, he is evil, and he is depressed, but you know what, folks? Mad, bad and sad don't equal crazy."

Although the jury sentenced Urdiales to death a week later—after hearing from a string of relatives of the victims, including Jack Reilley—then-Illinois Governor George Ryan declared a moratorium on the death penalty in 2003, automatically commuting Urdiales' sentence to life in prison. The following year, Urdiales stood trial in Livingston County for murdering Cassandra Corum. Again, he was convicted and sentenced to death. Urdiales appealed both convictions to the Illinois Supreme Court and lost. On October 29, 2007, the U.S. Supreme Court rejected his federal appeal of his first conviction. He currently sits on death row at Pontiac Correctional Center, although Illinois hasn't executed an inmate since March 17, 1999.

Although the Orange County district attorney's office issued an arrest warrant for Urdiales when he confessed a decade ago, there's no chance he'll be extradited any time soon to stand trial for the five murders he committed in California. Deputy DA Howard Gundy told the *Weekly* his office would love to prosecute Urdiales for murdering Robbin Brandley, Mary Ann Wells, Julie McGhee, Tammie Erwin and Denise Maney, but it may be more trouble than it's worth since Urdiales' attorneys could use the extradition to delay the eventual imposition of his Illinois death sentence.

"The irony in this case is justice may better be served if we let the state of Illinois complete the process, because if we don't do that, we may cause delay and a diversion he will look forward to having," Gundy says. "He's living in a very small cell out there. He's in perfectly good hands."

Gundy adds that he sympathizes with the Reilleys' anger at the lack of progress in the case. "I understand the frustration of the parents and other people, but part of that is you can never do anything for those poor folks unless you can bring their loved ones back. That's the quandary of a prosecutor."

Valerie Prehm, the woman whom the Reilleys suspected of being involved in their daughter's murder for 11 years, now lives in Seattle. She says Brandley's murder ruined her life. "I was one of the last people to see Robbin alive," she says. "We were really good friends on campus. She was an outgoing, beautiful person. Everyone loved her."

In 1991, Prehm's twin, Melanie, was brutally murdered in a Dana Point motel room. Although the police determined she'd been killed by an ex-boyfriend, Prehm says that shortly before Genelle Reilley came to her home and demanded she take a polygraph test, someone sent her a death threat. The message, sent with no return address, was assembled with letters cut out of magazines and newspapers and contained just five words. The first two—"Robbin" and "Melanie"—were crossed out. Beneath those words were "Valerie" and "You're Next."

Robbin Brandley's murder caused Prehm to experience severe depression and alcoholism. She is currently unemployed. "[Genelle] hired a private investigator and followed me for six years," she says. "At a time when I should have been getting jobs, I wasn't because she was placing reasonable doubt."

Echoing her videotaped polygraph statement in 1992—five years before Urdiales was arrested—Prehm still insists that, while the man doesn't match the description of Andrew Urdiales, a mysterious stranger did in fact approach her at the piano concert, asking about Brandley. "When Robbin and I were seating people, some guy tapped me on the shoulder," she says. "He had dark curly hair and thick glasses and an olive-green hunting jacket. It didn't match [Urdiales'] description, so I guess it's insignificant."

She vigorously denies playing any role in Brandley's murder, even as a witness. "I didn't leave the party with her," she says. "I wish I did."

Although Jack Reilley testified in the penalty phase of Urdiales' first trial, both he and Genelle refused to do so the second time around. They have cut off all contact with the Orange County Sheriff's Department and the DA's office. They believe their telephones have been tapped, that someone has repeatedly broken into their home and that these events have something to do with their daughter's murder 21 years ago.

"Our home has been broken into," Genelle says. "And guess what they're taking: hairbrushes, frequently worn clothing. Things with DNA are being stolen out of our house, and that freaks me out. [Jack] has a nice camera. Why didn't they take that?"

A decade after Urdiales confessed to murdering their daughter, the Reilleys still believe that while Urdiales may have been present at the crime scene, he didn't act alone. Because Brandley was the only victim who wasn't a prostitute and who wasn't shot with a gun, they're still haunted with doubts about his culpability.

"The question to us is, why was Robbin murdered one way and all the others another way?" Jack asks. "For all these other victims, he used a gun. There's no passion in a gun. How could a total stranger come up and stab her 40 times? You have to have a lot of anger."

Genelle, for her part, is convinced someone hired Urdiales to rob their daughter and didn't intend for him to murder her, only scare her into leaving the campus. "Brad Gates came to our house and told us this was robbery gone wrong," she says. "If you want money, you aren't going to go to a community college at 10 o'clock at night and maybe there's a rich student walking around. It's so stupid. It doesn't make any sense at all. And it's not the way it happened."

NICK SCHOU *has been covering crime and justice for* OC Weekly *since 1996 with stories that have resulted in the federal indictment and incarceration of Huntington Beach mayor Pamela Houchen, and the release from prison of wrongly convicted individuals. His writing has appeared in the* Los Angeles Times, LA Weekly, San Francisco Bay Guardian, *and other alternative weeklies. He is also the author of the book* Kill the Messenger: How the CIA's Crack Cocaine-Controversy Destroyed Journalist Gary Webb *(Nation Books, 2006). He lives in Long Beach, California, with his wife and son.*

Coda

The Orange County District Attorney officially has yet to extradite Andrew Urdiales to face trial for the murder of Robbin Brandley and four other California women. He remains on death row in Illinois, which has a moratorium on the death penalty. Unofficially, the DA seems to be hoping that the state reinstates its death penalty so it can avoid the expense and (for Urdiales) publicity and attention provided by a high-profile trial in Orange County.

James Renner

THE SERIAL KILLER'S DISCIPLE

FROM THE *Cleveland Free Times*

THE DEATH HOUSE at Lucasville Prison has a room for wit-nesses of executions, divided by a partition. When Akron *Beacon Journal* reporter Phil Trexler was ushered in one morning just over five years ago, he noticed three men sitting together on one side. Trexler had covered the case of the condemned man, Robert Buell, so he knew who these men were: the father and brothers of Krista Harrison, whose murder 20 years earlier, at age 11, was the crime the state was avenging that day.

On the other side of the partition sat Patricia Millhoff, Buell's attorney, and the Rev. Ernie Sanders, his pastor. Millhoff was crying. Not 10 minutes before, she'd had to tell Buell that his re-quest for a stay had been denied. She'd gotten to know Buell well. As the appeals process had wound down, there'd been little in the way of law to discuss, so they talked about mundane things. That morning's Diane Rehm show on NPR. Or what books Buell was currently reading aloud into a recorder for blind people.

Buell always insisted that he had not murdered the girl. Mill-hoff believed him.

Sanders also was grieving. He'd known Buell much longer, 17 years. Buell had heard Sanders speak at the prison, and wrote the reverend a letter, asking him to visit. Buell had a lot to confess— the rapes of two women, at least—but Sanders' God has grace enough for that. Grace enough to forgive even the murder of the child, he'd told Buell. But Buell never sought forgiveness for that. And in Sanders' mind, he didn't have to. Sitting there that night, Sanders believed he knew who really killed Krista.

The last time they spoke, Buell had said, "You were right all along."

The chairs on both sides of the partition faced a window that overlooked a gurney. On the other side, someone drew a curtain and when it was reopened, Buell was lying there, strapped down, facing the ceiling. He appeared calm. An IV tube snaked out of his arm and disappeared behind a wall.

Trexler observed Buell's Adam's apple bob up and down, up and down, counting off the seconds like a swallowed metronome. The witness room was silent except for the faint scratching of reporters' pencils on paper.

Buell was asked if he had any last words. He did, for Krista's parents.

"Jerry and Shirley," he said, though Shirley wasn't there, "I didn't kill your daughter. The prosecutor knows that . . . and they left the real killer out there on the streets to kill again and again and again."

Soon after Buell finished, Trexler noticed that Buell's breathing appeared more labored. Buell closed his eyes and died.

Buell's typewriter and small TV went home with Millhoff; he'd left them to her because the prison wouldn't let him donate them to fellow inmates. His personal collection of court transcripts, police files, letters, handwritten notes and newspaper clippings, collected over 18 years, left with Sanders. The contents of the box do not reflect well on Buell; there seems little reason to doubt that he belonged in prison. But they also raise a strange possibility: that he was telling the truth when he said he didn't kill Krista Harrison. And that he knew who did.

IN THE EARLY 1980S, someone was killing little girls in Ohio.

The first incident was the abduction and murder of 12-year-old Tina Harmon in the fall of 1981. Tina was a cute, round-faced girl from the small town of Creston with shoulder-length hair and a taste for Camel Light cigarettes. Back then, the only real entertainment was the game room at the Union 76 Truck Stop in Lodi, a few miles away. Tina was known to hang out there whenever she could hitch a ride.

According to police reports, on Thursday, October 29, 1981, Tina got a ride into Creston from her father's girlfriend, who dropped her off in front of a convenience store with a group of friends. Tina bought a fudgesicle and bummed another ride from her teenage brother, who took her only as far as the next Lawson's. Eventually, she made it to Lodi; several witnesses, including a local detective, remembered seeing her there that evening. Tina was last spotted in the presence of an unshaven man in a jean jacket, who appeared to be in his early 20s.

The girl's body was found five days later in Bethlehem Township, about 40 miles from her home, dumped beside an oil well in plain sight of anyone driving down the road. She was fully clothed and had been placed neatly on the ground. She'd been raped and strangled shortly after she was abducted. Oil well workers who had visited that access road the day before had seen nothing, and this supported the detectives' theory that Tina's body had been stored someplace else before being placed in the field.

In her pocket they found a book of matches from the Union 76 Truck Stop. On her clothes, the coroner found dog hair and several "trilobal polyester" fibers the color of nutmeg.

Less than a year later—July 17, 1982, a stormy Saturday—Krista Harrison was snatched from a baseball field across the street from her home. She had been collecting cans with a 12-year-old friend, Roy, who later told police that around 5 p.m., a dark-colored van pulled into the park. The van had bubble-shaped windows, black seats and a roof vent.

The driver climbed out and approached Krista. The man was white, and looked to be about 25 to 35 years old. He was skinny, with a mustache and dark brown hair that curled near his shoulders; he looked Italian, the boy thought. The man said something to Krista and she went and sat on the bleachers overlooking the diamond. The man then sat down next to the girl and reached underneath her blouse. When Krista started to cry, the man whispered something into her ear. Roy could not hear what was said, but Krista walked to the man's van, opened the driver's-side door, and climbed between the front bucket seats and sat on the floor. The man climbed in too and quickly sped away.

Witnesses later told police that a strange man resembling Krista's abductor had attended one of her summer softball games, photographing her with a 35mm camera. Classmates told police that on the afternoon Krista was abducted, she had gone to the Village Snack Shop game room and when she left, a strange man had blocked her way and tried to get her to dance with him. The man had dark hair that was curly on the ends.

And in the weeks leading up to her abduction, there had been several prank calls placed to the Harrison residence when Krista was home.

Krista was missing for less than a week. On July 23, two turtle trappers discovered her body next to an abandoned shed in a field in nearby Holmes County. She was fully clothed and wrapped in plastic. The coroner discovered carpet fibers on her, the same tri-lobal polyester fibers that had been found on Tina Harmon. Like Tina, Krista had been strangled to death shortly after being kidnapped, but her body had been stored somewhere before being moved to the field. Like Tina, she had been sexually assaulted, possibly with a vibrator.

The next day, a second crime scene was located in West Salem. In the weeds next to the road, police found a green plastic garbage bag covered in Krista's blood and hair. Beside the bag was a Budweiser blanket and pieces of blood-stained cardboard.

Then, a second sweep of the area where Krista's body had been found turned up a pair of dirty jeans, spotted with blood and specks of powder-blue paint. There was a hole in the left knee. A man's plaid shirt was also found.

The evidence was sent to the lab at the Bureau of Criminal Identification and Investigation, which determined that the bag and box had once contained van seats that had been ordered through Sears. And on the bag was a fingerprint.

Sears provided detectives with the names of everyone in the area who had ordered similar seats. The list was long, but every name was checked out. Bob Buell was on the list and was interviewed, but the detective did not feel that Buell was being deceptive and so he did not become the focus of their investigation.

The BCI&I lab also confirmed that the fibers found on Krista matched those found on Tina. The FBI commissioned a criminal profile of the perpetrator by Special Agent John Douglas, whose pioneering studies of the habits of serial killers inspired the book *The Silence of the Lambs*. Krista's killer should be in his early to late 20s, Douglas said. He is a latent homosexual.

"When employed, he seeks menial or unskilled trades," wrote Douglas. "While he considers himself a 'macho man,' he has deep-rooted feelings of personal inadequacies. Your offender has a maximum of a high school education. When he is with children, he feels superior, in control, non-threatened. While your offender may not be from the city where the victim was abducted he certainly has been there many times before (i.e. visiting friends, relatives, employment). He turned towards alcohol and/or drugs to escape from the realities of the crime."

Detectives from several jurisdictions and FBI special agents worked diligently to find the man who killed Krista and Tina.

But the evidence could not be matched to a likely suspect, and each new lead only led them to a different dead end. Then it happened again.

On Saturday, June 25, 1983, 10-year-old Debbie Smith disappeared from a street fair in Massillon. Later that day, Debbie called home. She sounded upset, but would not say where she was. On August 6 a canoeist found Debbie's body on the banks of the Tuscarawas River. She had been raped. She had most likely been stabbed, though the body also showed signs of blunt force trauma. Melted wax was found on her body, and the candles from which it had come were recovered nearby.

THESE MURDERS WERE STILL on the minds of police and area residents two months later when Franklin Township police received a chilling call from a Doylestown resident. There was a shaved, naked woman with a handcuff attached to one wrist standing in her kitchen, the caller said. The woman had shown up on her doorstep, claiming that she had been held captive in the house across the street—the little ranch house owned by Bob Buell.

The victim was a 28-year-old woman from Salem. She worked at a gas station, and on the night of October 16, 1983, she had been painting the office floor when a middle-aged man came up behind her with a gun and ordered her into his van. He pushed her between the front seats and handcuffed her hands behind her back. Then, he drove her to his house, into an attached garage and told her to go into the bedroom and undress. Inside, the man handcuffed her to a leather bench and spent the rest of the night raping, torturing and degrading the woman in increasingly vile and unique ways. When it was over, he shaved her head and tied her to his bed. In the morning he went to work, promising to return around lunchtime.

But the woman escaped, and when Buell returned home, a

Franklin Township cop was waiting. Buell was arrested and charged with multiple counts of rape and kidnapping.

At the time, Buell was 42 years old. He had a college degree and was employed by the city of Akron, writing loans for the Planning Department. He was dating an attorney. He had a daughter at Kent State. Those who knew him described a neat, clean, orderly man, almost to the point of obsessive-compulsive disorder. He didn't exactly fit the FBI's profile of their child killer.

But when other agencies got word of Buell's arrest and recognized his name from the list of men who had purchased van seats from Sears, police descended upon his home with an array of search warrants. They found everything they were looking for, and more.

In the master bedroom, they found all the evidence they needed to confirm the rape victim's story.

In a guest bedroom, painted powder-blue, detectives discovered a roll of carpet the color of nutmeg. The fibers were trilobal polyester and matched fibers found on the bodies of Tina Harmon and Krista Harrison. In the closet were jeans with a hole worn into the left knee—identical to the pair found near Krista's body. They also found dog hairs that matched those found on Tina, a newspaper clipping on the abduction of Debbie Smith, and candles of the same brand that were found near Debbie's body.

Investigators took Buell's van too, a 1978 maroon Dodge with new black seats from Sears. Inside was more of that same nutmeg carpeting.

Police put Buell's picture into a lineup which was shown to witnesses. Several people who had attended Krista's last softball game identified Buell as a stranger they saw watching the game. A check of Buell's timecards revealed he had taken time off from work the day Krista's body was dumped.

As Buell's face became a front-page and TV news staple, other women came forward claiming they had been abducted and raped by him, then released. One woman from West Virginia told a grim story almost identical to the Salem victim's, down to being handcuffed in the bedroom so that Buell could go to work.

But all of these women were in their late 20s or older. So FBI Special Agent Bill Callis commissioned a second criminal profile to help explain what is referred to as "the missing link" between Buell's practice of raping and releasing grown women and his presumed taste for killing young girls. Serial killers tend to stick to one sex and age group and tend to escalate in violence over time; they generally don't start just letting victims go. This second report was not prepared by John Douglas, but by another profiler in the FBI's Behavioral Science Unit. It blamed Buell's mother.

Buell pleaded no contest to the rape charges and was sentenced to 121 years in prison for those crimes. He was only charged with one murder, Krista's, even though police believe he murdered Tina Harmon and Debbie Smith and maybe more. But as one detective put it, "How many times do you need to kill a man?" Buell was convicted of Krista's murder on April 4, 1984. The jury sentenced him to die.

MARTIN FRANTZ WAS assistant prosecutor for Wayne County during Buell's lengthy trial and played a significant role in sending the Akron city employee to the Death House. Today, Frantz is county prosecutor and remembers the case well, down to the names of eyewitnesses, 23 years later. He has no doubt that Buell killed those girls.

"It wasn't in the trial," he says, "but we had someone figure out, mathematically, how many people in the world could possibly be connected to all of that circumstantial evidence that we found inside Buell's home. It was something like 1 in 6 trillion."

Actually, it's 2 in 6 trillion.

Bob Buell was not living at his ranch house during the summer of 1982. His nephew was. Ralph Ross Jr. was a skinny 20-year-old from Mingo Junction, a factory town just outside Steubenville. He had dark hair that curled near his shoulders and was growing a mustache. In February 1982, Ross moved to Akron to drive a truck for an auto-parts manufacturer. His uncle Bob let him stay in the powder-blue guest room. Usually Ross had the house to himself because Buell spent most nights at his girlfriend's place. In exchange for room and board, Ross did chores around the house. It was his job to take out the garbage.

Ross was Buell's ex-wife's brother's kid, but they shared a special kinship that was thicker than blood. For instance, they often fantasized about kidnapping women and doing things to them inside Buell's van.

"What are some of those things?" asked Wayne County Sheriff's Department Detective Dennis Derflinger, in an interview with Ross shortly after Buell's arrest in 1983.

"Tying them up, shaving their crotch, putting a gag in their mouth, using a vibrator, that's about all."

Ross went into a little more detail about these conversations when questioned by Frantz in front of a grand jury.

"Can you tell us what you remember about what Robert Buell said when he was talking of these fantasies and riding around in the van?" asked Frantz.

"I would like to say something," Ross replied. "It was me as well as him that was discussing whatever we were discussing."

Frantz: "So both of you were talking about it?"

Ross: "It was a two-way conversation."

Frantz: "Just tell us what Buell said."

Ross: "Well, he would talk about, if we would pass up a girl or something on the street, talked about wouldn't it be nice to have that girl for this evening, and I would say, yeah, sure would."

Frantz: "What else was said?"

Ross: "Well, I said I would doubt if she would go out with me or get together, that I didn't know her, just passed her up on the street. And he said well—or we both suggested—that we could get her into the van if we wanted to."

Ross specifically remembered cruising Marshallville.

When Ross moved into Buell's house, the roll of nutmeg carpet was still being stored in the living room, where it had been for years. It matched the color of Buell's old van, a golden-brown 1977 Dodge that Buell had sold to Ross in 1980. That van and Buell's new one were very similar, but Ross' had a sun roof and bubble windows. And Ross's van was a little dirtier; Buell had let his daughter's dog sleep in it before selling it to Ross.

But they didn't just share seats and vans, they shared women, too. Women like Buell's secretary.

Frantz: "And the three of you were in bed together?"

Ross: "Yes."

Frantz: "And at that time the vibrator was used?"

Ross: "Me and Bob both used it."

Ross' hair was a little curly and Buell's was straight, but otherwise the two shared an uncanny resemblance. In fact, when a police officer responded to a noise violation at the house in July 1982, he mistook Ross for Buell. (Ross may have shown him Buell's driver's license.) And a closer look at original interviews with bystanders at Krista's last softball game raises important questions as well. One who identified Buell in a lineup also said, "There was another man standing beside him with a camera and mirrored sunglasses on."

The detective asked her if she meant that Buell was taking photographs.

"No, the man beside him was taking photographs. [Buell] did not have a camera."

Roy, the boy who stood just a few feet away from Krista's abductor when she was taken, said repeatedly that the man he saw that day was not Buell, but that the man was similar in appearance.

Ross did not have an alibi for the day Krista was abducted. He told police that he was probably visiting his parents that weekend, but couldn't remember for sure, and this apparently was never confirmed. Detective Derflinger asked Ross to submit finger-prints and his photo, but he refused. Derflinger ends his written report with this note: "P.S. He has started to grow a beard, but I don't think that means anything."

When interviewed by Franklin Township Detective Ron Fuchs about whether Ross had ever helped Buell alter his vans, Ross was more evasive. "Ralph's answers are contrary to other information already gained and he appeared to be deliberately lying and trying to cover up the incident," Fuchs stated. In fact, Ross had helped his uncle move seats from Ross' van into Buell's new van.

A witness told police that he saw the jeans and shirt that were found at one of Krista's crime scenes lying near the road at around 11:30 the morning of July 23. Police believe Krista's body also must have been dumped that morning because the items strewn about the road were not seen before then. The jeans and shirt are assumed to have been dumped at the same time. But Buell was at work until noon that day. And, accord-ing to his girlfriend, the only reason he took the rest of the day off was to help her fix her clothes dryer. She produced a receipt that showed she had purchased a dryer belt that afternoon. By the time Buell had a chance to stop by his house, it was 4:50 p.m. In a letter to the Rev. Sanders during his incarceration, Buell stated that he remembered the time because he thought it was odd that his nephew was home so early on a work day, and Ross's hand was wrapped in bandages. "He told me he had in-jured his hand at work and had to go to the hospital to get his hand x-rayed and bandaged," wrote Buell. Ross's employer had no record of the injury, according to police records. Buell's girlfriend also told police that the last time she saw the boxes that had contained the van seats they were in the garage next to the garbage cans.

A week after Krista's body was found, Ross abruptly quit his job in Akron and moved home. He went to work at his mother's craft store and, for a while, managed small booths for her at area malls, flea markets and fairs.

And then there is the evidence that detectives didn't find. When they confiscated Buell's van, they vacuumed every inch of the interior, but did not find one hair or fiber from Tina Harmon, Krista Harrison or Debbie Smith. They never bothered to test Ross' van. The fingerprint on the plastic bag did not match Buell's, nor did DNA collected at the scene.

BY 1984, BUELL WAS BEHIND BARS, but young Ohio girls continued to disappear.

In 1989, 10-year-old Amy Mihaljevic was abducted from Bay Village. Like Debbie, she made a phone call to her mother when she was most likely already with her abductor. She resembled Krista Harrison. And even though Amy was from Bay Village and Krista was from Marshallville, two cities separated by 58 miles, Amy's body was discovered a short distance from where police found a bloody garbage bag containing part of Krista's scalp. Like Tina, Amy's body was found in a field, on an incline, placed so that it could be easily seen from the road. Amy's body had also been stored someplace before being moved to the "dump" site. On Amy's body, the coroner also discovered gold-colored fibers, but they were never compared to those gathered in the Tina Harmon and Krista Harrison homicides because Buell was already in prison. Wayne County Prosecutor Martin Frantz says his Sheriff's Department destroyed the evidence after Buell was executed, though some samples may still be kept by BCI&I.

The case of 13-year-old Barbara Barnes of Steubenville is similar too. Barbara disappeared in December 1995, on her way to school. She was found two months later, strangled to death. But Barbara's killer went to great lengths to hide the body, in a muddy embankment in Pittsburgh. She was discovered when the river level rose with the thaw.

"I UNDERSTAND the circumstantial evidence could be put to Ralph Ross as well as Robert Buell," says Frantz in his office today. The prosecutor is a gracious host and opens his files to the *Free Times* because he truly believes he sent the right guy to the Death House. He sees the Harrisons in public sometimes and can meet their eyes.

"I know that during the investigation, Derflinger had those feelings. We ruled [Ross] out, but I can't remember how. I've always felt in my heart that Buell was guilty."

Pastor Ernie Sanders disagrees.

"Buell never killed those girls," he says. "He was by no means someone you would call a perfect citizen, but I know he didn't do it. I told him I was suspicious of his nephew, but he just kept saying that [Ross] was not smart enough to pull something like that off. You see, Buell thought he was smarter than everyone he knew. He told me that when he talked to Ralph about kidnapping women, he specifically told Ralph not to cross the line. He said not to take kids. And Ralph never argued with him, but Buell said he wasn't happy about it. A month before his execution, he told me, 'You know what? You were right all along. Ralph set me up.' And I believe him. Ralph had access to Bob's clothes and the clothes found at the crime scene were too small for Buell anymore. He'd left them for Ralph."

Today, Ralph Ross Jr. lives in a small house just outside Steubenville, where he grew up. He works for a cable company. He was arrested earlier this year and charged with possession of marijuana.

He spoke to this reporter on the stoop in front of his house in 2007. "I don't think Buell did it," he says. "But I don't know who did. They never questioned me about the deaths. Why would they?"

When asked why he didn't allow the detective to take his fingerprints, he becomes defensive. "What if something come up?" he says. "I told them if they wanted it to get a court order and take it. If they needed it, they could have got a court order."

He puts his hands in his pockets and looks over the river that meanders below his house. Ross says he started talking with his uncle about kidnapping and brutalizing women when he was 13 years old, and the conversations continued until Buell was caught.

"Times were different back then," he says. "I was hanging out with my cool uncle. I thought it was just guys talking when we talked about taking those women. I should never have said anything about it to the cops."

Asked about Krista, he abruptly ends the conversation. "I don't have anything more to say," he says. He goes back inside, stands behind his screen door and glances up and down the sidewalk. Asked if he had anything to do with Krista's abduction, he shuts the door and disappears into the darkness.

Jack Swint, author of *Who Killed . . . Cleveland*, provided Buell's box of documents, which were cited in this story.

JAMES RENNER *is a staff writer for the* Cleveland Free Times. *He is also the author of* Amy: My Search for Her Killer, *a true crime book that chronicles his investigation into she unsolved murder of Amy Mihaljevic. Renner was named one of Cleveland's Thirty Most Interesting People by* Cleveland Magazine *in 2005, after he adapted a short story by Stephen King into a film, which Renner directed. It premiered at the Montreal World Film Festival later that year.*

Coda

I have spent the last three years researching the strange abduction and murder of Amy Mihaljevic, a crime that occurred in 1989, in Bay Village, the idyllic Cleveland suburb made infamous by the Sam Sheppard case. The FBI agents and police detectives that have worked Amy's case for eighteen years believe that her murder was the first and only one committed by her killer, because his "MO" does not match any subsequent crime. I began to wonder if that assumption was incorrect.

While it's true that there appears to have been no similar murder committed in northeast Ohio after Amy's, I quickly found three that occurred just a few years before. However, these murders were attributed to a man named Robert Buell, who had been executed in 2002. Still, I tracked down the original case files, to see—just for my peace of mind—that the police and prosecutor who sent Buell to the death house got the right man. After reviewing the files, I quickly came to believe that Buell was innocent of these crimes and that the real killer still lives among us.

Since this story was originally published in the *Free Times*, things have not gone well for Ralph Ross, Jr. He was fired from his job installing cable for Comcast after the article circulated around the office. FBI agents were seen at his office, questioning coworkers. However, Wayne County prosecutor Martin Frantz refuses to officially reopen the Krista Harrison case—the murder for which Buell was executed. Instead, detectives are "reinvestigating" the murder of Tina Harmon, which remains an open case, even though identical fibers were discovered on the bodies of both Tina and Krista. Those fibers have recently been compared to similar fibers found on the body of Amy Mihaljevic. They do not match.

Tom Junod

MERCENARY

FROM *Esquire*

THE PALISADES NUCLEAR PLANT in Covert, Michigan, is real. It produces 778 megawatts of electricity, and the electricity keeps the lights burning for about half a million residents. The nuclear reactor inside the nuclear plant is also real. It gets really hot, and anyone driving on Interstate 196 on his way to Grand Rapids or St. Joe can see thin clouds of steam rising from its cooling towers, as constant a presence as the weather. The steam is real; it's water from Lake Michigan, pumped in to keep the reactor cool. The nuclear power plant is on the shore of Lake Michigan, right next to the tourist town of South Haven and about eighty miles from Chicago as the crow flies. Lake Michigan is real, definitely, though it comes off as an illusory ocean, offering the horizon as its only boundary. South Haven is real, too, although it empties out in the cold of winter. And Chicago? As real as the millions of people who live there, and the strange American fervor they generate. Chicago is so damned real, and so damned American, that it's hard to imagine an American reality without it—it's hard to imagine an American reality if, say, a terrorist attack on Palisades Nuclear contaminated the big lake for the next thousand years or so and emptied out Chicago, not to mention St. Joe and South Haven and Covert.

Which is why it's a good thing that the security manager at Palisades Nuclear for the last year and a half is real, too, with real qualifications for the job. His name is William E. Clark, and he has been in the Army, he's been a cop, he's done some contracting work for the Department of Energy, he's gone to Kosovo on a diplomatic mission, and after Katrina, he worked for Blackwater, the security company, outside New Orleans. He started at Palisades in early 2006. He has a new house and a new wife and has told people, "I would shed blood to keep this job." As a statement of determination, this is reassuring . . . but what if he means it as a statement of fact? What if William E. Clark has told people—told me—that he has in fact shed blood many times, in many places, over the course of many years? What if William E. Clark says that he worked for Blackwater in Afghanistan and Iraq as well as in New Orleans and killed so many people that he considers himself a cold-blooded murderer? What if he says that his job as the security manager of a nuclear plant on Lake Michigan is both a reward for all the killing he's done and a means for keeping him quiet about it?

THE GUILT IS REAL. The shame is real. He is not proud of the things he's done, although that doesn't stop him from talking about them. He's not proud of what he had to do in Vietnam, his son says. He's not proud of having to kill someone in New Orleans, his ex-wife says. He wakes up with nightmares, his new wife says, because he's starting to see the faces of the human beings he once saw through the rifle scope. And so this story represents his attempt to come clean. He is a bad person, he says, but he wants to be a good person—he wants to be thought of as a good person. He wants to be *purified,* shriven. He is telling his story because he knows it will destroy him. He is telling his story because he knows it will set him free.

He has kept stuff, over the years, because he knows that nobody will believe him. He has kept the stubs from all the boarding passes, the keys from all the hotel rooms. There are hundreds of them, and he keeps them in thick wads and piles. He has kept a business card for one of his aliases, Zeke Senega, a reporter for *The Irish Times* in Dublin. He has kept his passports, including the diplomatic one that was required for the work he did for the State Department. And he has photographs. He has a folder full of photographs from what he calls an "operation" in Iraq—an operation that ended with two jihadists slumped dead in the front seat of an Opel, their car windows spiderwebbed with the ghosts of two precision gunshots. He also has a photo album, which he calls the Book. The Book is not very different from a lot of photo albums—it is a record, in snapshots, of the places he's been and the people he's met—except that the mostly unsmiling men staring at the camera are usually wearing camouflage and armed to the teeth. And in the middle of the Book, there is one photo, black-and-white and larger than the rest, of William E. Clark cradling a rifle to his chest in what appears to be a jungle. He does not seem to be posing, and indeed he looks a little sick—his mouth slightly slack and his long face droopy with exhaustion. And yet when he remembers the circumstances of the photo, he relishes them: "That picture was taken in El Salvador in 1996. I wasn't supposed to be there. Nobody was. Suddenly this UPI photographer shows up, taking pictures. I said, 'If you don't put that camera down and give me the film, I'll shoot you. I'll kill you and get away with it. Because I don't exist.'"

THE VOLUNTEER IS REAL— so real that her name cannot be disclosed, nor any identifying details. She is one of the Americans who volunteered their time after Hurricane Katrina flooded the

Gulf Coast in 2005. She worked at a makeshift shelter where people were very sick and couldn't be evacuated. There were drugs at the shelter, a store of narcotics, to keep the sick people comfortable. There had to be protection, and Blackwater USA supplied it, through a government contract. The volunteer was happy that Blackwater was there, because she kept hearing stories of what was happening in New Orleans—its descent into lawlessness. It was a very scary time. In fact, one night one of the Blackwater contractors at the shelter said he had received intelligence to the effect that a New Orleans gang had found out about the drugs at the shelter and was on its way. He assured her that she would be safe, because he had just come from Iraq, and after what he'd been through there with the jihadists, he wasn't about to be scared by American lowlifes. He was a senior member of the Blackwater team, and he made sure that if anyone so much as even parked around the block from the shelter, there was a Blackwater contractor in his face. Nothing happened that night, and nothing *ever* happened, for she had her own personal protector.

His name was William E. Clark, but he told her to call him what everyone called him—Zeke. She was struck by the apparent contradictions in him. He made her feel secure, but he seemed so terribly wounded, both literally and metaphorically. He had a problem with his neck, an injury that occasionally caused him to pass out. When she asked him how he got it, he told her that he couldn't say, that he was prohibited from saying. Little by little, though, it came out, because secrets come to light during the night shift, and stories get told in the dark. He'd done terrible things for his country. He'd had to do terrible things, but that was because of his willingness to do them. He wasn't so willing anymore. He was doing the worst thing someone like him could do: He was growing a conscience. No, worse than that: He was *talking* about it. He was talking to her. He had never talked to anyone about the terrible things he'd done, not even his wife of thirty years. He felt safe with the volunteer, as she felt safe with him.

He scared her a little, of course. She had never met anyone like him. He showed her how to use one of his guns. She had never fired a gun before and was surprised how much she liked it. But she also felt that he was watching her. He even said that he was. He would call her on her cell phone, in the middle of the night, when she couldn't see him. "I'm sick of just watching you," he would say and describe everything she was doing, so that she knew she was being watched. It was obsessive, and once they came together, they came together obsessively. She was in thrall to him, as he was in thrall to his stories and his terrible past. She didn't know whether to believe his stories, but when she got home, he sent her videotaped footage of people being executed in what he said was Iraq. There were voices on the video, and one of them sounded exactly like Zeke's.

DEATH IS REAL. Its reality is unsurpassed, and the people at the disaster-relief conference in Houston last July were on intimate terms with it. They were morticians, they were forensic anthropologists and forensic dentists, they worked suicide hotlines, and they handled the public relations when airplanes went down. Now they were all standing up and saying who they were and where they came from and why they were interested in doing work that few people wanted to do—why they wanted to take care of the dead left behind by mass disasters. As the attendees were introducing themselves to one another by both name and profession, a man stood up and said, "My name is William Clark, and I'm a designated marksman for Blackwater."

He stood out as soon as he stood up. He was lean and he was lanky, with his face and everything else about him aligned on a vertical axis—he had a full head of springy hair rising straight up off his scalp in a kind of modified brush cut and a Fu Manchu mustache bracketing his rabbity front teeth. There was an arrogance in his military bearing and a desire to shock secreted in the monotonal nonchalance of his voice. I was one of the people who gave him the reaction he was looking for, and when I asked him if I could speak with him, he seemed as though he'd been waiting for me to ask the question.

We met in a small room away from the main auditorium and away from the other attendees of the conference. I was well aware of Blackwater and its reputation as a private security company whose armed contractors had changed the rules of engagement in Iraq and elsewhere, even in New Orleans. I was also well aware of the reputation its contractors had for not talking, and so I was surprised when William Clark sat down and, in the same manner he used when he was introducing himself in the auditorium—a manner at once matter-of-fact and challenging—he started not only talking but confessing. Yes, he said, he was one of *them*—a "merc," or mercenary, for Blackwater. He was a sniper. He had been a countersniper for the security details assigned to protect Hamid Karzai in Afghanistan and Paul Bremer, the former American proconsul, in Iraq. He did overwatch, which meant he sat up on rooftops and shot people who looked dangerous. "Hey," he said, "thirty-seven Al Qaeda and twenty-one Baathists can't be wrong." At first, he was blithe on the subject of killing, saying that the Blackwater contract was "perfect for a guy like me—a thousand bucks a day, and you get to kill people legally." Then he said that he must be "missing a chromosome or something—I don't have the moral firewall that keeps normal people from killing." He had met people doing body-retrieval work when he was in New Orleans for Blackwater, and when they told him what they did, he said, "You're a taker-outer? That's funny—I'm a putter-inner. Maybe we can work together." It was a joke, of course—the kind of bitterly defensive joke he liked to make—but then he'd started giving the matter some thought. He was fifty-three years old. He was old for the kind of life he led, the life, in his words, of "an operator," "a shooter," "a trigger puller." In effect, he had given his life to take lives, and it had cost him almost everything, including, he said, as he held up his left hand and displayed a denuded ring finger, his thirty-year marriage. He was trying desperately to adjust to civilian life, but a lifetime habit of chasing headlines didn't die easily. He was at the conference because he was hoping that maybe there was a way to chase headlines without having to kill anybody.

I CALLED THE NUMBER he gave me a few days later and asked for William Clark.

"Who?" a voice said.
    "William Clark."
    "Who is this?"

I told him I was the reporter he met at the disaster-relief conference. "Oh, yeah," he said. "I remember. You just threw me off, asking for William."

"Your name isn't William?"
    "It is. But everybody calls me Zeke. The only person who doesn't is my mother, and she calls me Billy."

THERE WAS A STORY HE TOLD about his first day at Palisades. He was already at his desk when his boss came in. His boss said, "I just want you to know you're not my first choice for the job, so if you're in over your head, please tell me." Zeke couldn't help himself. He answered, "Well, you're my first choice to throw out the window." The boss beat an immediate retreat, and later, it had to be explained to Zeke that threats are taken very seriously in the modern corporate workplace. "But yeah, he knew who he was hiring," Zeke said when I asked him if his boss at Palisades knew what he had done for a living. "He knew he hired an assassin."

He had been screened, and the screening was real. He had been checked and vetted. The screening was standard but rigorous—it was the same screening everyone got when they were applying for a job that gave them complete freedom of movement and access at a nuclear power plant. His piss was checked, and so were his finances. He was given a psychological test and a polygraph. His references were called. Zeke claimed to have extremely high-level security clearances—a TS/SCI with the Department of Defense and a Q clearance with the Department of Energy—but Randy Cleveland, who's in charge of employee screening for the company that operates Palisades, said that he doesn't generally check security clearances, because he's in the business of granting security clearances of his own. Besides, he said, "I don't know how much work Zeke did that by its nature you wouldn't be able to validate. Some of these operations, he tells us, were of such a covert nature that you have to do an extreme amount of digging to find out about them, if you can find out at all."

So they knew. What's more, they *all* seemed to know. On the first day I visited Zeke at Palisades, some of his security guards were receiving special-operations training at the plant's practice range, and all day long the people who came to observe the training seemed to know not only Zeke but also his history. The idea for the training was *based* on his history—based on his certainty that the jihadists he'd fought against in Afghanistan and Iraq would be able to take Palisades without much of a fight if the security guards weren't given the proper training. He wound up convincing the owners of Palisades to pay $50,000, he said, for the creation of an elite strike force from the ranks of his security guards, which he would call the Viper team. He wound up inviting Aaron Cohen, a former Israeli commando Zeke had seen giving commentary on Fox News, to come to Michigan and provide Viper training. He wound up convincing a local agent from the FBI and a local agent from the Department of Homeland Security to participate in the training and become members of the Viper team. He wound up convincing representatives from the Nuclear Regulatory Commission to come and observe the training, which he called the first-ever partnership between a private security team and federal law-enforcement agents for the purpose of critical-infrastructure protection. And so they all came to the practice range, and they all gave Zeke credit for making Viper training happen, although a senior manager at Palisades confided that Zeke was far better at creating elite strike forces than he was at doing paperwork and dealing with corporate politics. But this was not surprising, the manager said, given who Zeke was and where he'd been—given that Zeke had gone to Afghanistan and Iraq looking to die and had instead wound up a security manager at Palisades.

HE WAS STILL NEW TO HIS HOUSE. On his refrigerator door, he still had a drawing a little boy down the block had sent him, a stick figure emblazoned with the words MR. ZEKE, WELCOME TO THE NEIGHBORHOOD. He hadn't met the little boy yet, nor any of his other neighbors. After all, he had not bought the house because he wanted to make friends but rather, he said, because it was at the end of a dead-end street and offered an advantageous line of fire. The house was two stories, with dormer windows, and contained a small arsenal. There were bullets everywhere—in boxes, in the bathroom, on bookshelves, a few scattered on the floor—like candy in the home of a fat man. There were a lot of knives, too, the fighting kind, with handles like brass knuckles. There was a handgun secreted away in the couch that faced the forty-three-inch TV screen, another next to the computer keyboard, and another on top of the refrigerator. In Zeke's bedrooms, there were two handguns on his nightstand and a black pump-action shotgun propped in the corner. In one of the spare bedrooms, there was an empty black case, very long and designed to carry the long rifle—Zeke said he preferred a Remington 700—that snipers use.

There was a Ruger .22-caliber Mark II long-rifle target pistol. There was a scope next to a pair of black gloves. There were a dozen empty magazines, a magazine half filled with bullets, and three magazines that were fully loaded. There were a couple of holsters, a stock, a shooting brace, and a metal case filled with 7.62 mm shells. On the floor, there was a pair of handcuffs and a big box filled with smaller boxes of bullets. On the shelf bracketing another wall, there were two Kevlar helmets, a set of pads for a shooter's knees and elbows, and a long coiled rope. In the corner, there was a backpack, ready to go, and then a duffel bag, olive-green and already packed with clothing and gear, so that if Zeke ever got called on a mission, he would be able to leave—and leave everything behind, including his new house and his new wife and his very real job at the nuclear plant—at a moment's notice.

HE LIVED IN FEAR, because he was not in control of his life. He had a handler, he said. Did I know what a handler was? A handler was a person who handled him and who handled things for him. He'd had a handler since 1984. He'd been in the Army, been in Vietnam, been a Ranger, with marksman as his particular skill set. He'd gotten into some trouble, so he'd gotten out in 1977. He'd become a cop, outside of L.A. He was SWAT. He was, by his own description, "hard charging," maybe too aggressive. He made a lot of arrests. He also spent a lot of time at the range. One night, he said, the phone rang at his house. "Friend of a friend. 'We hear you're a hell of a shot. Why don't you come and talk to us?' I told him I had a job. He said, 'Don't worry, we'll pave the way.' The next day I got to work and was told to take a leave of absence. I went for training in northern Virginia, and six months later I was in Honduras. 'There's your target. Handle it.'"

He handled it, and from then on he had a handler. It wasn't always the same guy, and one time, about five years ago, it was a woman. But the handler always did the same thing. Made sure he was current on his piss test. Made sure he was current on his polygraph. Made sure he could get insurance and a mortgage. Made sure that Zeke had a reference when he went for a job and had to explain the gaps in his résumé. Made sure that Zeke knew where to go and knew what to do once he got there. Made sure that Zeke followed orders. Made sure that Zeke was still handling it, which meant that he wasn't talking to anyone—whether wife or friend or shrink or reporter. Handling it was what Zeke was good at, until he wasn't. Now, for the first time in his life, he was scared. He couldn't sleep at night. He had nightmares. He was afraid that he was too old. He was afraid that no one was going to call him with another mission. He was afraid that he *was* going to get called on another mission tomorrow. He was afraid that he was never going to go back to Afghanistan or Iraq. He was afraid that he *was* going to go back to Afghanistan or Iraq and die there. He was afraid of losing his job at the nuclear plant and winding up on a park bench. He was afraid that he was going to spend the rest of his life at the nuclear plant, a washed-up old operator "with a lot of stories that no one believes till they see the scars." He was afraid of being betrayed, afraid of disappearing, afraid of being afraid forever. "I've hurt a lot of people, Tom," he said. And he knew he would hurt a lot of people again if he didn't burn his bridges to the handler who ordered him to hurt them. "And there's only one way I'm going to burn my bridges, and that's by talking to someone like you."

He had the most amazing things to say about hurting people, about the reality of sitting up on high and hunting them, about the quiet deliberation of it, about the stillness of it, about watching a man "through the glass"—the scope—about watching him smoke and drink coffee and talk to friends even as you know the order is in and he's already dead, about taking aim at his lip or his teeth—"teeth are always good, because you can always see them"—or between his buttons and concentrating only on the shot, on the tumbling piece of paper that helps you determine which way the wind is blowing, and then on the soft squeeze of the trigger, only that, before the kick of the rifle brings you back to life with almost more adrenaline than you can bear.

He's always lived for the adrenaline. We were watching an NFL game one night at his house, and he got up and assumed the stance of a defensive back, but with his elbow up high, as if ready to drop the hammer. He said that he'd been a cornerback in high school, all county, and that he still remembered what it was like, watching a play develop, watching the whole field, the movement of the ball both chaotic and marked by a sense of inevitability, because it had to come to an end, and it came to an end when he made the hit. He was the end. He was a hitter, and nothing could match that feeling of intervention—that feeling of being the instrument of inevitability—until later in his life, when he felt the kick of the Remington 700 and heard his spotter say, "Man down."

ONE NIGHT HIS MOTHER CALLED his cell phone. She called him almost every day. He was closer to his mother than he was to anybody, and once, when I asked him if he had any code of conduct, he said, "No women. No children. And I don't lie to my mother." Now he talked to her for a few minutes and handed me the phone. "Well, I'm glad someone's finally writing about Billy, because he's an American hero," she said, in a strong old-woman's voice. Then I handed the phone back to Zeke, but he was sitting on the couch, looking sick to the soul. "She's so happy that I have this job at the plant," he said. "I don't have the heart to tell her that I hate it. So I lie to her, like I lie to everyone else."

I STAYED AT HIS HOUSE THREE TIMES. The first time, last August, I stayed with him for two nights. I stayed with him for two nights again in September. When I visited in December, I cut my trip short—I stayed one night instead of two—but by that time the process of revelation that he'd started in the summer threatened to go out of control. He had revealed secrets about himself from the moment I introduced myself to him, and yet over the course of four months he had always managed to up the ante, to suggest that behind every secret there loomed another whose revelation would prove dangerous not only to him but to me.

In August, he told me about his handler and about the remorselessness his handler expected of him. He detailed his methods as a sniper and called himself an assassin. And he told me that he lived in fear of being arrested for what he'd done for Blackwater—and, by extension, his country—in Afghanistan and Iraq.

In September, he said that it was in Iraq where he had crossed the line that had made him lose "the stomach" for killing. "In all my years as a professional, I've seen a lot of conflicts," he said. "I never committed murder until I went to Iraq." When I pressed him about what he meant, he said, "You're going to get me indicted, Tom." And when I asked him why, he replied, "War crimes, man. War crimes."

And yet he kept talking, driven by his guilt and his compulsive need to tell me that he was not like mere contractors—that he was both better and far worse. In November, I sent him a book about Blackwater and asked him to read it. When I called for his comments, he said that it was accurate, but only so far as it went. "The guys in that book are really sort of knuckle draggers," he said. "I operate on a much higher level."

"What do you mean?" I said.

"I'll tell you the next time you come up."

And so I visited him again, one last time, in December. It was 12 degrees in Michigan, and the phone books and old cardboard boxes that had littered his driveway in the summer were now stuck there, frozen solid. He was wearing all black, black jeans and a black ribbed mercenary sweater, and he told me that something had changed since the last time I spoke to him. He told me that he had gotten married.

THE PEOPLE WHO LOVE HIM ARE REAL. He has a mother and father, still alive. He has two brothers. He has an ex-wife, Linda, to whom he was married for thirty years. He has a son, Rick—Linda's son, whom Zeke adopted when he was four years old. And he has a new wife, a woman he calls Baby Doll. They all love him, but he is afraid they wouldn't if they knew who he really was and what he had really done.

Does he love them in return? He said he did, while acknowledging that a man who couldn't tell the truth about himself to those closest to him was going to have trouble with his relationships. He had, for instance, a photograph of one of his brothers on his bookshelf, but he said that he hadn't seen or spoken to him in years. And he hadn't spoken to his son, Rick, since the divorce, and although Rick lived on an Air Force base not five hours away, Zeke had never met his grandchildren. And although he still spoke to Linda as often as twice a day—as often as he spoke to his mother and Baby Doll—he viewed his divorce from her as the ultimate cost of his lifestyle and its necessary secrets. In his darkest moments, he even intimated that his handler had gotten to her, had called her and told her, well, everything, for why else would he have come home from the hell of

New Orleans and heard from his wife that she wanted out after thirty years?

He had met her in high school, in Tulare, California, in the Central Valley, south of Fresno. She was his English teacher his senior year. She was eleven years older than he was. They got married in 1975, when he was still in the Army. They did not live together at first—he was at Fort Stewart, in Georgia, and she remained in Tulare, teaching—but she was always available to him, as she had to be, for even as a young man he was haunted by his past, he said, and in this case his recent past was Vietnam. These were the last shadowy years of the war. There was a period when he just *disappeared*—when neither his mother nor Linda knew where he was—and when he resurfaced, he had a story to tell, except that he couldn't tell it. He was bound not to tell it, though of course it leaked out over the years, both to Linda and to Rick, as did all the others. It was hard on Linda, Zeke said, because she had to guard his secrets as closely as he did. She was even liable to be polygraphed, as he was, and so after a while he made it easy for her—he stopped telling her things, and she stopped asking questions. She just *knew*—and it was her unspoken knowledge of who he really was that led him to say that she was his "real wife," no matter what, and to keep the gold band from his wedding with Linda up on his bookshelf, right next to the picture of Baby Doll.

Baby Doll was his nickname for a woman he met on eHarmony in 2006. Her real name was Terri, but she had a small, breathy voice, so he called her Baby Doll. She was divorced, living with two teenaged sons, and she described herself as a "wounded soul," for she had multiple sclerosis. Zeke was a wounded soul, too, she said, and their relationship seemed to enter a new stage with each visit: In August, they met; in September, she'd just visited him in Michigan for the first time, and he was deciding whether to "take on" a woman with such a debilitating illness; in December, he'd just married her, because she'd saved his life. He'd been all alone on Thanksgiving 2006, eating a frozen pizza, waiting for the phone to ring and determined to "eat the barrel" of one of his handguns if it didn't. It did, and it was Baby Doll. Her voice gave him something to live for, and he married her a week later. She wasn't living with him, but she called his cell phone all day long, and one night, when we were out to dinner, he passed the phone to me. Terri's voice was just as Zeke said it was, and in answer to my question, she confirmed that she had met Zeke on eHarmony. Then she said that she had a question of her own: "Is he wearing his ring?" I told her that he was, although as soon as she hung up, he said he was going to take it off when he got home and put it on the bookshelf next to the ring from his marriage to Linda.

ZEKE TRIED TO CONTINUE the affair with the volunteer he met in New Orleans after they both returned home. One day, she even received an e-mail from Zeke's wife, Linda, while Linda and Zeke were still married. It was an admission of failure—an admission that Linda had never been up to the adventure of living with someone like Zeke, an admission that she simply wasn't as passionate as he was. Linda wished the volunteer luck and expressed hope that Zeke had finally met a woman who was his equal. How extremely gracious, the volunteer thought, and how extremely odd, for the e-mail was marred by elementary misspellings and grammatical errors. Wasn't Linda Clark an English teacher? Then she realized something, in a flash of alarm: The letter had been written by Zeke, from his wife's account and in his wife's name.

She began trying to extricate herself from the relationship, but there was a problem: He threatened her and he threatened her husband. He said that he had no qualms about killing women—that when he was in Iraq, the locals had been prohibited from doing so by their religious scruples, and that the dirty business had fallen to him and had become a specialty. He even told her exactly how he'd kill her, sticking the knife above her collarbone and flicking it toward her feet, so that, with just the barest nick, her jugular and carotid would bleed out.

And then, when threats failed, he said he was going to kill himself. He told her he was spending Thanksgiving 2005 alone, eating frozen pizza, and that he was going to eat the barrel of one of his handguns if he didn't get a call from the volunteer, whom he called his Baby Doll.

HE MADE A LOT OF THREATS. Some of them were just avowals of lethal capacity—"Hey, I'm a trigger puller," he said when I first met him. "I'll put a round in your eye." Others were the result of him playing around, as when I was watching TV in his living room in August and the red dot of a laser pointer started dancing around the walls. He was standing behind me, in the kitchen, pointer in hand, and when I said, "Um, Zeke?" he answered, "Oh, sorry. But don't worry—if I ever wanted to kill you, you'd never see the red dot." Others were more specific. When he first told me about his handler, he said that he'd told his handler about me—with the assurance that if I revealed information he didn't want revealed, "I'll hunt you down and kill you." Another time, on the subject of journalistic betrayal, he said, "Never betray someone who can kill you from a thousand yards away."

And yet for a long time I was not scared of him, because on some level he was not a scary guy. He was a lonely guy. He was a pathetic guy. He was a recently divorced guy who, like every other recently divorced guy in America, had a George Foreman grill in his kitchen and a stack of DiGiorno pizzas in his freezer. He was too hangdog to be threatening, and when he finally did scare me, it was not because he threatened me. It was because I thought he was going crazy.

He had a photograph of a sniper on his living-room wall. It was poster sized, and it was framed, and the man it portrayed was carrying a gauze-wrapped long rifle and wearing a hood that hid everything but his eyes and the bridge of his nose. He looked like a primordial executioner, rising out of the swamp, and as soon as I saw the photo, I thought it was Zeke. He had always said that I would never be able to trace him to Afghanistan or Iraq— that his participation there, though ostensibly part of a Blackwater contract, was a "black op," with no paper trail. Now there was a poster in his living room whose copyright line—"Steve Raymer, National Geographic Image Collection, 2005"—made me think that I had found an image linking Zeke to Iraq, right there on his wall.

He was cagey when, during my September visit, I asked who it was. "A friend," he'd said. "Misunderstood. You'd like him if you got to know him, but not too many people get to know him." And so I went home and did a search for Steve Raymer. His name came up right away, and so did the photograph, which was available for sale, tagged with the following information: "French Soldier, 13th Demi-Brigade of the French Foreign Legion, Djibouti, Horn of Africa, 1988." I called Steve Raymer, and he said yes, he was sure of the photo's provenance—that he remembered being out in the desert on a Foreign Legion training exercise and all these snipers rose up all around him, in terrifying silence. Raymer didn't say a word to the sniper, and the sniper didn't say a word to him—he just took his picture, and eventually *National Geographic* put it up for sale.

It was the first thing I asked Zeke about when I visited him in December, because—even though he'd made no claims for the photo—now I thought I'd somehow caught him in a lie. "Tell me about the guy in the poster," I said.

"You don't want to know that guy," he answered. "He's a guy going through a very bad time."

"Zeke, I know who it is."

"You do?"

"It's a soldier with the French Foreign Legion in the Horn of Africa."

He didn't miss a beat. Standing in front of the poster, he said, "Second Para, out of Corsica," meaning the Legion's Second Paratroop Regiment, which is indeed out of Corsica. "That's where we mobilized out of."

"You were in the French Foreign Legion?"

"Among other things," he said.

"So that's you?"

"That's me."

"I don't get it. I don't get why you're so coy about it."

"I don't like talking about Africa. Those were the bad years."

"Zeke, what are you afraid of?"

"I'm afraid of going to *jail*, man. Have you ever been arrested?"

"No."

"Well, I have. I was arrested for attempted murder when I was a Ranger. McIntosh County, Georgia. You can look it up if you want to. It's a matter of public record."

He was defending a friend, he said. The friend had gotten beaten up at a notorious brothel called the S&S Truck Stop. With a few other soldiers, Zeke had gone back and put an incendiary device on the roof, with the intention of "burning up everyone inside, including the whores." The bomb didn't go off, he said, but he and the others were arrested anyway and spent nine days in jail before an FBI agent investigating the S&S for drug trafficking set them free. The incident ended his career as a Ranger, but he said it also might have played a role in the call he received a few years later: for he had demonstrated a willingness not only to kill but to incinerate a room full of undesirables.

"DO YOU HAVE THINGS in your life that you're ashamed of?" Zeke asked. He had gone from the photo of the sniper to the couch and was stretched out on it, with his hands covering his face. I told him I did; of course I did. He said, "Well, you probably don't *do* them anymore. But I do. I keep doing them. I seek them out." He was finally paying the price; he'd had a mild heart attack the month before, on account of the stress of living with his secrets. I told him that maybe he had received a sign that he should begin talking, starting with Africa. He said, "You might not like me very much after I do," and asked if I thought he was a bad person. "I think you're trying to be a good person," I said, "or else I wouldn't be here." He got up and told me to follow him. He opened the door to his basement and turned on the light. He went halfway down the stairs and then stopped and looked at me over his shoulder. "Have you ever been around pure evil?" he asked. I paused. I'd been around pure evil before. I had just never followed pure evil down to the *basement,* and when I got there, I expected to be greeted by the grinning ricti of other journalists who'd pursued Zeke's story and wound up preserved in pickle jars. But no: It was just a basement, and Zeke couldn't find the photographs of the evil he had done in Africa. He did find, however, a big cardboard box full of the plays and screenplays he'd been writing since he got out of the Army, some of them faded with the passage of time.

THE WIND WAS MAKING NOISES The noises were making Zeke jumpy. He was sitting up on the couch, doing what he was always doing—watching Fox News on the big-screen TV and revealing his secrets. On this night, however, he was saying that everything had changed since he'd married Baby Doll. "I have something to *lose* now, man," he said, by which he meant Baby Doll, by which he also meant his house, his job, his life. He had told me about everything. He had told me about Africa, about Afghanistan and Iraq. He'd also told me about the Philippines, about Indonesia, about Somalia, about Yemen, about Angola, about Nigeria, about Guatemala, about Haiti and El Salvador and Honduras. He had continued raising the stakes on his secrets until they all bled together. Indeed, he really had only one secret, because over the last twenty years he'd had only one job. He did not really work for Blackwater, and he did not really serve in the French Foreign Legion, and he wasn't a missionary for World Vision, and he wasn't a diplomatic observer for the State Department. Those jobs were just covers for his real job, which was something he called "direct sanction." No matter where he was, he worked for his handler, and his handler paid him to kill people. He was, in his words, "a national-security asset," "one of the best in the world at what I do"—a one-man death squad.

He had revealed his secrets in order to survive them, but now he thought he had made a mistake. He wondered if I had endangered him, and if it was the revelation, not the secrets, that would be impossible to survive. I told him that he had no choice now but to go all the way—that going public was the only way he could protect himself. "Do you mean *testify*?" he said, like a snake handler who had fallen from his trance and realized what he had been holding. "No way, man. I have nightmares about Charles Schumer asking me questions. You ever raise your right hand? I have, and it's a life-altering experience. My mother couldn't stand it. . . ."

Suddenly he stood up. The wind had gusted, and there was a noise. He went to the refrigerator and came back with a handgun. He cocked it and went to the garage door, peeking outside while standing next to the jamb, his back pressed against the wall.

When he returned to the couch, he did not uncock his gun. Instead, he started transferring it from hand to hand and told me that I didn't know who I was dealing with: "If they want to get you, they get you. Or they don't get me. They get Baby Doll. They rape her, they sodomize her. It's called a break-in. Random violence. But it's not, and I know it's not. So no fucking way. I'm not going to get my Baby Doll raped and sodomized so Charles Schumer and Hillary Clinton can make political hay!"

HIS HANDLERS WERE REAL, Zeke was talking to them on the phone. I was sitting across the table from him. It was the next day, and we were having breakfast at a restaurant in South Haven. At 9:30, he picked up the cell phone and dialed. He said, "Clark, William," and then a number, 553. Then he said what sounded like a last name. And then he was talking to his handler, whom he called Larry. He was telling Larry that he was sitting with the writer from *Esquire*. He cringed at his handler's response. Then, as he explained later, he was transferred immediately to his handler's subordinate, who read him his secrecy oath and threatened him with the penitentiary. The subordinate's name was Kyle. Zeke complained about the way he was being treated by Kyle, then he began complaining about the way he was being treated by Larry. When he was finally transferred back to Larry, he said this: "Hey, Larry, thanks for the kick in the balls." He said that if he ever saw Kyle in the street, he'd "take him out," and then he promptly apologized for the threat. He hung up, and when he called back, a secretary answered and told him that Larry was at a meeting. "I just talked to him two minutes ago," he said, and she put him through. "Larry, how much longer do I have to be in purgatory?" he said, and accused Kyle of selling him out years earlier. His tone softened after that; he said, "Hey, I'll do it, I'm a good soldier," and hung up. He finished his coffee but not his eggs, and when we got back to the car, he said, "I fucked myself.

I stayed in too long, now they have their hooks in me. I have a new house, a new wife, a new job, and it's all fake. They can punch through it whenever they want to, and they just did. The thing is, you don't know what they can do—so they can do anything. If you ever hear that I've committed suicide, investigate the hell out of it."

A FEW DAYS LATER the phone in my home office rang at eight o'clock in the morning. I didn't run to get it, though I knew it was Zeke. All that week I'd been on the phone with him, trying to get him to go public with his story, trying to convince him to allow me to use his name. He kept saying that he was going away. He was going back to Afghanistan. He was taking a job with a company that provided security for firms trying to do business in Kabul. He was leaving in January and didn't know when or if he was going to be back. He hadn't told Baby Doll, he said, then asked: "Do you think she's going to be mad?"

When the phone rang, I knew I'd lost him. And sure enough, when I checked the message, this is what it said: "Hi, Tom, this is Zeke. Hey man, I couldn't sleep at all last night, thinking about this story and stuff. And I gotta tell you, man, I have nothing to do with Iraq or Afghanistan, I have no operational knowledge of Iraq and Afghanistan, I have no knowledge of any operational plans that have taken place in Iraq or Afghanistan, there's no record of me ever being in Afghanistan or Iraq, I'm a nonentity, I just don't exist in any of that kind of thing, I have nothing to do with Iraq or Afghanistan. Anything else is fine, but I have no knowledge of, there's no witnesses, there's nothing that ties me to Iraq or Afghanistan, never been to Iraq or Afghanistan, I just don't have anything to do with that, I can't have anything to do with that, and I'm sorry, I don't want to have anything to do with my name at all with Iraq or Afghanistan, I don't exist in that arena, never have, never will, and I just had a sleepless night last night, so I wanted to call and tell you that I don't know anything about Iraq or Afghanistan and never have been and never will. I hope you're okay, your family's okay. I just had to tell you that. So. Thanks, Tom. Bye-bye."

WAS IT A DENIAL or a confirmation? Was it the lie that told the truth or the truth that told the lie? I called Blackwater, and it was exactly as Zeke had foretold: A spokeswoman said there was no such thing as a "designated marksman" for Blackwater: "It's not a term we would use, because all our missions are defensive." She confirmed that a William E. Clark had worked for Blackwater in Louisiana in the wake of Katrina, but that he was "never, ever, ever in Iraq or Afghanistan for us. He was never there on a Black-water contract." And then she said, "My understanding is also that he is prone to give false information and is not to be consid-ered a trustworthy source."

BLACKWATER, OF COURSE, had an interest in proving him a liar, since he'd come home from Louisiana and told his wife and son that he'd killed someone there. Zeke was still married to Linda then. He was still talking to Rick. He pulled both of them aside and told them that some dope addict made a play for the narcotics in storage, and he'd shot him. It wasn't something he was proud of, because it wasn't clean. It wasn't precise. He'd shot him in the dark, and he'd hit him without killing him. The ad-dict died eventually, but still. He was pretty shaken up about it, Rick said—and that's what gave the story its legitimacy. Rick had grown up with his father's stories. He'd come to doubt a lot of them, but there were certain ones he believed, because his father wasn't playing the hero. Ever since Rick was a little boy, his father had told him stories about Vietnam—but the story he believed was the one where the Vietnamese captured and broke him. Why, Rick thought, would someone tell a story like that if it wasn't true? What kind of man would try to make you believe what he was ashamed of?

DENNIS COLLINS MET William Clark in El Salvador in the mid-nineties. He will not say what he was doing there; he is, he says, prohibited from saying what he was doing there. All he will say is that he was there, and that when he was there, he met William Clark, who called himself Zeke. They were in El Salvador for different reasons, he says, but they became friends, and when they came home, Collins started getting Zeke work. Collins was associated with Nuclear Security Services Corporation, or NSSC. It provided security training for nuclear facilities, and it employed a lot of former operators. Zeke was a perfect fit, because he was so enthusiastic, such a great motivator and storyteller—when clients gave their evaluations, "the number-one guy they talk about is Zeke," Collins said. Zeke's success with NSSC led him to find work with DynCorp, the security company that provided manpower for the Kosovo Diplomatic Observer Mission in 1998. And his success with DynCorp led him to find work with a company that contracted with the Department of Energy to provide assault teams—adversary teams, as they're known—that would stage mock attacks on nuclear facilities for the purpose of exposing their vulnerabilities. Zeke never would have gotten any of these jobs without Dennis Collins—Collins was a critical reference—nor would he have gotten the security-manager job at Palisades, for it was one of Collins's associates who recommended Zeke for the position.

Zeke called Collins "my best friend in the business," and Collins knew that Zeke was struggling at Palisades. Zeke was a "shooter and operator," he said, and like a lot of shooters and operators, he was having trouble accepting that he had become "a desk jockey." That was why Zeke was so desperate to get to Iraq. He and Collins had gone to Camp Pendleton, California, for counterterrorism training about five or six years ago, and Collins had seen how some of the young marines had responded to Zeke's stories—they were enthralled. A few years later, when they went back, everything had changed. There was a war on. Now there were young marines who had been to Fallujah, and when Zeke told his stories, they were like, You don't know what you're talking about, old man. Zeke couldn't take it. He became obsessed with getting to Iraq, but then, during one of the training exercises, he hit his head against a wall and passed out. People thought he was playing around, but he wasn't. He had a neck injury that occasionally cut the flow of blood to his brain. And so he washed out. Nobody's going to hire a guy with an injury like that. "Believe me, he's not going to Iraq," Collins said. "Because if he does go, he's either going to get killed or get somebody else killed. But it's tough, because he's having a real hard time. If you ask me, what happened at Camp Pendleton cracked him."

LAST OCTOBER. Zeke flew to Washington, D.C., and gave a presentation to the Department of Homeland Security. He went with one of his superiors from Palisades, and with Al DiBrito and Mike Moll, the agents from the FBI and the DHS who had become part of Zeke's Viper team. That's what the presentation was about: Viper. It was Zeke's brainchild, and now he was proposing to create Viper teams at every nuclear power plant in the United States. The presentation was attended by Craig Conklin, the head of the DHS's nuclear-hazards branch, as well as by other representatives from the FBI and the Nuclear Regulatory Commission—"about ten people in all," Conklin says. Zeke did most of the talking and was impressive enough for some of the participants to consider Viper training as a "best practice," in which case Zeke would be able to take his program nationwide.

ZEKE GOT SHOT IN KOSOVO. Everybody knew about it: He told some of the shooters and operators he'd met when he was staging the mock assaults on nuclear plants. It was part of Zeke's legend. He'd gone to Kosovo for DynCorp, which had contracted to provide personnel for the State Department's Diplomatic Observer Mission. He had a diplomatic passport. But he says he was also there as a cover. He was an operative whose mission was to determine the war-fighting capacity of the Kosovo Liberation Army. He would hike into KLA camps with not much more than a box of Marlboros and a medical kit. He should have been shot, but people would line up as soon as they saw him. He would spend all day stitching wounds and get the information he needed. Then he did get shot, and the only thing that saved him was his flak jacket. When he got home, he showed Linda the sweater with the hole in it. Did she believe him? Well, she loved him, she said. And besides, she'd seen the sweater; she'd put her finger in the hole.

THAT WAS THE FIRST THING Linda Clark said to me, the first thing she wanted me to know. They were divorced, but she still loved him. She had known him for so long that being married to him "was almost like raising another child." He used to ride motorcycles with her first husband, and when she was divorced and became a single mother, he protected her. "He always made me feel secure," she said. They were baptized together before they were married. But around 1984, he lost his job as a policeman in Visalia, California, for having an affair with another officer's wife, and they struggled. They struggled financially, as he wrote the six novels that never got published and wrote the stack of plays and screenplays that never got produced—well, one did, at a community theater. And he did make a movie. Did I know that he made a movie? He did, he really did, in the early nineties, with a friend's workmen's-compensation check. But of course it never went anywhere, and what kept Bill and Linda afloat, she said, was Bill's job as a chimney sweep. For twelve years, from '84 to '96, he worked as a chimney sweep in his hometown of Tulare, down the road from Visalia. "I'll bet Bill didn't tell you about that, did he?"

No, I said, he didn't. It's not on his résumé, either, those twelve years representing the gap only his handler could explain. But wait a second—didn't he go by Zeke?

"Oh, I don't know where he got that," she said. "Everybody I know calls him Bill. But then he went on that trip to El Salvador and everything changed. He was always big into skydiving, and though we didn't have a lot of money, he wanted to go skydiving with the El Salvadoran army. I let him go, because it was so important to him, and that's where he met Dennis Collins. And when he came home, he wanted me to call him Zeke. I couldn't do it. He's still Billy to me."

Their finances got better after that, Linda said, because Bill started doing work for Dennis, and the work for Dennis led to work for the DOE, and the work for the DOE led to work for security companies like Vance and Blackwater. What got worse was Bill's . . . well, his *problem,* Linda said. He has to make himself more interesting than he is. He can't bear to be just plain old Bill Clark from Tulare, California, because plain old Bill Clark had dyslexia, and really suffered in school. . . .

"Did he ever play football?" I asked.

"Junior varsity," she said. "He was too small for varsity."

Well, was he ever in Afghanistan or Iraq? I asked.

"Oh, heavens no," Linda said. "He told you that?"

"He also told me that he was in the Horn of Africa with the French Foreign Legion."

"Well, he did go to Nigeria, back in the early eighties. A Nigerian minister came to Tulare, and Bill went to Nigeria with him as a missionary. He didn't like it very much, though. He came back in about two or three weeks."

She said this without malice. Indeed, she was praying for him to see the error of his ways, so that their marriage could be repaired and they could reconcile. She still loved the man. She still spoke to him. As a matter of fact, she had spoken to him just the day before, and he was saying that he wanted to break off his engagement with Terri so that he could remarry Linda.

"Linda, I hate being the one to tell you this, but he and Terri aren't engaged. They're married."

"Oh, my God," Linda Clark said.

AN OFFICIAL at one of Zeke's former employers confirmed that he did have a Q clearance with the DOE, which gave him access to top-secret information at nuclear plants. But when two officials with access to Department of Defense databases—one in the DOD, the other a screener for a private security company—checked Zeke's TS/SCI clearance, they found no record of William E. Clark having DOD "eligibility or access." That is, they found no record of William E. Clark holding the high-level DOD security clearance he included on his résumé at Palisades Nuclear.

HE HAD NEVER TALKED about his life before, Zeke said, and he was always disdainful of people who did. He was always disdainful of both the "cowboys" who liked to brag and the "wannabes" who were endemic to the world of covert operations.

Real operators, he said, never talked about their exploits when they got together. They talked about their wives, they talked about their families, they talked about how much they missed home. It was strange, then, that about seven years ago he held the ultimate wannabe job—he was an auxiliary cop in Kingsburg, California, an unpaid position that called on him only to "assist officers on duty." And it was even stranger when, last year, he called a cop he knew from Kingsburg named Kevin Pendley. "He tried to recruit me to go to Iraq," Pendley says. "He called out of the blue. He said he'd been over there for Blackwater and that he'd just gotten back. He said he killed sixty-nine people."

RICK CLARK KNEW instinctively that his father had remarried. He had, in fact, warned his mother that his father had remarried, although he hadn't spoken to his father in a year and a half. It was just something he felt, from a lifetime of experience—the familiar vibrations of his father's falsehoods. "He's living a movie in which he's the flawed but sympathetic central character, a really deeply interesting central character," Rick said. "He's smart enough to show his flaws, because when he does, he becomes believable, and you become an accomplice in the movie of his life."

Was Rick one of Bill Clark's accomplices? "I grew up with the mythology and to some extent defined myself by it," he said. "One of the reasons I went into the military was to carry on the tradition." Rick is thirty-five now, about to leave the Air Force, and he doesn't consider himself an accomplice anymore. "If my father told me the sun was shining, I wouldn't believe him—even if I lived in the next town over, for God's sake." But he did want to know one thing. He wanted me to find out the truth of one story, because he'd been hearing it since he could remember and had built his life around it. He wanted to know if Bill Clark had been a Ranger and had been in Vietnam. "I really need to know that, Tom," he said. "Because I need to know whether *everything* has been a lie."

THERE WAS NO INCIDENT on Zeke's first day at Palisades; no threat to throw his boss out the window. That's what the senior manager said, the same one who had told me that Zeke had gone to Afghanistan looking for a high-velocity round between the eyes. When I told him that Zeke had never actually been to Afghanistan or Iraq, he said, "He *wasn't?*" And then he said, "You know, I'm really glad you called, because he's been trying to get me to quit my job and go into business with him. He said that I had the know-how, and he had all the contacts from his years in covert operations."

THE MOVIE WAS CALLED *Team Dragon*. Bill Clark got the idea for it when a B-movie company came to Tulare to reshoot some footage on the cheap, and he went out to get some stunt work. He thought it looked pretty easy, making a movie, so he started watching movies obsessively on his VCR, with a notebook in his lap. When he felt ready to direct, he began shooting bits of a script he'd written, featuring guys he knew from Tulare. One of them, Ken Washman, was bothered by the suspicion that if what Clark was shooting ever did become a movie, he wouldn't get paid a dime, and so he began asking Clark what it would cost to get cut in—to make a real movie whose profits he could share. Clark came up with a figure, which happened to be the amount of the check Washman had recently received in compensation for a workplace accident. And so, in 1990 and 1991, Bill Clark shot *Team Dragon* in and around Tulare, with Ken Washman as his star. It was about a Vietnam veteran who had to face his demons when he found out that the NVA was selling opium in California, and it cost $25,000 to make. "My wife wasn't real happy about it,"

Washman says now. "She didn't really like me spending that much time with Bill Clark, and she wanted me to put the money in a piece of property or something. I guess I would have had a better return on my investment if I did, but I wouldn't have had as much fun as I did running around and shooting guns out there in Tulare. And it was a real movie, you know. We had a premiere at the Elks club in Tulare. Bill showed it and said, 'Well, Ken, what do you think?'

"I said, 'Well, Bill—it's a movie.' There was not a whole lot much more you could say about it, other than that."

ZEKE DIDN'T KILL anyone in Louisiana. A former marine who was on Zeke's Blackwater team said that no one even discharged his weapon, because it was well known that if you did, Blackwater would fire your ass. Besides, they were in the sticks. They weren't in New Orleans. It was quiet where they were, really sort of boring, except when Zeke told the story that a gang was coming to get at the narcotics. Even then, the former marine listened with half an ear. That guy was always telling stories.

THE VOLUNTEER FROM the shelter in Louisiana received a call one day from Linda Clark. Linda told the volunteer that she'd been speaking to the Lord, and the Lord had instructed her to forgive the volunteer for breaking up her marriage to Bill. By this time, the volunteer was living in fear of the man she knew as Zeke, and so she asked Linda the one thing she really wanted to know: Is he dangerous?

Oh, I don't think so, Linda said.

But what about the video footage he sent? the volunteer asked. What about the footage of him executing people?

And that's when the volunteer found out about *Team Dragon*. That's when she found out about *everything*, including the fact that he had never been to Afghanistan or Iraq. She was hoping that she could keep the affair from her husband, but she wound up confessing it all, and once she did, he forgave her, as the victim of a skilled predator.

"So I dodged a bullet," she told me. "And so did you."

It was embarrassing to think of it that way, of course—embarrassing to think that Zeke had singled me out the way he'd singled out so many others, embarrassing to think that I was one of his victims.

"Hey, look at it this way," the volunteer said. "At least you didn't have sex with him."

THE OLD SOLDIER was surprised to hear Zeke's name when I called him on the phone. "William Clark from California?" he asked, and when I told him what I was calling about, he responded immediately. "Well, if he's the security manager at a nuclear plant, he bullshitted his way into it. He was like that as a teenager. He was one of the most grandiose, storytelling individuals I've ever met."

Indeed, in May 1975, the soldier had been arrested for the sake of one of Clark's stories. At the time, the most famous mercenary in the world was a man named Michael Hoare, who had raised private armies in the Congo and the Seychelles. Clark said he had been a Ranger, but now, like the soldier, he was in the 34th Infantry. He and a friend told the soldier that they knew somebody who worked for Michael Hoare, and that Hoare was looking for new recruits. First, though, they had to prove that they were brave and that they were ruthless. And so one night, Clark convinced the soldier to throw a bomb at the window of the S&S Truck Stop. It bounced off the bulletproof glass and exploded in the parking lot. They were arrested, along with three others, and spent the night in jail, before their CO got them out the next morning. There was no friend they were defending; there was no

FBI agent. There were only a bunch of ignorant kids beguiled by a shot at glory, and in the story the old soldier tells, "I disassociated myself from William Clark as soon as I got back to the base."

So he was living it, even then—the fantasy that has consumed his life, as well as the lives of everybody who has trusted him. Court records from McIntosh County indicate that there were no charges of attempted murder, as Zeke had said; the charge was "criminal attempt," and it was dropped when it came to the docket. His military records indicate that although he might have gone to Ranger School, he did not graduate, and although he was assigned to a Ranger battalion, he finished out his career in the 34th Infantry, with an undistinguished rank and without a Ranger tab. There was no career as a Green Beret, as he had told his son; nor had he ever served in Vietnam. The gooks had not broken him, but he had come damned close to breaking Rick, who, when I told him the military records confirmed that he'd been lied to since he was four years old, said simply, "I want to put my head through a wall."

When Zeke had the cell-phone conversation with his handlers in the restaurant, I knew that his story had only two possible outcomes, and that both were monstrous. If Larry and Kyle were real, then Zeke was an assassin in the employ of a secret governmental agency that had seen fit to give him a job at a nuclear plant just as he was starting to go crazy with guilt and shame. If they weren't real, then Zeke was not just a liar; he was a liar who was willing to engage in complicated three-way public conversations with people who didn't exist. He was a liar with an alias and fake passports, a liar who maintained extensive stocks of boarding passes and hotel-room keys, a liar who packed a duffel bag and kept it in his house in order to further the fiction that his next mission was one phone call away. He was a liar who conflated his lies with threats so that skepticism would be conflated with fear. He was a deranged liar, and he was the security manager of a nuclear plant on Lake Michigan.

I have a pretty good idea of what the answer is. After all, Zeke told the volunteer the exact same things about the handler that he told me, with the exact same proviso: that this was the first time he had talked about him to another living soul. And Linda Clark said that when Zeke got phone calls from his girlfriends, he often told Linda that his handler was on the line, and that he had to take the call in private.

There is no handler. There was no Larry or Kyle. And yet sometimes I find myself wishing that there were, because the alternative is harder to accept. In the four months I spent with Zeke, he told me exactly two significant facts, two plain truths uncomplicated by falsehood and fantasy: first, that he was security manager of Palisades Nuclear. And second, that last October he had gone to Washington, D.C., in the company of two federal agents and presented his vision of nuclear security to the head of the nuclear-hazards branch of the Department of Homeland Security.

HE WAS WONDERING if he should tell her. He was wondering if she would love him if he did. I urged him to. It was last December, and he had been married less than two weeks. I was saying goodbye to him for what turned out to be the final time, and I urged him to tell his new wife who he really was, so that he wouldn't make the same mistakes he'd made with Linda. And then the phone rang. It was Baby Doll. He handed the phone to me, and I asked her why she'd married him. She told me that he was tall, that he was not fazed by her multiple sclerosis, and that he was, in her mind, "a gentle protector. He's afraid that if I found out what he did, I wouldn't love him. But that's not the part of him that I care about. The part that I care about is the courageous part, the part that came to Michigan to start a new life without knowing a soul. The rest—he did what he had to do, what he was asked to do for his country. Others did it, too, and are still doing it. I know he has bad dreams about it. But I want to hold him through his bad dreams. He told me when we first met that we're both wounded souls, and he's right. But that's why I love him."

IT IS EASY TO THINK OF LYING as a victimless crime, akin to storytelling, akin to performance—after all, wasn't Zeke performing when he was speaking to his handlers? All those unpublished novels, all those unproduced plays and screenplays; and now, at fifty-three, the chimney sweep finds his true métier, telling tales to a complicit reporter. And yet his victims number more than those whose feelings he's hurt, whose lives he's wrecked. When I called Blackwater about William E. Clark, I asked if Blackwater prohibited its contractors from having sex with the people they were supposed to be protecting. *"What?"* the spokeswoman answered, in disbelief. "Yes. Of course. It's the first thing they're prohibited from doing. It's the worst thing they can do. Does that answer your question?" When I called DynCorp to see if William E. Clark was part of Dyn-Corp's Kosovo Mission—he was, but he wasn't shot; no diplomatic observers were—the spokesman was chiefly concerned with Zeke's claim that he was really in Kosovo for American intelligence. "He's saying DynCorp was his *cover?*" he said. "You have to understand—that's the kind of claim that can put all our guys in jeopardy." And when I called an FBI agent who until recently had been one of the chief liaisons between the bureau and the CIA, he listened to what I told him about Zeke, then said: *"Fuck* this guy. Expose him. He's an asshole.

Guys like that make it much, much harder for the guys who are legit."

A STORY ABOUT A LIAR always turns out to be about one thing: He lied. Zeke says he doesn't talk to his brothers anymore? He lied. Zeke says that he threatened a UPI photographer who took his picture in El Salvador? UPI says it never had a photographer in El Salvador at the time in question.

And yet what haunts me are not Zeke's lies but the truths he told, or tried to tell, from the moment I met him. He was confessing, after all, and though his confession was a failed one, the impulse behind it brought a psychological truth—the momentum of a man unraveling—to his most outrageous falsehoods. He said that he was a nobody. He said he lacked a moral firewall. He said he lied to his mother like he lied to everyone else. He said that his life was a fake. He said that he'd been a lot of people, and that he'd hurt a lot of people. He even said, at length, in a phone message, that he'd never been to Afghanistan or Iraq. I listened, but I didn't believe him, because as invested as I was in telling his story, I was even more heavily invested in proving him a killer and not just a liar. I was aware, all along, that he was one or the other, but somehow I could not bear to think that he was just a liar, and neither could he. It was too shameful. So he said he was a killer instead, because he knew that somehow human sympathy extends to killing even as it ends at lying.

He said that he was talking to me because he needed to burn his bridges; because he needed to be stopped; because he didn't want to hurt any more people. I believed him then. I believe him now.

TOM JUNOD *lives in Marietta, Georgia, with his wife, his daughter, and his pit bull, a rescued fighting dog named Carson. Though Junod's been writing for* Esquire *for ten years, he was shocked by the extent of "Zeke's" lies, and to a certain degree still is.*

Coda

Bill "Zeke" Clark resigned from Palisades Nuclear in early May 2007, the day "Mercenary" was posted on *Esquire*'s website. The story itself prompted several investigations into the question of how someone like Clark was hired in the first place, and one of his former colleagues at Palisades said, "I suspect it's going to change the way the entire industry works, when it comes to hiring people." Then he added, "If you ever talk to Zeke, tell him he didn't have to lie. We'd have liked him anyway."

I have not spoken to Clark since the story's publication, so I have no way of knowing if he's still lying. I have, however, remained in contact with his ex-wife and his son, who told me that after he resigned from Palisades, he left Michigan and moved to the state where his parents are living. There, he "hit bottom," sustaining himself as a laborer and a construction worker, until November 2007, when he was contacted by a British security company. Then, as Rick Clark says, "he finally got to Iraq. He was doing security for vehicle convoys. But he got over it pretty quick. He didn't want to be a trigger puller. He said it was a young man's game. He even got wounded. He took a piece of shrapnel in his back. All he got was a bad bruise. But if he didn't have body armor, he's toast. He's in Nigeria now. He's training troops. There are troops all over the world, and they need trainers. It's what he wants to do; it's what he's best at."

This all sounded uncannily familiar, and I asked Rick Clark if he believed his father. "I decided to believe it," Rick Clark said. "I have no logical reason. But we've pretty much reconciled, and if after everything we've gone through he's still spinning . . . Well, I want what he's saying to be true."

At this writing, Bill Clark is still married to Baby Doll.

Jonathan Green

MURDER AT 19,000 FEET

FROM *Men's Journal*

THE FIRST GUNSHOT went largely unnoticed by the climbers. Most were still in their tents—the sun had risen, but it hadn't been up long enough to blunt the knifing cold—and no one expected to hear small-arms fire on a mountaineering expedition, much less at 19,000 feet in the Himalayas. Later, though, a few climbers would recall that the ravens that hung around camp had suddenly lifted from the snow in a small, black, squawking cloud, a missed omen.

Earlier on September 30, 2006, the first clear day in a week, the Sherpas in camp had conducted a ritual for the safety of the climbers. There were at least 100 at Cho Oyu advanced base camp; most had not yet made their attempts on the summit because of the poor weather. The world's sixth-tallest mountain, Cho Oyu is the second most popular Himalayan peak, and it's often used as a test run for those who aspire to climb the most popular one, Mount Everest, 19 miles to the east. As part of their ritual the Sherpas had uttered incantations beneath fluttering Tibetan Buddhist prayer flags and burned juniper, which left a resinous aroma around the 70 or so brightly colored tents.

Among those the Sherpas blessed was Luis Benitez, a 34-year-old commercial guide from Colorado who was getting his three clients ready for the four-day summit push. When the first rifle shot was fired, his crew were in their tents packing, sorting, and repacking, and could have mistaken the gun's report for a snapping tent flap.

A few minutes later, near 8 AM, Benitez's team had gathered at their dining tent for breakfast. Moments later two of Benitez's Sherpas burst in: "Chinese soldiers are coming, very bad!" This time they all heard the distinctive, percussive cracks from Type 81 assault rifles, the Chinese answer to AK-47s.

Benitez and the others dropped their mugs and ran outside. They were shocked to find a handful of Chinese soldiers belonging to the People's Armed Police, or PAP, a mountain paramilitary unit, lined up on a shelf of ice over the moraine about 500 yards away. They were doing most of the firing. Others, hefting matte black rifles, marched toward the camp. Still other soldiers, in small clusters, perhaps three or four in each, were farther down along the icy, hummocky terrain, about 200 yards. As they popped off rounds, the smell of cordite had replaced juniper in the air.

At first some of the climbers thought the gunmen might be shooting at animals. Then, to their horror, they realized that the soldiers were actually taking aim at two snaking lines of 20 to 30 people moving up a glaciated slope at least 100 yards away. Against the aching white expanse of snow the figures were tiny black silhouettes, but even at a distance of several hundred yards, the climbers could make out that many of the figures were smaller still—children—and stumbling as the bullets thudded around them. At that range, the Type 81s—street-fighting weapons, not sniper rifles—are woefully inaccurate, so the gunmen were essentially taking potshots.

Benitez heard cries of anguish drifting across the glaciated pass, punctuated by the crack-popping of the Chinese Kalashnikovs, which made his ears ring. Taking a grave risk, Romanian climber

Sergiu Matei, 29, took out his Sony DCR170 video camera. "They are shooting them like dogs," he uttered. Then what looked to be three figures dropped to the snow. Two struggled up and staggered on. One figure tried to crawl, but then collapsed in an immobile heap.

CHO OYU, ELEVATION 26,906 FEET, lies just north of Nepal in Tibet. Sherpas know it as the Turquoise Goddess, while some Tibetan Buddhists believe that Padmasambhara, who brought Buddhism to Tibet, buried instructions on how to save the earth from chaos somewhere on the mountain. At the height of the main climbing season, in autumn, the slopes of Cho Oyu are as cosmopolitan as an olympiad, as climbers from around the world make for the top of the sacred massif, the easiest of the earth's 14 peaks that rise above 8,000 meters (or 26,247 feet). In September 2006, advanced base camp had alpine athletes from the U.K., France, Australia, New Zealand, Romania, Slovenia, Russia, and the U.S., among others.

With foreign mountaineers and guides like Luis Benitez, Cho Oyu is an international crossroads because of the Nangpa La Pass, not far from where advanced base camp is established most years. Because it is remote, hard terrain, Nangpa La Pass is a difficult part of the border for the Chinese to patrol, and thus it's one of the few places where Tibetans looking to leave their occupied homeland undetected risk the elements for freedom abroad. In 1959 the Dalai Lama used a route like this one to escape into exile; Xinhua, the government-run Chinese news service, has dubbed it a "golden route" for Tibetans seeking asylum from Chinese rule.

It's also a trade route; some of the traders using the Nangpa La Pass had stopped in camp to sell their wares, including knockoff name-brand parkas from Beijing. But the people the Chinese were shooting at now didn't look like traders, and they weren't.

Many were nuns and monks, unable to practice their faith freely in Tibet. While a few Tibetans are able to obtain passports to travel abroad, fleeing refugees violate Article 322 of the Chinese criminal code, are jailed immediately, and, according to Human Rights Watch, are often tortured and then monitored by authorities for years after.

As the shooting erupted around him that morning, Benitez says he contemplated a "Rambo move" to try to disrupt the Chinese soldiers. Only Benitez is no commando; he's a sunny, sincere mountain guide. To his self-confessed shame, Benitez did nothing to stop the soldiers as they used the Tibetans for target practice.

On the one hand, this most recent Himalayan disaster had a familiar ring to it, as the mountaineers had to choose between their own selfish goals and helping others in distress. Several of the climbers, including Benitez, continued up toward the summit after the Chinese soldiers stormed their camp, rounding up refugees.

But in most other respects this incident stood alone: A cold-blooded murder by the host nation's own police left foreign witnesses not knowing at all what to do. Confusing matters further, a handful of commercial outfitters and their guides allegedly told climbers not to tell anyone outside of camp about the shooting. Fearful the Chinese authorities would revoke their permits to operate on Cho Oyu and the Chinese/Tibetan side of Everest, or that they'd seek revenge on the Tibetan cooks and porters in their employ, two of the top Everest guide operations allegedly suppressed news of the shooting.

The incident made headlines, especially in Europe, when it reached the media in October 2006, but drawing on more than 30 interviews, transcripts of interviews conducted by the Washington, DC-based International Campaign for Tibet (ICT), and visits to Cho Oyu and India, this is one of the most complete accounts yet compiled. Before the climbers spoke out, and Sergiu

Matei aired his video, the Chinese claimed the shooting was in self-defense. Meanwhile, climbers were left to contemplate what it meant for their sport that peers would put personal and commercial goals ahead of reporting an atrocity. The episode could play as farce if it hadn't cost at least one young woman her life and if it hadn't exposed, on the eve of the Beijing Olympics, the brutal contempt the Chinese authorities continue to have for Tibetans.

LIKE MANY OF THE ESTIMATED 2,500 to 3,500 Tibetans who flee their occupied homeland each year, Kelsang Namtso wanted the freedom to practice Tibetan Buddhism. A serious young woman who dressed in the traditional long skirts of a Tibetan nomad, Kelsang, 17, and her best friend Dolma, 16, rosy-cheeked and more jovial than her friend, left Nagchu, their home in a rural area northeast of Tibet's capital, Lhasa, with the intention of seeking out the Dalai Lama, their leader in exile, in Dharamsala, India.

Kelsang and her five brothers grew up with parents who struggled to make ends meet as semi-nomads, Dolma told me. Forced to recite paeans to Mao Tsetung, Kelsang dreamed of becoming a nun. (In Tibet it's an honor for one child from every family to follow a Buddhist calling; it accrues "merit" for the whole family.) But Kelsang's parents were against it. Her mother had arthritis and felt that her only daughter should be at home helping her. "Her mother didn't want her to be a nun because she was the only girl," says Dolma. "She said she had to help her mother."

Undaunted, Kelsang took vows with lamas in secret, stopped listening to music and dancing, which she loved, and maintained a strict vegetarian diet. Eventually, she left under the cover of night for a free life, on September 18, 2006.

After dodging Chinese army patrols in Lhasa, Kelsang and Dolma were crammed into the back of a truck with 75 other refugees numbering monks, nuns, and children as young as seven. Dolma. Kelsang, and the others had paid around $500 each—two years of wages for rural Tibetans—to two men, illegal guides, who were secretly stowing everyone in the truck. Even before they left, one man's courage deserted him. He jumped off the truck and fled home. As they lurched on into the night, another started vomiting with fear.

As the vehicle rumbled out of Lhasa, sliding past Chinese checkpoints, the mood inside was desperate. Inside the juddering, dark, and airless interior, children began to cry, cries that risked everyone by alerting Chinese border guards. The guides urged them to be silent with hoarse whispers. Guides face up to 10 years in prison for leading refugees out of Tibet.

The guides pushed hard, getting angry if anyone faltered. Temperatures dropped to well below freezing. Dolma and Kelsang walked with the hems of their skirts sodden and caked with snow, their arms folded across their chests to keep their fingers warm as they stumbled and fell. They had left with a store of *tsampa*, roasted barley flour, to sustain them, but their supply ran out; worse, they found themselves without water. At one point they came across herders, who charged them 70 yuan (about $9) for plastic bags of water.

Kelsang, with Dolma at her side, was faring badly. The altitude and lack of food gave her splitting headaches. Finally, 12 days after leaving Lhasa, a monk in the group spotted orange and yellow climbers' tents, incongruous against the dazzling white.

Figures clad in long coats clambered down the rocks toward them. The monk thought they might've been Tibetan monks in religious dress and waved. The refugees embraced one another as relief swept through the group. Then they realized the long coats were actually fur-lined Chinese army-issue, known as *dayi*. The smiles froze on the refugees' faces. Some in the group shouted warnings, "They are soldiers!" and urged everyone to run.

Pandemonium erupted. A soldier started screaming, *"Thama de!"* which translates as "Fuck your mother." Puffs of snow erupted around them as bullets tore into the ice.

"I heard the bullets zinging past my ears," says Dolma. "The noise was like, *tag, tag*. And then when they came past my ears, they were like, *pew, pew*."

Refugees split off running in different directions, which at that altitude is a superhuman feat. A few escaped. Somewhere in the melee Dolma lost Kelsang. Her back to the soldiers, woozy from the altitude, Kelsang presented a slow-moving target. She was a few yards from cresting a ridge and getting out of range when a 7.62mm round tore into her back, just under her left arm. She slumped in the snow and, 20 minutes from freedom, died.

BACK IN CAMP SERGIU MATEI, the Romanian climber, switched off his camera. "I didn't want to film her dying," he said. He had nearly 30 minutes of film that would have a devastating worldwide impact—if he could get it out of the country. Immediately Matei felt a lingering gaze from a soldier nearby. He waved to the soldier and swallowed hard, trying not to betray his fear before walking back to his tent to stow the tape.

Minutes later the Chinese police marched the first of several groups of refugees they'd captured into camp. One group included about a dozen kids.

"The children were in single file, about six feet away from me," Steve Lawes, a British climber, later told the International Campaign for Tibet. "They didn't see us—they weren't looking around the way kids normally would; they were too frightened. By that time advanced base camp was crawling with soldiers. They had pretty much taken over, and the atmosphere was intimidating. We were doing our best not to do anything that might spark off more violence."

The soldiers marched the kids into a big green tent flying a Chinese flag, a tent that was off-limits to foreign climbers. About an hour later a PAP soldier entered the camp with an injured

Tibetan on his back. The Tibetan appeared to have been shot in the leg, but the soldier dumped him on the snow like a sack of grain. In all, nearly 30 refugees were brought to the green tent, then herded off to a detention center. There, according to testimony given to the ICT, several were severely beaten.

The climbers were appalled but felt helpless to intervene. A few of the PAP soldiers were actually friendly to the climbers; in their late teens, the soldiers took breaks in camp, lit cigarettes, and carried on as if everything that had just happened was routine, a morning's work.

Four hours later a Tibetan kitchen boy came running to Matei. Someone was hiding in the toilet tent, he said. Matei went to investigate. Hunkered in the latrine, his hands shaking, was a man called Choedron, a poor farmer in his 30s. He had tried to bury himself in rocks, pathetically using a toilet paper bag to cover himself. As the tent zip ripped up, he nearly retched from fright; he feared that a Chinese prison cell, torture, and shame awaited him. Instead, he was confronted with Matei, whose red goatee and shaved head lend him the look of a death metal bassist. Unable to speak Tibetan, Matei repeated the one thing Choedron said: "Dalai Lama." Choedron put his hands together in veneration. They understood each other.

Matei acted quickly. First he tried to convince the Nepali base camp manager to help the terrified refugee. He refused. "The Chinese will shoot us if we are caught," he said. "It is much too dangerous." Over the manager's protests, Matei took Choedron from the tent and fed him. Starving after nearly two weeks in the snow, he devoured any food set in front of him. Afterward Matei gave him all of his spare clothes and then hid him in his tent.

As darkness fell Matei wanted to videotape Kelsang's body as evidence of the murder. But he had noticed that the PAP soldiers had night-vision equipment, and he feared being shot in the dark.

By 2:30 AM Choedron was ready to leave. The stress of hiding

Choedron, along with the tape he had of the shootings, had turned Matei into a nervous wreck. With the pass below them glistening in the moonlight, they looked at each other awkwardly. Matei clapped Choedron on his back, and said, in Romanian, "God will be with you."

Out in the night a group of refugees was hiding in a snow hole, waiting for their turn to run under the protective cloak of darkness. A few crept to Kelsang's body. One nun crouched by her side, lifted her arm, and saw congealed blood, now frozen.

The next day a small detachment of Chinese soldiers and officials returned to Kelsang's body. There they posed for pictures, with the body in the foreground and Cho Oyu in the background. According to one eyewitness account, they wrapped the corpse of the 17-year-old nun-to-be in a red blanket or body bag and hurled it into a crevasse. It is believed that later they returned to take the body into custody.

AMID DOUBTS THAT he should be doing more to help the captive Tibetans, Benitez had reflexively returned to his clients and their summit preparations. "My first responsibility is to my team," he recalls thinking. Besides, focusing on what he knew helped calm his nerves. It was a decision, he says today, that "I'll regret the rest of my life."

Matei, watching as Benitez and other teams carried on to the summit, was disgusted. "No one was saying, This is bad," he says. "Everyone was just like, Where's my coffee? Let's have some tea and get ready."

Benitez didn't make the summit. Nor did two of his clients—one was suffering from symptoms of altitude sickness; the other was simply exhausted, mentally and physically, after the events in base camp. One turned back on the first day, returning with one of Benitez's Sherpas. The other lasted a second day before Benitez took him down after assessing his condition.

"On that climb I've never had such heavy feet," Benitez says. "The summit push is meant to be where all your hard work pays off; it was the final fight of the mountain, but at that point it felt like I didn't want to go to the top. My heart wasn't in it. We were fighting to reach the top, but we felt that we were fighting for the wrong thing. All we had were questions about what we had seen. We had no fight in us."

When Benitez returned to camp he was surprised to learn no one had reported the shooting to anyone outside the camp. "I really thought all the climbers would be standing up for human rights," he says.

Instead, climbers were being urged by at least two guides not to tell anyone what they had seen. Renowned Slovenian climber Pavle Kozjek, 48, who witnessed the aftermath of the shooting, said, "For many people in the base camp the most important thing was to be able to come back again. They decided not to tell what had happened because of this." And, he said, "I heard some expedition leaders forced their clients not to report these events."

But Benitez couldn't live with himself. He sent an e-mail to ExplorersWeb.com, an expedition website, just after 7 AM on October 2. The header of the e-mail read: "story not being told here in tibet." He detailed the shooting, asked for his name to be kept out of it, and ended by emphasizing the need to "tell the world about this little corner of the planet, where people are dying attempting to reach for a better life."

A few hours later Kate Saunders, from the International Campaign for Tibet, alerted governments worldwide, which took the issue up with China. "Over those few days I was trying to speak to as many climbers up there as possible," she says. "Luis was the only climber who would speak to us from Cho Oyu, inside Tibet."

Meanwhile, as Benitez was ordering yaks and packing for the trail down, he confided to his assistant guide, Paul Rogers, that he'd sent the note. Immediately afterward, Benitez claims, Rogers "did a Judas." (Rogers declined to comment.)

According to Benitez, Rogers went straight to Russell Brice, owner and operator of Himalayan Experience, the biggest commercial climbing operator on the north side of Everest. Brice, hero of Discovery Channel's *Everest: Beyond the Limit*, dropped the sage, avuncular manner of his television persona and became enraged. Brice works closely with the Chinese, depending upon them for climbing permits to run his business; all told, he pulls in, by some estimates, as much as $10 million a year. "And that's a low estimate," says Tom Sjogren, who runs ExplorersWeb.com with his wife Tina and is a known critic of Brice. "Just about any business on Cho Oyu or Everest somehow has Russell Brice involved in it."

Brice, with Rogers at his side, stormed down the hill at around 3 PM. "Paul told me you sent an e-mail to ExplorersWeb," Brice accused Benitez. "Are you trying to get us kicked out of the country?" He began jabbing his finger at the younger guide. "Are you fucking crazy?"

"This 'free Tibet' thing is bullshit," Rogers jumped in. "The Chinese have done more for Tibet than you know. These people they shot at were human traffickers. It's a girl-smuggling ring to Mumbai. The only reason you want to tell everyone is that you want to be famous."

Benitez was shocked. If he were out for fame, as Rogers claimed, he was going about it the wrong way, requesting that ExWeb keep his name out of it.

Then Brice stunned Benitez further. Not only had Brice harangued him for sending the e-mail; he and his team had treated the Chinese soldiers who killed Kelsang for snow blindness shortly after the shooting. Now Benitez went on the offensive: "So, basically, you've been treating the people who were doing the shooting?"

Benitez retreated to his tent, but 45 minutes later Brice and Rogers returned with a third man, climbing operator Henry Todd. During his whole career Benitez had always had "great respect" for Todd, and had often sought his advice.

"You should be fucking hung out to dry for what you have done," Todd yelled at Benitez. Todd, a.k.a. the Toddfather, is a large, ruby-faced man known for his vicious temper; he's an ex-con, having served seven years in jail for possession of LSD as part of a massive drug sting in Britain in the late 1970s. In 2000 Todd violently assaulted one of his own clients, an American reporter named Finn-Olaf Jones, who felt so threatened by the incident that he took a helicopter out of camp a few days later. Nepalese authorities banned Todd from Nepal for two years. Since then he changed the name of his company from Himalayan Guides to Ice 8000, and is now in operation in China. Having been cast out by the Nepalis before, Todd didn't want to get banned by the Chinese, too.

"I think your name has been given to the Chinese," Todd hissed, trying to intimidate Benitez. "If I were you I would leave ahead of your group, or you will get them into trouble." Eventually the three left, but from that moment on, Benitez kept to himself. (Neither Brice nor Todd responded to repeated requests for comment.)

Benitez and his clients made it to Kathmandu. Border guards didn't detain them, but Benitez was indeed a wanted man. Word was, the Chinese embassy wanted to talk to him, along with two other British climbers, including Steve Lawes. Hoping to leave Nepal without further confrontations, Benitez holed up in the Radisson hotel in Kathmandu. On October 7, doubts assailing him—*What if these people really were people traffickers? Maybe I put my career on the line for nothing . . .* —his phone rang. Unsure of who knew he'd checked in to the Radisson, he didn't know if he should answer.

THE ROMANIAN WHO'D TAKEN THE VIDEO of the shooting, Sergiu Matei, faced his own anxious journey to safety. He knew that he had incontrovertible proof that Chinese riflemen had shot an unarmed teenager in the back. He stashed the tape in a belt pouch, and burned a hole in the casing of the cassette with a cigarette to make it look like an ashtray.

At the New Delhi airport a man with a gun under his coat approached Matei, saying he was with the Austrian embassy. He asked him what his occupation was and if he'd been on Cho Oyu. "I'm a dentist," Matei lied. "I was on Annapurna." It seemed to satisfy the man, whoever he was, and he left. "I was shitting my pants," said Matei. "On the mountain, if they had caught me with that tape, I thought I would be shot on the spot, and the Chinese would have said a Romanian had died in an avalanche. It made me hate communism and the idea of communism."

On October 12, 2006, the Chinese released a statement citing an unnamed official who claimed that soldiers had found "stowaways" and tried to "persuade them to go back to their home. But the stowaways refused and attacked the soldiers." The official said that "the frontier soldiers were forced to defend themselves and injured two stowaways." The report added: "One injured person died later in hospital due to oxygen shortage on the 6,200-meter high land." (In August 2007, the top Chinese general in Tibet was reportedly forced into early retirement over the incident.)

On October 13, Matei's footage aired on Pro TV in Romania and was quickly screened by the BBC, CNN, and other networks worldwide. (It can now be seen on YouTube.) Diplomats from around the world condemned the Chinese actions—none more forcefully than Clark Randt, the U.S. ambassador in Beijing.

Away from news cameras, says the International Campaign for Tibet, some of the captured refugees reported being beaten with rubber hoses and electric cattle prods. Police questioned the children, and Chinese officials later claimed that they had been sent to India to be "trained" by the Dalai Lama, then sent back to China as "splitists," who want to see Tibet independent. Some of the youngest children were not collected by their parents and so remained in custody for three months. When their parents came they were fined 100 to 500 yuan ($13–$66).

Dolma, who witnessed her best friend's death, made it to freedom in Dharamsala, India, where the exiled Tibetan government is based. She met the Dalai Lama and is today pursuing a secular education; she may later join a nunnery. She sat in a green park and gazed out at the Himalayas. Her hands clasped under her thighs, she rocked back and forth as tears rolled down her cheeks. "Kelsang would have been pleased that I made it," she said. Kelsang's body was never returned to her family.

AFTER SEVERAL RINGS, Benitez snatched the telephone from its cradle. Instead of a Chinese agent, it was Kate Saunders, from the International Campaign for Tibet. She offered to assuage his fears that he'd been misinformed by letting him meet 43 Tibetans.

In an SUV with smoked windows, Benitez and a Tibetan ICT representative drove along Kathmandu's bustling backstreets to the Tibetan Refugee Reception Center, on the eastern edge of the city. There he saw monks sitting in prayer alongside families with children in cheap, tattered sneakers. He looked at snapshots covering an entire wall outside of the medical clinic. Many were painful to see, as they depicted the horrific frostbite many Tibetans suffered, their toes and fingers blackened, as they made it over the Nangpa La Pass. He met many of the refugees; any doubts he'd had about interfering with policing human traffickers quickly dissipated. He wept for a moment before regaining his composure.

In May 2007, Benitez made it to the top of Everest for a sixth time, and he did it from the Nepal side. Normally wasted but ecstatic atop the roof of the world, Benitez says that this time he experienced disappointment.

"I realized I'm not a fireman or a policeman or anyone else

who saves lives," he says. "I'm just a mountaineer, part of a sub-strata of society that people can't peg. What happened on Cho Oyu made me realize that there's something more important than just reaching the summit. So I stood on top of Everest and thought, What's the point of this?"

JONATHAN GREEN *is an award-winning journalist who has reported on jihadist militias in Sudan, corruption in oil-rich Kazakhstan, the destruction of the rainforest in the Borneo jungle, and Tibetan refugees in the high Himalaya, among other subjects and places. He has won several journalism awards, including the American Society of Journalists and Authors award for reporting on a significant topic for his piece "Hooked on the Gold Rush," an investigation into human rights violations connected with gold mining in west Africa.*

He has *written for* Men's Journal, *the* New York Times, Best Life, Reader's Digest, British GQ, *and* Esquire, *among many other publications. He is writing a book based on this piece,* Murder in the High Himalaya, *which will be forthcoming from PublicAffairs.*

Coda

Shortly after the shooting, my editor at the *Mail on Sunday* espied a small newspaper item on the incident. She called me to see if there was a deeper story worth investigating. I knew nothing about Tibet, but discovered that the murdered nun was just one of thousands of refugees fleeing oppression to freedom along a well-trodden trail. What was extraordinary was that while many wanted to flee the oppression, others would risk everything to meet the Dalai Lama in exile in northern India only to return to Tibet. For some Tibetan Buddhists, meeting the Dalai Lama for even a few short seconds is worth risking their lives on the high passes and against the guns of Chinese soldiers.

Roughly two months after the shooting, I was in the high Himalaya on assignment. I had been on the trail in Nepal's Himalaya for days, trekking up to fifteen thousand feet along knife-edge ravines and scrambling over rocks and boulders attempting to avoid the Maoist insurgents who controlled the mountains and had killed thirteen thousand so far in their bloody campaign for power in this tiny, poverty-stricken country. Heaving for oxygen in the thin air, we had hiked to the Chinese-occupied Tibetan border from Namche Bazaar, a mountain village at eleven thousand feet and a hub for the Sherpa communities. It's the last place to hire porters and supplies before Everest base camp.

My Sherpa guide Ramesh, Tibetan translator Kunchok, and I were all trying to blend in as tourists and mountaineers. But while others went east to Everest base camp from Namche, we scurried west toward China. We were searching for Tibetan refugees escaping the murder, torture, and ethnic cleansing that were driving them from their homeland to the relative safety of neighboring Nepal, and then into safety in exile in northern India.

High up in the mountains in a hamlet called Thame, I was ushered into some traders' tents under cover of darkness. I met two brothers, their faces lit by a flickering yak-dung fire, who were helping their three sisters, quietly observing me, escape from China to live peacefully as Buddhist nuns. The same two brothers were camp cooks with the expedition that observed the killing at Nangpa La Pass. After the shooting, they realized Tibet was becoming increasingly dangerous under the Chinese, so they wanted their sisters to have the chance of a better life.

The brothers also told me that two years ago they had worked with a climbing expedition and encountered a seventeen-year-old girl who had fallen down a crevasse while fleeing Tibet. "The people she was with tied clothes together and tried to pull her out but it wasn't long enough," said one brother, Tsering. "The other refugees could only string prayer flags over the hole, drop some barley for her to eat, and watch as the girl was swallowed alive as her body heat melted the ice and she slipped further and further into the crevasse. The climbers watched through binoculars and did nothing," says Tsering. "They had ropes but they climbed the mountain instead."

It disgusted me. When I returned home I also dug into the story of the climbers who witnessed the shooting.

After the story was published, the mountaineering community polarized around the issue. Some readers wrote in to cheer Luis's brave whistle-blowing. But privately, still more attacked him for speaking out against his fellow climbers and the "brotherhood of the rope." "This is a very dark secret at the heart of our community," said Benitez. "I have been getting flak from a lot of people to keep my mouth shut. But this is a story that needs to be told. It's just sad that more aren't rallying around the cause. I have no regrets. I would do exactly the same again if I had to."

Permissions

THE BEST AMERICAN
CRIME REPORTING SERIES

Otto Penzler and Thomas H. Cook, Series Editors

THE BEST AMERICAN CRIME REPORTING 2008
Jonathan Kellerman, Editor

ISBN 978-0-06-149083-5 (paperback)

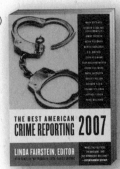

THE BEST AMERICAN CRIME REPORTING 2007
Linda Fairstein, Editor

ISBN 978-0-06-081553-0 (paperback)

THE BEST AMERICAN CRIME WRITING 2006
Mark Bowden, Editor

ISBN 978-0-06-081552-3 (paperback)

THE BEST AMERICAN CRIME WRITING 2005
James Ellroy, Editor

ISBN 978-0-06-081551-6 (paperback)

ABOUT THE EDITORS

JONATHAN KELLERMAN received his Ph.D. in psychology at the age of twenty-four. In 1985, his first novel, *When the Bough Breaks*, became a *New York Times* bestseller, was produced as a TV movie, and won the Edgar Allan Poe and Anthony awards for best first novel. Since then, he has written twenty-seven bestselling crime novels, including, most recently, *Compulsion*.

OTTO PENZLER is the proprietor of the Mysterious Bookshop, the founder of the Mysterious Press, the creator of Otto Penzler Books, and the editor of many books and anthologies, including the annual Best American Mystery Stories.

THOMAS H. COOK is the author of twenty-one books—two works of nonfiction and nineteen novels, including *The Chatham School Affair*, which won the Edgar Allan Poe Award for Best Novel, and the recent *Master of the Delta*.